# Christian Child-Rearing
# and Personality Development

# Christian Child-Rearing and Personality Development

*Paul D. Meier, M.D.*

*Baker Book House*
Grand Rapids, Michigan

Copyright 1977 by
Baker Book House Company

ISBN: 0-8010-6014-1 (cloth)
0-8010-6016-8 (paper)

Library of Congress
Catalog Card Number:
76-057501

First printing, April 1977
Second printing, July 1977

Printed in the United States of America

to my parents

**Alexander and Elizabeth Meier**

who brought me up, with love, in

the "nurture and admonition of the Lord"

# Foreword

The parenthood job market is depressed. Not that unemployment lines are long, but old-timers and on-the-job trainees alike are frustrated. Quality control is off—not very many really good products. We parents are seriously in need of some good advice—medically, psychologically, and spiritually—that tells us what to do after we've paid the obstetrician.

For the concerned parent (or teacher) Dr. Paul Meier has concocted a large helping of common sense know-how for the job of planting a young life in the rather unfriendly soil of our society. Many of us do a far better job at raising chrysanthemums and cabbages than children. Over-the-fence conversations about high fevers and low self-images are fine, but secretly we would like to know from somebody with professional training and experience how to do what—and *why*. It has to be more than "an apple a day...."

*Christian Child-Rearing and Personality Development* is a well-crafted manual launched from a platform of deep respect for children—God's creation in His own image. With the expertise of a seasoned practitioner, the author pierces the clouds that disguise reality in childhood and proceeds to defog many of the "unmentionable" trouble spots. Knots are untied with liberal use of both medical and Biblical insights.

The table of contents looks like a treasure hunt. With tongue in cheek, as if to travel with the wind at our backs, and avoid heaping guilt on the already troubled parent, our teacher uses the clever device of negative suggestion. You want to know how to avoid this trap? All right, read this chapter. By explaining how problems develop, he steers the reader around them.

Beyond professional competence, Dr. Meier comes through more as a man than a mentor—a caring, understanding fellow-father along on the hard climb through the growing-up years. His words sound like a sympathetic player-coach as he spurs us on near the finish line: "If you feel that you have made a great many mistakes in the past, well, welcome to the human race!"

Directions are simple and chatty, yet technical and profound. For example, "If the blood cells of an average human were lined up in single file, they would reach all the way to the moon and halfway back." Dr. Meier makes childhood seem logical, uncomplicated, and manageable.

An appropriate subtitle for this volume could well be: "Everything You Always Wanted to Know About Children, But Didn't Know Enough to Ask." It comes very close to being a counselor-in-residence for the Christian parent, and may well find itself comfortably at home on the reference shelf beside Webster, Betty Crocker, and the Living Bible.

HOWARD G. HENDRICKS
Chairman, Department of Christian Education
Dallas Theological Seminary

# Preface

As a Christian psychiatrist, I have been appalled by the number of psychologically disturbed Christians I have seen who were reared by relatively normal Christian parents. These normal Christian parents, however, had used very poor judgment in their child-rearing practices. Their judgment was not only psychologically unsound, but even more importantly, Scripturally unsound.

In seminars I have given across the country, I have frequently had middle-aged parents come up to me privately to say, "Oh, how I wish I had known these things about Christian child-rearing twenty years ago." For this reason, and with a sense of urgency, I have written this book integrating scores of Scriptural passages with hundreds of findings from psychiatric research on healthy and unhealthy child-rearing techniques. I have also included lessons I have learned from my twelve years of training, as well as from my private practice. Many of my students have found the information in this book valuable for gaining insights into their own personality development. I have seen many dramatic changes in the families who have put these Scriptural and psychologically sound principles into practice. It is my sincere hope that young married couples, in particular, will read this book before their children are too old to change. It is my firm belief that approximately 85 percent of one's adult personality is formed by the time he is six years old. Those first six years, therefore, are obviously the most crucial. This is not to say that after six it is too late to correct emotional defects. No, it's not too late, but it becomes increasingly more difficult.

Praise God that He can work miracles and dramatically alter troubled lives.

The purpose of this book is to further the cause of Jesus Christ through preventative Christian psychiatry which is based on the absolute authority of God's divine revelations to man in Scripture.

PAUL D. MEIER, M.D.

# Acknowledgments

I would like to especially thank my wife, whose graduate degree in early childhood development complemented my own training in child and adult psychiatry. She brought three children into this world for us to love and learn from firsthand. She also struggled at my side through many months of living as houseparents in a youth home for delinquent and disturbed teenagers, so we could learn about teenage problems firsthand and not have to rely primarily on books.

I also want to thank the following pastors, friends, and educators who have contributed significantly to the attitudes, ideas, and data I have assimilated for this book: Rev. Joseph Balbach, Rev. Eugene Williams, Rev. James Abrahamson, Rev. Ralph Hart, Rev. Richard Meier, Rev. Stuart Briscoe, Rev. Gene Getz, Mr. Richard Case, Mr. Don Meredith, Mr. Tim Timmons, Mr. Bill Gothard, Mr. Paul Brown, Mr. and Mrs. Mel Goodenough, Mr. and Mrs. David Brown, Mr. and Mrs. John Festa, Dr. and Mrs. Frank Minirth, Dr. Gary Collins, Dr. Joseph Hensen, Dr. Walter Fremont, Dr. Thomas Emerson, Dr. Roscoe Dykman, Dr. John Peters, Dr. Robert Shannon, Dr. William Reese, Dr. Irvin Ringdahl, Dr. Eaton Wesley Bennett, Dr. William Glasser, Dr. William P. Wilson, Dr. Basil Jackson, and Dr. Carl Wenger.

I also want to acknowledge the graduate students in my personality development course who eagerly participated in sixty hours of dialogue on the rough draft of this manuscript and made a number of suggestions which have been incorporated. Their names are: Keiko Anno, Carl Balsam, Jim Bedell, Steve Berger, Jim Evans, Chieko Fukushima, Lee Hotchkiss, Bill and Mindy Meier, Roger Parnham, Alan Reber, Dave Riemenschneider, Rick Ringler, and Larry Tornquist.

Last but not least, I want to thank my secretaries and typists who helped me with the various drafts of this manuscript: Jenny Wiers, Georgette Sattler, Nancy Brown, and Doris Brown.

# Contents

**Part Three**

**Part Four**

# PART | ONE

*The Budding of the Self-Concept*

# The Child's Self-Concept

1

We have all been told in many ways, throughout our lives, that we are inferior. This includes both verbal and non-verbal messages. Some of these messages have been intentional, while many have been unintentional. I will discuss some of the ways that we can minimize the development of inferiority feelings in our children. I believe very firmly that our first and most important calling from God, if we are parents, is to be the kind of parents to our children that God would have us to be. I don't care if you're a doctor, pastor, businessman, or traveling salesman—your family comes first! Whatever time you have left over from being the right kind of parent—*that's* the time you can use to accomplish whatever other callings God has given you! And one of the most important things we can do for our children is to develop within them an emotionally healthy and Scripturally accurate self-concept. Without self-worth, our children will not only have a miserable life, but they will also be unable to reach the potential God has called them to reach. I firmly believe that all emotional pain ultimately comes from three root sources: (1) lack of self-worth, (2) lack of intimacy with others, and (3) lack of intimacy with God. A poor self-concept can significantly hamper us in all three of these essential areas.

One of the most important facts I have learned in my psychiatric training is that approximately 85 percent of a person's

ultimate personality is formed by the time he is *six years old*. This
fact alone has given me great insights into people and their problems. During those first six years of life, children really are inferior
in many ways to the other persons in their environment. They
are much smaller physically, more clumsy, more ignorant of the
facts, and more concrete and naive in their interpretation of the
meager facts they have accumulated. And on top of all that, they
are inferior in authority, with parents ruling over them and older
siblings bossing them around. That's what goes on the first six
years. Then they go off to school at age five or six, and what happens
there? They may get all 80 and 90 percents on their papers and
tests, but what does this mean to them? It means that they got
10 or 20 percent wrong, and all they see and hear about are the
parts of their work that the teacher marked with red ink! Instead
of the emphasis being on what they have learned and accomplished,
the emphasis in American schools today is usually a negative
one—on what they have done wrong![1]

Another serious influence on the development of self-worth in
our children is the influence of our parental value systems. What
do we as parents place the most value upon in our own everyday
life? I'm not talking about the values we tell our children they
should have, but the values they see us actually living by when
they analyze why we do the things we do and say the things we
say. Is our focus on materialism? Athletics? Sinless perfection? Good
looks? Intelligence? Humanitarianism? Or *godly character?* Perhaps
your own parents went through the depression of the 1930s, and
have reacted by overemphasizing material gain in their daily life
experiences and conversations. Now you have grown up in that
home, and, as an adult, have become very successful at a very
worthwhile profession that only pays average wages. You will
probably have conscious (or unconscious) inferiority feelings because you have not lived up to the materialistic expectations that
were built into your way of thinking. At this point your own
children detect your inner dissatisfaction and frustrations about
not having more money and material possessions. They see these
frustrations eat away at your own self-worth, and, step by step,
they learn from you to measure their own self-worth in terms
of their own material possessions—motorcycles, mod clothes, ten-

---

1. William Glasser, *Schools Without Failure.*

speed racing bikes, and spending money. If they don't have these things, they feel worthless. And even if they do have these things, they will compare themselves with others their age who have more, and they will still feel inferior. That's human nature. From this example I hope you can understand how faulty value systems can be passed on from generation to generation.

I want to make it clear that I am in no way condemning being rich. It is not a sin to be rich. But it *is* a sin to base our self-worth on our riches. Some of the godliest men in the Bible were also the richest men on earth in material terms—Abraham, Isaac, Jacob, Joseph, Job, David, Solomon, and many others. But their self-worth was based on their faith in God, wisdom, and godly character traits. God simply chose to bless them tremendously with material possessions.

Other great men of God had similar virtues but God chose for them to live in financial poverty. Take, for example, the disciples and the Apostle Paul. Paul said he had experienced both riches and poverty, both popularity and abasement; but Paul based his self-worth on godly character traits, and could therefore say, "I have learned, in whatsoever state I am, therewith to be content" (Phil. 4:11). Paul's sense of values is reflected in his counsel to early Christians:

> Let this mind be in you, which was also in Christ Jesus: Who, being in the form of God, thought it not robbery to be equal with God: But made himself of no reputation, and took upon him the form of a servant, and was made in the likeness of men: And being found in fashion as a man, he humbled himself, and became obedient unto death, even the death of the cross. Wherefore God also hath highly exalted him, and given him a name which is above every name: That at the name of Jesus every knee should bow, of things in heaven, and things in earth, and things under the earth; And that every tongue should confess that Jesus Christ is Lord, to the glory of God the Father.          —Phil. 2:5-11

Christ Himself told us, "But seek ye first the kingdom of God, and his righteousness; and all these things shall be added unto you" (Matt. 6:33). If God has blessed you financially, I think that's great! But be aware of the fact that your life here on this earth is a temporary pilgrimage and a mission, and that developing godly character in children who will live forever is millions

of times more important than devoting yourself to business opportunities so you can provide them with so-called financial security. I'd rather have eternal security than financial security
any day. Of course, there's nothing immoral about having both,
if God so blesses.

The proverbial Jewish mother puts a lot of emphasis on good
grades, 100 percents on test papers, and things like that when
she praises her children. This is in contrast to the average American
mother who praises her children for hanging their clothing up
or being quiet in the restaurant. My own parents, even though
they weren't Jewish, rewarded me for good grades and punished
me for poor grades when I was in elementary school. After I got
to junior high, they continued to reward me for good grades and
would frown at occasional not so good grades. They also rewarded
me for reading Spurgeon's sermons and drawing architectural de-
signs of houses. My father, who is a retired home builder, even
built one of the houses I designed and moved our family into it,
an event which I'm sure contributed to my own self-worth. My
parents also attended all the elementary school open houses to
see and praise the good work their children had done. But mixed
with all this were regular church and Sunday School attendance,
and daily devotions around the supper table. At these devotions,
we would sing a hymn, read a chapter or so from the Bible, and
then get down on our knees beside our chairs and pray for each
other's needs. It was this background that influenced me to continue my education for twenty-five years (thirteen before high
school graduation, counting kindergarten, and twelve after), and
become a Christian psychiatrist whose desire is to design spiritual
homes rather than physical ones.

But I have seen this emphasis on education get out of hand
in some of the families I have dealt with. I had a patient with
a Ph.D. from Duke University who frequently felt like a failure
because he didn't go after an M.D. degree, as his parents had
wished. I know another man with a doctorate in economics from
Harvard, who is very successful professionally and a brilliant
scholar. But he still carries around bad feelings about the one
course in which he didn't get an "A" as an undergraduate in
college. His parents had taught him that anything less than an
"A" is a dishonor to the entire family. His uncle even flew in
from out of state to talk to him about it when it happened. If we

as parents have unrealistic expectations for our children, they will feel like failures, no matter how much they succeed in the world's eyes.

Some parents go to the other extreme too, caring nothing about the accomplishments of their children. I know of many doctors and preachers who were so busy serving humanity or furthering the cause of Christ that their children developed terrible feelings of worthlessness, feelings from which they ran by taking drugs or committing suicide. The Bible tells us that the only men who should be ministers, elders, or deacons in a local church are those who have "faithful children not accused of riot or unruly" (Titus 1:6). There was a time when one of my sisters was going through a temporary rebellious stage, so my father resigned as deacon and did not assume his duties as deacon again until she had passed through it. Now that same sister is a godly woman who is happily married to a fine Christian, has two beautiful children, conducts Bible studies in her home, and is a real prayer warrior for God. She has the highest regard for the father she rebelled against earlier. He admits now, when he looks back, that he was spending too much time doing church work and not enough time with his family. He was holding several church offices at the same time.

It's interesting to note that my sister now attends church where the minister will not allow any individual to hold more than one position in that church. He says he would rather have each individual do one job well and devote the rest of his time to his family. I think that's a great idea. One of the most important abilities I have learned is the ability to say no to well-intentioned people who ask me to do things when I know my time is already stretched as far as I want it to be. A minister who can't say no sometimes for the sake of his family should serve the Lord in some other profession. As church members, we can also be of assistance to our pastors by such little things as not calling him at night, hiring people to relieve him of mundane chores, and participating in the evangelistic work of the church ourselves, as was the case in the early church.

Let's discuss our value systems regarding athletics for a moment. Overall, I think athletics are a great tradition for a number of reasons. A school-age child's self-worth is influenced a great deal by how he is regarded and valued by his peers. And being average or better than average in athletic skills is one good way to gain the respect of his peers. Sports will teach the child teamwork, enthusiasm, how to compete with himself, how to compete with others, how to win graciously, and how to accept defeat and frustrations. He will see himself improving with practice, and apply this concept to other areas of his life. He will learn to play by the rules, and he'll learn the consequences of disobeying rules. It is to be hoped that he will apply these concepts to the "game of life." Sports can help your child gain self-confidence as his ability increases, and he can use athletic teams to develop close friendships and to learn to relate to others.

But before you decide that athletics is a cure-all, I feel that it is my duty as a Christian psychiatrist to show you the other side of the coin too. Athletics, if misapplied, can be used to destroy a child's self-worth, or even to teach him sociopathic values. When you play baseball with your children, do you praise them when they do something right, or do you remain silent when they hit or catch the ball and criticize them when they miss it? Are you continually correcting and showing them how they should have done it? To become good athletes what they really need is your *acceptance,* your *companionship, repetition, repetition,* and *repetition,* mixed with some genuine praise for what they do right. Then there is the problem of coaches. There are good coaches and there are bad coaches. There are coaches who are emotionally healthy, who help develop character in youngsters; and there are emotionally disturbed or spiritually depraved coaches who need to win so badly that they teach their athletes to cheat, to injure other players, and to do whatever else is necessary to win. This is the "win at any cost" philosophy. If your child accepts this "win at any cost" philosophy in sports, he will apply it to other areas of his life as well. An intense desire to win is quite healthy, but not if it is at any cost. I want my children to be assertive and competitive, but not sociopathic.

Another thing to watch for is expecting too much of your children in athletics. Don't forget that much of athletic ability is inherited, and your child may be getting social benefits from simply warming up the bench. If you're proud of him for making the team, or for having the courage even to try out, he'll have self-worth. If you express disappointment that he is not the quarterback or shortstop, he'll lose some self-worth. I am 6'4½", but I don't have very much natural athletic ability. I'm good at some sports and poor at others. I had a basketball backboard on the garage when I was growing up, and spent hundreds of hours there shooting baskets—but I never made a single basketball team. I didn't even make my fraternity basketball team in college. Basketball is definitely not my spiritual gift! I'm fairly good at tug-of-war and arm-wrestling, and I was a fairly good goalie in soccer, but definitely not basketball. For that reason, there is nothing that would build my self-worth more than to have my son become a professional basketball player. I could build his whole life around basketball and place all sorts of demands upon him if he wants to be accepted by me. And this is exactly what a multitude of parents do—expect their children to succeed in areas that they were weak in when they were growing up. So if my sons inherited my basketball-playing ability, I ought to give God the freedom to develop the talents He chose for them to have. I would rather have my children meet the needs of the Kingdom of God, and their own personal needs, than to feel obligated to make up for my own personal deficiencies.

I don't believe sports are the exclusive possession of the male gender either. Girls can benefit from them just as boys can, but I would not advise you to encourage in any way your daughter to be a boy or to try out for left tackle on the high school football team! Some fathers prefer sons so much that their daughters become boys to gain their acceptance. This can result in a wide variety of emotional conflicts, including difficulty relating sexually in marriage. But this is only if the problem is severe, and most girls go through somewhat of a tomboy stage in pre- and early adolescence.

We have touched on a few of the faulty value systems that we parents frequently have: overemphasis on materialism, education, or athletics. There are dozens of others we could discuss, but there is one more that I feel I must cover. It is the one I have probably seen misused more than any other in my experience as a psychiatrist, with materialism taking a close second. That faulty value system is the overemphasis in American society today on physical appearance.[2] A great deal of the inferiority feelings experienced by millions of Americans today comes from compar-

2. Bill Gothard, Seminar: Institute in Basic Youth Conflicts.

ing various physical defects with the physical attributes of others. I have seen this commonly in both men and women. I'll describe briefly how it is developed in girls, and some of the consequences of it, but remember that this occurs in boys too in a very similar way. This particular faulty value system usually develops when a pretty little girl is born into a family that overemphasizes physical appearance, so they praise her over and over again for how pretty she is, but never praise her for anything else. There is nothing wrong with praising your children *occasionally* for how nice they look—I'm not talking about that. I'm talking about praising good looks at the expense of other more important things, like godly character traits. These parents are also constantly bragging to others about their child's good looks in the child's presence. The parents certainly mean no harm, but if this is overdone (and it frequently is in today's society), the child will learn to measure her own self-worth for the rest of her life on the basis of her physical attractiveness or sex appeal. As she grows older, especially during her teens, she will *always* find somebody who has a prettier face, a better figure, less knobby knees, or whatever else she considers her main physical defect. It is interesting to note that it is nearly always her physical defects that she will compare with others, not the physical attributes that are satisfactory. In many cases, the more attractive the girl, the more inferior she may feel deep down, partially because her parents naturally tended to place more emphasis on her looks than they would have had she been an average-looking girl. *What a difference it would make if parents would primarily praise their child's good character and behavior!* Character and behavior defects are correctable! Physical defects usually are not. A child whose parents value and praise good character and behavior will strive to improve his or her character and behavioral weaknesses in order to gain both parental approval and feelings of self-worth, which are vital to good mental health.

Many of us fail to recognize the hidden bitterness and resentment we carry toward God for not designing us the way we would have designed ourselves. We don't realize that God designed us the way He did because He loves us and wants to develop within each of us a Christlike character, so that we can experience the abundant life. How foolish we sometimes are, thinking that we are wiser than God. Let's take a close look at what God inspired David to write about this subject:

> For Thou didst form my inward parts; Thou didst weave me in my mother's womb. I will give thanks to Thee, for I am fearfully and wonderfully made; Wonderful are Thy works, and my soul knows it very well. My frame was not hidden from Thee, when I was made in secret, and skillfully wrought in the depths of the earth. Thine eyes have seen my unformed substance; and in Thy book they were all written, the days that were ordained for me, when as yet there was not one of them.          —Ps. 139:13-16, NASV

I especially appreciate this beautiful portion of Holy Scripture from my point of view as a physician. David, under God's divine inspiration, does a fantastic job of describing medical embryology. David knew nothing about DNA and RNA, but he knew that before we were even born, *God designed us!* While our bodies were being skillfully differentiated within our mothers' wombs, each of our "inward parts" was designed exactly as God intended. This includes the strengths and weaknesses of each of us. It includes areas of special talent, and areas where the talent just isn't there. It includes basic intelligence potential, some basic personality characteristics, and hereditary predispositions to certain physical and mental illnesses. Manic depression, for example, is primarily a genetically predetermined mental illness.[3] Psychiatrists put patients suffering from mania on lithium salts and they frequently are back to normal within ten days. Other examples will be discussed later. In contrast, many people, probably all of us, have changeable defects, such as being overweight, overanxious, or overly dependent upon others. These are things that we are responsible for ourselves, and I believe we should make every effort to correct our correctable defects. This will improve our self-worth as well as our usefulness to God as far as our testimony is concerned.

Let's take a brief look at the Apostle Paul. Paul was probably the greatest missionary of all time. Why did Paul make himself so totally available to God while so many other Christians make themselves available to God only a portion of the time, thinking that they can run their own lives better than God can? Note what Paul had to say about this:

> And because of the surpassing greatness of the revelations, for this reason, to keep me from exalting myself, there was given me a thorn in the flesh, a messenger of Satan to buffet

3. Merrill T. Eaton and Margaret H. Peterson, *Psychiatry*, p. 199.

me—to keep me from exalting myself! Concerning this I en-
treated the Lord three times that it might depart from me.
And He has said to me, *"My grace is sufficient for you, for
power is perfected in weakness."* Most gladly, therefore, I
will rather boast about my weaknesses, that the power of
Christ may dwell in me. Therefore I am well content with
weaknesses, with insults, with distresses, with persecutions,
with difficulties, for Christ's sake; for when I am weak,
then I am strong.                                —II Cor. 12:7-10, NASV

God gave Paul the gift of healing, and with that gift Paul
healed all kinds of illnesses in others. But God said no to Paul
when he requested the power to heal himself. God said no for
a reason. I believe God answers every one of our prayers, but
to expect God to always answer them affirmatively is not only
naive, it is an attempt to take over the omniscience and omnipotence of Almighty God. God gave the Apostle Paul an uncorrect-
able defect for Paul's own good and for the glory of God, and
He may do the same for some of us, like it or not. *True Biblical
Christianity is extremely practical. It works! Living according to
God's wise concepts, as outlined in His Holy Word, will result
in the abundant life of love, joy, peace, and the other fruits of
the Spirit.*

It doesn't surprise me that many non-Christian psychiatrists
think that all religion is hocus-pocus magical thinking, since so
many of their mentally disturbed patients are hysterical and trying to play God, telling Him what to do and how to do it. The
more inferior a person feels, the more superior he will probably
act; this is to compensate for his feelings of inadequacy. If his
inferiority reaches psychotic proportions, he will likely make up,
and actually believe, grandiose delusions about himself. These are
frequently paranoid delusions which make him feel more important.

I have had several patients (including one woman) who actually thought they were Jesus Christ. I interviewed one such patient
in a locked room, and when I asked him if he knew why he
was there in the mental hospital, he told me God had sent him
there to take me home to heaven. At that point I began sweating
profusely! I was afraid that he might get up right then and there
and try to send me home to heaven! He asked me for a sip of
my coke, and I told him I didn't share my cokes for fear of spreading germs. He responded that if I would give him a sip of my

coke, he would give me eternal life. So I said, "Here, take the whole thing!" With proper medication, he improved from his acute paranoid schizophrenic episode in a few weeks. I found out later that he had lived a very wicked life, but had accepted the Lord a couple of years prior to this illness and joined a very negativistic local church. He already had an abundance of inferiority and inadequacy feelings because of his past. To make matters worse, this church kept pounding negative and legalistic thoughts into him right and left. His self-worth finally reached such a low ebb that he convinced himself he was Christ, so he could bear the severe pain of his low self concept. I encouraged him when he was sane again to dwell on God's grace and his importance to God, and God's total forgiveness for his entire past. I wanted to tell him to quit his church and get into a healthier assembly of believers. In fact I hinted at this to him, although I don't believe it is my place as a psychiatrist to tell people what church to go to—just what type of churches I think are health-producing.

The local church you choose for your children to grow up in will become one of the major influences on their self concepts. If you're in a negativistic, legalistic church that neglects God's grace, you're in the wrong boat! It will permanently damage your child's self-worth. Or if you are in a liberal church, supposing it to be a sinking ship you can save, your children will probably sink with it. I would recommend that you get your family into a church where the Bible is accepted as the errorless Word of God, where souls are being saved, where genuine Christian love is practiced, where God's grace, love, acceptance, and forgiveness are preached (as well as God's justice), and where healthy entertainment and youth activities are available for your children.[4] I am genuinely grieved in my heart when I see the potential so many children have to live the abundant life and to further the cause of Christ, and then realize that thousands of them will never reach that potential because they are being ruined by rigid churches that stand for the wrong things or liberal churches that don't stand for anything!

Solomon said, "Take away the dross from the silver, and there

---

4. For a good description of a spiritually and psychologically healthy church, read Gene A. Getz's book, *The Measure of a Church.*

shall come forth a vessel for the finer" (Prov. 25:4). As Christians, each of us is a silver vessel, made according to God's divine plan. Each of us also is covered, to various extents, by the dross of human error. And each of our children is covered to some extent by the dross of our errors as parents. Underneath that dross, each of us (and each of our children) is a unique silver vessel. Not a single one of us is inferior to any other, though we may each have a different, unique design. We must all strive for spiritual and emotional maturity, placing ourselves and our children in God's hands, so He can remove that dross and use our children and ourselves as vessels of honor rather than vessels of dishonor.

Each human being is extremely important to God. Christ said, "Are not two sparrows sold for a farthing? and one of them shall not fall on the ground without your Father. But the very hairs of your head are all numbered. Fear ye not, therefore, ye are of more value than many sparrows" (Matt. 10:29-31).

Christ also showed us how important we are to Him when He said, "My sheep hear my voice, and I know them, and they follow me: And I give unto them eternal life: and they shall never perish, neither shall any man pluck them out of my hand. My Father, which gave them to me, is greater than all; and no man is able to pluck them out of my Father's hand. I and my Father are one" (John 10:27-30). What security that brings! So many unhealthy churches believe that God is a mean old man holding a whip, just waiting for us to dare to break one of His rules, so He can snap us with the whip or take us out of His hand and flick us off. When these churches read John 3:3 and John 3:7, they stutter, so that it comes out, "Ye must be born again, and again, and again, and again." But the God of the Bible is a God of perfect love and perfect justice, who sent His Son, Jesus Christ, to die on a real cross in order to save us from a real hell. He is a God who loves us so much that He gave us His love letter, the Holy Bible, which contains the principles He wishes us to live by if we want the abundant life. And Christ says He takes those who put their faith in Him and puts them in the palm of His hand, giving them eternal life. And the Father puts His loving hand around Christ's hand, and neither of them will let us out of that secure position that we have in Him by His grace. "For by grace are ye saved through faith; and that not of yourselves: it is the gift of God: Not of works, lest any man should boast" (Eph. 2:8-9).

We may have a long way to go as far as emotional and spiritual maturity is concerned, but we are definitely not inferior, and neither are our children. Several years ago, a friend of mine wore on his coat a button with the letters BPGIFWMY. I asked him what it meant, and he told me, "Be patient, God isn't finished with me yet!" There is a real lesson to be learned from that. We should be as patient with ourselves and with each other as God is.

> O LORD, Thou hast searched me and known me.
> Thou dost know when I sit down and when I rise up;
> Thou dost understand my thought from afar.
> Thou dost scrutinize my path and my lying down,
> And art intimately acquainted with all my ways.
> Even before there is a word on my tongue,
> Behold, O Lord, Thou dost know it all.
> Thou hast enclosed me behind and before,
> And laid Thy hand upon me.
> Such knowledge is too wonderful for me;
> It is too high, I cannot attain to it. . . .
>
> How precious also are Thy thoughts to me, O God!
> How vast is the sum of them!
> If I should count them, they would outnumber the sand.
> When I awake, I am still with Thee.
>
> Search me, O God, and know my heart;
> Try me and know my anxious thoughts;
> And see if there be any hurtful way in me,
> And lead me in the everlasting way.
> —Ps. 139:1-6, 17-18, 23-24, NASV

# 2

## *The Importance of Genuine Love Between Parents*

I want to begin this second chapter of my book with a few comments on love itself—its meaning, its development, and the importance of a healthy husband-wife love relationship in the development of their children's self concepts. A definite majority of the neurotic children I have treated come from homes in which there are *a weak, passive father and a domineering, smothering, overprotecting mother*. Also, in preparation for this book, I have sat for many days in the library of Duke University Medical School pouring over research findings on parent-child relationships—what types of parents produce what types of children. The research literature describes hundreds of syndromes, and in a majority of them, there are a weak, passive father and a domineering, smothering, overprotecting mother. In the bibliography I have listed several hundred of the research articles I have studied and used as primary sources for this book. I have studied these articles with a view to the findings of objective research. I have discarded the non-Christian philosophies and interpretations that clearly disagree with Scripture. In the process I did not have to discard the results of any objective, documented research. I believe the Bible is the totally inspired Word of God, and that it contains no errors whatsoever in its original manuscripts. As a Christian psychiatrist, I use the Bible as the foundation for all my beliefs and practices. I consider my Bible to be God's revealed truth to me. But there are many things that the

Bible does not talk about. The Bible doesn't tell us how to treat
bedwetting, or stuttering, what to do with Mongoloid children,
or how to treat childhood schizophrenia. These are things that we
learn from experience and research.

I have emphasized the first six years the most, because 85
percent of the child's eventual personality will be formed by the
time he is six years old. After age six, all we can do is to try to
modify the other 15 percent of his personality development. Dr.
Gary Collins has stated,

> Developmental psychologists have conducted literally thou-
> sands of studies and the results of these investigations have
> substantially increased our knowledge and understanding of
> the nature of childhood. A survey of some of these psycho-
> logical conclusions could be of value to church leaders and
> Christian parents as they seek to "train up a child in the
> way he should go" (Prov. 22:6).[1]

I have attempted to follow this suggestion by Dr. Collins, a dedicated Christian psychologist and seminary professor. The reader
may be asking how this relates to the importance and meaning
of love. I have mentioned the commonness of the weak father/
smothering mother syndrome in the families of neurotic children.
One of the main reasons that neurotic parent-child relationships
develop is that there already exists a neurotic husband-wife relationship. I don't know how many times I have had a mother bring
her neurotic child to me, and I have put the mother on tranquilizers and the child got better!

The treatment for most child psychiatry problems almost
always involves helping the parents learn better ways to live and
love. If the husband and wife are not getting their love needs
met by their mates, they will look elsewhere for satisfaction. The
husband traditionally gets involved in an outside affair, and the
wife develops a neurotic need for her child to love her. So desperate
is she for her child to love her that she is afraid to spank him
when he needs it—spanking would cause him to stop loving her
for a few minutes or hours. Many of these mothers sleep in separate bedrooms, or even sleep with their children, rather than with
their husbands. They don't want the child to grow up because
of their intense fear of the child leaving them eventually and

---

1. Gary Collins, *Man in Transition,* p. 32.

taking away the only relationship they have. That's why they smother the child, spoil him, make all his decisions for him, and discourage independence. When these children are six, they're afraid and unable to go to school because they are so neurotically involved with their mothers. In their teens, they realize their inadequacies, turn to drugs or alcohol, hate their mothers, and seldom mature. When they eventually marry and have children of their own, the mother extends her attempts to dominate into the new home, smothering the grandchildren and dividing their parents. Generations can be affected by a husband and wife who do not love each other as they should.[2]

What is love, anyway? This is an ancient question the answers to which usually bring little satisfaction. Is it a feeling? Is it an action? Or is it just a figment of our imagination? I believe true love is real, even though the love people *think* they have is frequently imagined. Many people mistakenly think that love is an automatic sensation that comes and stays forever when a person performs some magical ritual, like saying, "I do." Love is more than a mere emotion, even though it has a large emotional component. Love involves an individual's entire spirit, soul, and body. By "spirit," I refer to the part of us that yearns to know God's love and also longs for the love of others. By "soul," I refer to the mind, emotions, and will. Thus emotions are a large component of love, but true love is more than just an emotion. By "body," I refer to the various practical and sometimes physical ways in which we express true love and concern for others whom, over a period of time, we have learned to love on the levels of spirit and soul.

I believe strongly that God has designed us to share our love with others on all three planes: the spiritual plane, emotional plane, and physical plane. It is also important to develop our love relationships in that order. In today's society, the trend is to "love" physically first, which is really not love at all. It's just old-fashioned lust. Unfortunately, our society has cheapened sexual relationships. Sexual communion is a beautiful thing, created by God for the dual role of procreation and the godly person's enjoyment. It provides tremendous relief from sexual tensions. But God intended this physical, sexual communion to be a regular part of married

2. Paul D. Meier, "Self-Acceptance Leads to Mate-Acceptance."

life, warning specifically against fornication, adultery, and homosexuality. He warned that those who commit these sins, just like
those who commit any other sin, will suffer the natural consequences. As a psychiatrist, I have seen many patients whose psychological problems were influenced greatly by these specific sins.
And as a psychiatrist, I have also seen numerous Christian patients
who had sexual hang-ups because of Victorian misconceptions about
what the Bible really says concerning the sexual relationship in
marriage. And what is really sad is the effect of the Victorian
ethic on the children of these husbands and wives. Many Christians
are shocked to find out that the Apostle Paul warned husbands
and wives never to turn each other down for sexual relations,
except during prayer:

> Let the husband fulfill his duty to his wife, and likewise also
> the wife to her husband. The wife does not have authority
> over her own body, but the husband does; and likewise also
> the husband does not have authority over his own body, but
> the wife does. *Stop depriving one another,* except by agree-
> ment for a time that you may devote yourselves to prayer,
> and come together again lest Satan tempt you because of your
> lack of self control.                          —I Cor. 7:3-5, NASV

It is obvious that when marriage partners turn each other down
for sexual relations, and don't seek fulfillment in this area of
their lives, they will have less resistance to the temptations offered by Satan to meet those needs in unscriptural and neurotic
ways. In a Christian marriage, anything the couple mutually
enjoys, in a physical way, that is not harmful to either partner,
is beautiful in the eyes of a Holy God who created them for each
other. It is the physical expression of the true love that exists on
a spiritual and emotional level. It promotes good mental health
in the entire family. Very few people ever reach their true love
potential in the marriage relationship.

Love is not something that is restricted to the marriage relationship. As Christians, we are to love God with all our heart,
soul, and mind, and to love our neighbor as much as we love
ourselves (see Mark 12:30-31). True healthy love of God, self,
and others is essential for good mental health.

True love is not a natural thing. It is learned. It requires
emotional and spiritual maturity. A newborn babe, though loved
by his mother, does not yet know how to love in return. Warmth,

stimulation, and food are his concerns. For the infant, "I love you" really means "I possess you." And yet, an infant's love is a beautiful thing, as primitive as it may be. It feels good to want to be possessed by someone so young. As the infant becomes a young child, his primitive love also grows. He strives to please his parents —most of the time, anyway. The son identifies with his father, and the daughter with her mother, taking on their personality characteristics. But this immature love is still quite selfish, and frequently a technique to manipulate and to avoid punishment. When I saw this one time in one of my sons, I wrote a brief poem about it:

> Who taught my child to love so selfishly?
> "Surely not I!" I quickly say,
> But then when I face reality,
> Part is from Adam, and much is from me.

An adolescent's new-found puppy love, when described in honest terms, frequently means something like, "I want to use you to prove what I am, and to satisfy my physical and ego needs." A naive person feels flattered by this adolescent form of love; an emotionally mature and realistic person may feel physically flattered, but knows that this type of love won't satisfy his or her soul and spirit. *Mature love is patient. Mature love is kind. Mature love seeks the other person's benefit, expecting nothing in return, though appreciative when true love is returned. That's true love!* Most individuals, families, groups, and even nations have learned (and chosen) to love only on the infantile, childish, or adolescent level. Mature, intimate love is found in a minority of adults, some adolescents, and a few exceptionally mature children. These individuals have sought, and acquired, the help of the God of love in reaching this blissful state. God gave the Apostle John the following words to pen for us: "Beloved, let us love one another: for love is of God; and every one that loveth is born of God, and knoweth God. He that loveth not knoweth not God; for God is love" (I John 4:7-8).

Dr. O. Quentin Hyder, a Christian psychiatrist from New York City, has aptly stated:

> It is not surprising that, as they get older, children from Christian homes tend to rebel and fall away from the faith of their parents. They can see the hypocrisy, the inconsistency,

and the prejudice in their parents' lives. Unhappily, they then tend to equate these with the church, and in rejecting their parents' faith they also reject Christ in their own lives. By contrast those Christian homes in which love is paramount produce sons and daughters who themselves devoutly propagate the faith to their own children. *Christian love* is unselfish and unprejudiced. It is patient and humble, tolerant and understanding. It is giving and giving again. It is the opposite of hostility, resentment, and jealousy. It is the gift above all others which fills lives with happiness, satisfaction, security, and inner peace. It is given by God to all who desire that their time in this world should be spent in a higher dimension. "A new commandment I give unto you, That ye love one another; as I have loved you, that ye also love one another. By this shall all men know that ye are my disciples, if ye have love one to another" (John 13:34, 35).[3]

---

3. O. Quentin Hyder, *The Christian's Handbook of Psychiatry*, p. 96.

# How to Teach Your Child
# to Love Himself in a Healthy Way

**3**

The title of this section may sound alien to many Christians who have, unfortunately, been brought up in churches where they were taught that self-hatred is a virtue rather than a sin. Many were taught that salvation is acquired by obeying denominational rules and regulations, self-punishment, tithing, hiding all emotions, attending all church services, and by constantly reminding yourself of how worthless you really are. These Christians become chronically depressed, and that's why I see so many of them in my office. Dr. O. Quentin Hyder talks about perfectionism, legalistic Christians, and forgiveness when he states:

> Perfection in this life is categorically impossible. If it were possible, we would need no redemption in Christ. But striving toward perfection in the sense of trying to live a life in conformity with the will of God is not only possible but our aim as a Christian.... We cannot attain perfection but we must strive toward it, not in the sense of trying to earn our salvation by good works, but as an act of gratitude to Christ for having already saved us by His atoning death. Unhappily, legalistic Christians cannot see this. They have heard it a hundred times from the pulpit, but they have great difficulty accepting forgiveness. They are often people whose parents were very demanding, never satisfied with their efforts, and unforgiving of their failures. These emotional pressures, especially on impressionable, sensitive, and vulnerable children, lead to an inability in adult life to believe that it is possible

to be forgiven. They think that forgiveness is something for
nothing. This is erroneous. Indeed it costs nothing to become
a Christian initially, but it costs everything to *be* a Christian
and live up to the pledge made at the moment of commitment to Christ. It costs absolute surrender of the will to God
to live the sort of life, albeit imperfect, which God intended
for us in this present world. Paul specifically admonished the
Galatians against legalism and perfectionism in his letter
to them. They were teaching the heresy that good works were
necessary to supplement the redemptive work of Christ in salvation. Paul wrote: "Received ye the Spirit by works of law,
or by the hearing of faith? Are ye so foolish? having begun
in the Spirit, are ye now made perfect by the flesh?" (Galatians 3:2-3). To the Romans he wrote: "... by the deeds of
the law shall no flesh be justified in his sight" (Romans 3:20)
and to the Colossians: "... ye are complete in him, which is
the head of all principality and power" (Colossians 2:10).[1]

A majority of all the depressive neurotics I have treated personally have been Christians from legalistic, negativistic churches.
They have the basic position in life that transactional analysts
call the "I'm not O.K. and you're not O.K." position, or else the
"I'm not O.K., but you're O.K." position, the latter being somewhat less severe than the former. "I'm not O.K. and you're not
O.K." is the most emotionally harmful position a person can have.
Christians who have been taught (and believe) this position withdraw from others and have neither self-worth nor genuine love
relationships with others, the two main requirements of mental
health. Many of them have a nervous breakdown and become
psychotic because reality—or at least reality as they see it—is too
painful to bear. If they don't obey all the laws of the denomination, they are told that they will lose their salvation. What an
unbearable, frustrating life that must be—to gain and lose one's
salvation and never know for sure if heaven or hell is waiting
at death's door.

The Apostle John told us, "And this is the record, that God
hath given to us eternal life, and this life is in his Son. He that
hath the Son hath life; and he that hath not the Son hath not life.
These things have I written unto you that believe on the name
of the Son of God; *that ye may know that ye have eternal life,*
and that ye may believe on the name of the Son of God" (I John

---

1. O. Quentin Hyder, *The Christian's Handbook of Psychiatry*, p. 116.

5:11-13). The Apostle Paul told us, "For by grace are ye saved through faith; and that not of yourselves: it is the *gift of God: not of works,* lest any man should boast" (Eph. 2:8-9). He also said, *"All things are lawful unto me, but all things are not expedient: all things are lawful for me, but I will not be brought under the power of any"* (I Cor. 6:12). And so I would like to ask legalistic churches the same question Paul asked the church at Galatia, "Have ye suffered so many things in vain?" (Gal. 3:4).

I know a Christian physician who suffered more than a year of mental anguish and depression in spite of my best attempts to help him, until he finally accepted the principle of God's grace. What a difference in him now, as he continues life as a confident Christian physician, eager to serve God out of love rather than obligation.

Is it really God's plan for us to love ourselves, and our children to love themselves? If by love of self you mean vanity and pride, the answer is, "Definitely not!" When God lists the seven sins He hates the most, He leaves off such sins as adultery and divorce; but number one on his "top seven" list is the sin of having "a proud look" (see Prov. 6:16-19). This is referring to a "better than thou" attitude. It is the "I'm O.K., but you're *not* O.K." position of sociopathic criminals and drug pushers.[2] No, I am not referring to sinful pride and vanity when I talk about the importance of self-worth. I'm talking about loving ourselves in a healthy way—in a way that pleases God because it makes us more useful in His service, and because He loves us and wants us to experience the abundant life.

Mark 12:28-34 tells of a legal expert—a scribe—who came to Jesus and asked Him which of the commandments is the most important. Jesus answered, "The foremost is, 'Hear, O Israel; The LORD our God is one LORD; and you shall love the LORD your God with all your soul, and with all your mind, and with all your strength.' The second is this, 'You shall *love your neighbor as yourself.'* There is no other commandment greater than these" (Mark 12:29-31, NASV). The Apostle Paul tells us, "So husbands ought also to love their own wives as their own bodies. He who loves his own wife *loves himself"* (Eph. 5:28, NASV). A person who has a negative attitude toward himself will also be

2. Thomas A. Harris, *I'm O.K.—You're O.K.,* pp. 48-50.

quite critical of others. A person who doesn't love himself in a healthy way will find it impossible to develop genuine love relationships with others. Two of the most important concepts I learned from my psychiatric training, both of which agree totally with Scripture, are: *(1) You cannot truly love others until you learn to love yourself in a healthy way; (2) Lack of self-worth is the basis of most psychological problems.*

One important aspect of loving yourself in a way that will please God involves taking care of your body. If you want your children to take proper care of their bodies, you need to take care of your own. The Apostle Paul asked, "Know ye not that ye are the temple of God, and that the Spirit of God dwelleth in you?" (I Cor. 3:16). And further, "What? know ye not that your body is the temple of the Holy Ghost which is in you, which ye have of God, and ye are not your own? For ye are bought with a price: therefore glorify God in your body, and in your spirit, which are God's" (I Cor. 6:19-20). Paul called our bodies "the temple of the living God" (II Cor. 6:16). These passages of Scripture make it quite plain that our bodies are very important to God. In fact, "the very hairs of your head are all numbered" (Matt. 10:30).

The fact that our bodies are God's temples has some serious implications. It implies that our families, including ourselves, should have healthy eating and sleeping habits, as well as adequate exercise and recreation. When a person becomes more and more irritable and gets angry over seemingly trite circumstances, his personal physician knows that he is probably either anemic or psychologically depressed—or both. Anemia is especially common in females, because of their monthly menstrual cycles. Iron supplements are frequently all that is needed. If your teenager starts fad-eating or crash dieting, leaving protein out of his diet, he may become anemic and more irritable and rebellious although this is not the usual cause of adolescent rebellion. Overeating can be just as detrimental to our physical and emotional health. The incidence of heart attacks and other fatal illnesses takes a sharp rise when we weigh about 20 percent more than our recommended weight. If we overeat, we also have increased feelings of guilt and loss of self-esteem. It is somewhat contradictory to tell our children to exercise self-control in their lives while they watch us exercising poor self-control in areas such as eating.

Taking care of God's "temple" also implies healthy sleeping

habits. I have seen many zealous Christians totally ignore their need for sleep, only to find themselves burned out a little while later. God made sleep for the healing of both our bodies and our minds. Sleep is much more important for mental health than it is for physical rest, although it serves both functions. The average adult dreams approximately twenty minutes out of every ninety minutes that he sleeps. Children spend an even higher percentage of their sleep-time dreaming. We remember dreaming, however, only when we happen to wake up during a dream. That's why it may seem to us that we seldom dream, even though we do several times every night. It has been theorized, and I think correctly, that in our dreams, bizarre as they may be, we symbolically reduce emotional tensions, satisfying our unconscious conflicts.[3] Going without sleep for two or three days, many normal people will begin to exhibit psychotic tendencies, such as delusions and paranoid ideation.[4]

Our dreams are believed to be mediated by a chemical in the brain known as serotonin. Before entering medical school, I was a graduate student in human physiology at Michigan State University, spending much of my time doing research on various effects of serotonin.[5] Among the things I learned about this chemical which God created to help us stay mentally healthy is that tryptophan—which our bodies use to make serotonin—is found in high concentrations in milk, certain fruits (bananas, for example), and certain meats (like liver). Through electroencephalograms I learned that babies spend about nine of their sleeping hours dreaming. Maybe that's one reason why babies need so much milk. I also learned that LSD is a serotonin antagonist—interfering with the serotonin in the brains of drug users who are foolish enough to take it. I have seen a number of psychiatric illnesses which were precipitated by LSD, including a sharp, B+ average college student whose roommate talked him into taking LSD just so he would know what it was like. He had a normal response to it, so he tried it again sometime later. But this time it disordered his brain chemistry to such an extent that he had to drop out

---

3. Walter Bonine, *The Clinical Use of Dreams*, pp. 229-30.
4. S. R. Clemes, et al., "Effect of REM Sleep Deprivation on Psychological Functioning."
5. Paul D. Meier, "The Cardiovascular Effects of 5-Hydroxytryptamine (Serotonin)."

of college, and several months later, when I saw him, he was
still unable to concentrate long enough to even enjoy reading a
newspaper.

In graduate school, I also learned that the average adult needs
about eight hours of sleep a night, although some can get by on
six hours, while others require ten hours. Teenagers need about
nine hours a night, elementary school children about ten, preschoolers about twelve hours, and babies about sixteen to eighteen
hours of sleep per twenty-four hours. If an individual, at any age,
continually gets less than his required amount of sleep, he's headed
for trouble. The best way to get straight A's in school—if that happens to be one of your ambitions—is to study every day in a quiet
room, get some exercise and recreation, eat the right foods, stay
in tune spiritually, get some fellowship with others, memorize
Bible verses for mental exercise (and for spiritual maturity as well),
and get eight hours of sleep every night, especially the night before
a big test.

Recreation is also important. Many Christians are overly strict
on themselves. They think watching a weekend football game,
hiking in the mountains, or even playing games with friends, is a
waste of time. They are very wrong. "All work and no play
makes Jack a dull boy" applies to parents as well as to children.
If a person spent all of his time in recreation, he would, of course,
accomplish nothing for the Lord. But there needs to be a happy
balance, and God intended it that way. Christ Himself spent a
great percentage of His three-year ministry camping out in the
mountains, sometimes with His disciples (especially Peter and
John), and sometimes alone. There in the mountains, Christ could
get away from the demanding crowds, relax, meditate, commune
with the Father, enjoy the world that He Himself had created,
and share intimately with His chosen disciples. Christ spent most
of the first half of those three years just selecting and building His
disciples. That is how Christ, who was God in the flesh, decided
He would have the most effective ministry.[6]

I have studied the life of Christ carefully in order to plan
my own activities in accordance with Christ's teachings and the
example of His life. We can see from all this that even such

------

6. For an interesting discussion of how Christ budgeted His time during His
three-year ministry, see Robert E. Coleman, *The Master Plan of Evangelism*.

mundane things as being sure you and your children get enough recreation, a proper diet, and adequate amounts of sleep are vitally important to the development of self-worth. The kinds of spiritual food you feed your children, of course, are even more important than the kinds of physical food. The overall spiritual atmosphere of the home, including family devotions, the music played, the type of TV shows watched, the neatness and cleanliness of the home environment, the regularity of bedtime and meals, spiritual insights shared, scriptural plaques on the walls, the parental attitudes—all enter into the development of spiritual self-worth.

One extremely important area that we will discuss in some detail at this point is how we, as parents, should handle sin in the lives of our children. This includes some important concepts we can pass on to our children about how *they* can handle temptations in their own lives. In psychiatry, we learn that an adult's attitudes toward God are influenced greatly by his attitudes toward his own father while he was growing up. This places a great deal of responsibility on those of us who are fathers. For quite a while at Duke University I followed a patient whose father was a dedicated cardiologist—so dedicated, in fact, that he was away from home practically all the time taking care of his medical practice. When he was home, he was cold, indifferent, and tired. About the only comments my patient ever received from his father were negative ones, correcting him for being imperfect. My patient, a brilliant young Ph.D. now, still went back home from time to time, wanting so badly for his father to accept him, but he continued to receive primarily criticism, that is, if his father was home at all. My patient carried around tremendous guilt feelings all the time for not being perfect. He falsely blamed himself for the lack of acceptance by his father. Several times I shared my own personal faith in the God of love, as well as God's offer of salvation and forgiveness, but to no apparent avail. This patient was a devout atheist. And I would have expected him to be, given the kind of father image he grew up with. In general—and this is with some exceptions, of course—my experience has been that patients whose fathers were gone a lot, and negativistic when they were home, or patients who had no father at all, tend to be atheists. In their subconscious minds, they want to believe there is no God because they resent the fact that they had no father, or one who was nearly always absent and negativistic. Oftentimes they would like to repress their fathers right out of their minds. But since they can't totally repress the existence of their earthly fathers, they fool themselves into thinking there is no God, or heavenly Father.

Patients who had cold, passive, and frequently absent fathers tend to believe that God is some cold, indifferent being out in space somewhere. Their earthly fathers knew their children existed, but were neither positive nor negative with their children—they more or less ignored them. And so these patients believe there is a God who knows they exist, but doesn't really care or even pay attention to mere earthlings. Patients who had rigid, demanding, negativistic, overly punitive fathers have tended to fall into two categories: some of these patients hated their fathers so much that they became atheists as an unconscious rebellion against the existence of their fathers; on the other hand, most of them believe that there is a God, but that God is a mean old man up there, holding a whip and just daring us to break one of His rules· so He can snap us with it! Many of the latter group, surprisingly, are Christians. These are the Christians who tend to migrate to legalistic, negativistic churches, where it will be easier for them to live up to their unrealistic concept of God's standards, based upon the standards of their earthly fathers. These patients wanted their earthly fathers to accept them, so they became rigidly perfectionistic in order to win their fathers' approval, which they seldom won anyway. In the same manner, they are afraid of God and His punishment, but they want His acceptance and the only way they think they can get it—deep down anyway—is by becoming rigidly perfectionistic and denying their own natural feelings of anger and aggression. They never really feel forgiven. They project their own anger outward, convincing themselves that people are angry at them. This is their usual way of lying to themselves about their own anger. In psychiatry, this is called paranoid ideation. They withdraw from all the people they imagine are so angry at them, criticizing these other people excessively, to justify in their own minds withdrawing from them. They have to believe they are correct—probably because the real God of love is convincing them that they are wrong—so they associate only with other legalistic, negativistic people. Many of them join extremely right-wing, semidelusional political organizations and "religious" groups. I know of thousands of Christians, whom I believe are genuine, born-again believers, who are like ostriches with their heads in the sand, thinking they are the only ones who are right, or the only ones going to heaven. The pent-up anger they have frequently causes them to become chronically depressed.

On the other hand, patients who have had a father who loved them, accepted them in spite of imperfections, spent time with them, and punished them when they did things that he knew were bad for them in the long run, generally have a healthy concept of God. They believe in the existence of a God who loves them, accepts them, listens to them, and disciplines them out of love. If they haven't already put their faith in Jesus Christ, they do so readily when I show them God's simple plan of salvation.

I have also had a group of patients whose fathers were the overly sweet type, who pampered them, bought them whatever they pointed at in stores, seldom contradicted them, and hardly ever punished them. These people tend to be religious liberals who are quite idealistic, deny the sinful nature of man, and pretend that there is no literal hell, in spite of the fact that Christ spent more time (as recorded in the New Testament) warning people about the reality of hell than He did discussing heaven. In Christ's teachings, there are nearly twice as many verses about a literal hell as there are verses telling us about heaven. These people are a traveling salesman's delight, because they are so naive and believe in the basic goodness of all mankind. Sociopaths and alcoholics will get everything they can from these people, including room, board, and financial support for their bad habits. To be aware of the fact that someone is being blatantly selfish and lying to them would ruin their deluded belief in man's basic goodness, so they use a tremendous amount of denial to lie to themselves about such situations.

I hope those of us who are fathers, or who someday will be fathers, will grasp the heavy responsibility that God has given us. I sometimes wake up at night, and go to my children's bedrooms. I pull their covers up to be sure they're warm, and bend over to give them a soft kiss. Then I frequently get down on my knees beside their beds and rededicate myself to God, to be the kind of father He wants me to be, because I know God loves them even more than I ever could. And I thank God for trusting me with that responsibility.

Let's look at some more right and wrong ways to respond

to guilt, temptations, and sin in the lives of our children. First, I want to differentiate between true guilt and false guilt. Freud seemed to think that all guilt is false guilt—that guilt itself is a bad thing. Most of the psychiatrists I have studied under and worked with agreed with the Freudian view—that guilt is always an unhealthy thing. I disagree strongly. True guilt, in my opinion, is the uncomfortable, inner awareness that we have violated a moral law of God. It is produced partially by the conviction of God's Holy Spirit, and partially by our own conscience. Our conscience is what Freud called the superego. Our conscience is molded by many influences in our environment, such as what our parents taught was right or wrong, what our parents practiced as being right or wrong (which isn't always the same as what they taught), what our church taught was right or wrong, what the people in our church practiced as being right or wrong, what our friends thought was right or wrong, what our teachers thought was right or wrong. If we studied the Bible, our conscience would also be molded by what the Bible says is right or wrong, but even that is influenced by our own interpretations and sometimes misinterpretations. No two consciences are exactly alike. God's Holy Spirit is always right, but our consciences are frequently wrong. Someone with an immature conscience can do something wrong and not know that it is wrong, in which case his conscience will not bother him. Or we can have an overgrown conscience if we have been taught that everything is sin, and our conscience in that case will bother us even when we do things that God Himself does not consider wrong. This is what I call false guilt: feeling guilty for something that God and His Word in no way condemn.

On the other hand, true guilt is valuable. God uses it to influence us to change our minds about what we are doing. That's what repentance is all about. Then when we do what is right, instead of what is wrong, we will be in fellowship with God, and we will like ourselves more too. Doing what is wrong lowers our self-worth. Doing what is right greatly improves our self-worth. In my experience as a psychiatrist, when people come to me and tell me they feel guilty, it has usually been true guilt. They feel guilty because they *are* guilty. And straightening out what they were doing that is wrong sometimes is all that is needed to straighten out their feelings of depression. But I have also had many Christians come to me, especially from the legalistic churches, to express feelings of guilt for things that the Bible in no way condemns. They may feel guilty for being tempted, for example. It's no sin to be tempted. But it *is* a sin to dwell on that temptation and yield to it. Christ Himself was tempted—"For we have not an high priest which cannot be touched with the feeling of our infirmities; but was in all points tempted like as we are, yet without sin" (Heb. 4:15).

The Apostle Paul talked about Christians who believed it a sin to eat meat that had been offered to idols (see I Cor. 8). Back in Paul's day, the people would bring sacrifices to the pagan temples. Then the priests would cut up the meat and sell it to earn some spending money. They would sell this meat at a discount, compared to meat prices at the nearby butcher store. In some towns Paul preached in, the Christians thought it was immoral to buy that meat, since it had been offered to idols. I can see why they would think that, and I admire them for wanting to do what they thought was right. Christians in other towns thought it was perfectly fine to buy meat that had been offered to idols. It was much cheaper, and they could invest their money in better ways than to waste it on the expensive meat at the butcher shop. The Apostle Paul said that God Himself had revealed to him that eating meat that had been offered to idols was all right. God told him there was nothing immoral about it in His eyes. But He told Paul not to show off his liberty in front of Christians with weaker consciences (weaker in the sense of being more easily offended), so whenever Paul was in a town where Christians thought it was wrong, he wouldn't eat meat which had been offered to idols. That was diplomacy, not hypocrisy, and I'm sure Paul did it out of love and empathy. He had more important things to teach them, and he didn't want to hurt his testimony. That would diminish his effectiveness. He knew that when people make up their minds something is wrong, not even a direct message from God can change their minds!

Paul Tournier, the Christian psychiatrist from Switzerland, calls true guilt "value guilt," and he calls false guilt, "functional guilt."[7] Tournier says:

> A feeling of "functional guilt" is one which results from social suggestion, fear of taboos or of losing the love of others. A

---

7. Paul Tournier, *Guilt and Grace,* p. 64.

feeling of "value guilt" is the genuine consciousness of having betrayed an authentic standard; it is a free judgment of the self by the self. On this assumption, there is a complete opposition between these two guilt-producing mechanisms, the one acting by social suggestion, the other by moral conviction.... "False guilt" is that which comes as a result of the judgments and suggestions of men. "True guilt" is that which results from divine judgment.... Therefore real guilt is often something quite different from that which constantly weights us down, because of our fear of social judgment and the disapproval of men. We become independent of them in proportion as we depend on God.[8]

Dr. O. Quentin Hyder states that:

The causes of false guilt stem back to childhood upbringing. Too rigid a superego or conscience can only be developed by too rigid expectations or standards imposed by parents. For example, parents who excessively blame, condemn, judge, and accuse their children when they fail to match up to their expectations cause them to grow up with a warped idea of what appropriate standards are. Unforgiving parents who punish excessively increase guilt. Adequate and proper punishment given in love and with explanation removes guilt. Some parents give too little encouragement, praise, thanks, congratulations, or appreciation. Instead they are never satisfied. However well the child performs in any area of school, play, sports, or social behavior, the parents make him feel they are dissatisfied because he did not do even better. The child sees himself as a constant failure, and he is made to feel guilty because he failed. He does not realize at his young age what harm his parents are doing to his future feelings of self-worth. He grows up convinced that anything short of perfection is failure. However hard he tries, and even if he actually performs to the maximum that he is capable of, he grows up feeling guilty and inferior.

As an adult he suffers from neurotic or false guilt, low self-esteem, insecurity, and a self-depreciatory pessimistic outlook on all his endeavors and ambitions. He then blames himself and this leads to anger turned inward. He attempts to inflict punishment upon himself because of his feelings of unworthiness. His failures deserve to be judged and punished, and since no one else can do it for him, he punishes himself. This intropunitive retribution, part anger and part

---

8. Ibid., pp. 64-70.

hostility, leads inevitably to depression. It can also cause psychosomatic complaints and inappropriate sorts of actions.[9]

Dr. Hyder says the only treatment for false guilt is understanding it and evaluating it for what it really is. Feelings of bitterness and pride need to be separated from what the patient interprets as feelings of guilt. The patient needs to understand that he has no right to condemn himself—only God has that right, and Christians should leave judging and condemning to God alone. Then he needs to set new goals for himself that are realistically attainable, and no longer compare himself to others who are more gifted than he is in specific areas. Instead, he should compare his performance with what he believes God expects of him. God doesn't expect us or our children to achieve sinless perfection in this life. But He does want us to seek His will in our lives to the best of our abilities.[10]

The Apostle Paul compares entering the Christian life to entering the Sabbath Day rest (see Heb. 4:1-9). God wants us to rest in Him, and in His power. Martin Luther struggled for years with the legalistic expectations of his religion, until he learned that "the just shall live by faith" (Rom. 1:17), and that "man is justified by faith without the deeds of the law" (Rom. 3:28). Then he trusted God's grace rather than his own good works to save him. In 1529, Luther penned the famous hymn, "A Mighty Fortress Is Our God." In this hymn, Luther expresses his appreciation of the fact that our God is an all-powerful God and that we should let Him win our battles for us, resting in His power rather than our own. In the second verse of that hymn, Luther refers to God by the Old Testament name, *Lord Sabaoth,* which in Hebrew means "Lord of Hosts," and refers to God's omnipotence. Let's take a look at that second verse:

> Did we in our own strength confide,
> Our striving would be losing;
> Were not the right Man on our side,
> The Man of God's own choosing.
> Dost ask who that may be?
> Christ Jesus, it is He;
> *Lord Sabaoth His Name,*

---

9. Hyder, *Handbook,* pp. 121-22.
10. Ibid.

> From age to age the same,
> And *He* must win the battle.

We have already discussed the notion some Christians have that God is a mean old man, holding a whip, who is just waiting to crack us with that whip whenever we break one of His rigid rules. But the God of the Bible is not like that at all. God is perfect love, and perfect justice. God didn't make rules so He could whip us when we break one. God gave us principles to live by so we can enjoy the abundant life and the fruits of the Spirit. God has set up natural laws for human nature just as for physical nature. If we do not abide by God's principles, we will suffer the natural consequences He has established. Sin is the transgression of those laws or principles which God has set up (see I John 3:4). All of us have sinned many times. Paul tells us that "all have sinned, and come short of the glory of God" (Rom. 3:23). He tells us that the ultimate reward for those sins is eternal death in hell, but that in perfect love and grace, God offers us the free gift of eternal life and forgiveness for all of our sins—past, present, and future (see John 1:12; 3:16; Rom. 6:23; 10:13; Eph. 2:8-9).

When a person becomes a Christian, he is a new creation. Paul tells us that "if any man be in Christ, he is a new creature: old things are passed away; behold, all things are become new" (II Cor. 5:17). But this does not mean he has reached sinless perfection. Far from it. *Sanctification,* which is the process of gradually becoming more and more like Christ, now takes place in the growing Christian's life. Just as a newborn babe needs milk, the newly reborn spiritual babe—the new Christian—needs a lot of spiritual milk. The Apostle Peter said, "As newborn babes, desire the sincere milk of the word, that ye may grow thereby" (I Peter 2:2). The "word" means God's Word, of course—the Bible. Daily devotions are a must for continued growth in spiritual and emotional maturity. I began reading my Bible every day when I was ten years old. There's no reason why our own children can't start even sooner. We began using an illustrated Bible story book for our oldest son when he was two years old, and when he turned four, my wife started to teach him short Bible verses. Recall the time Christ's disciples were getting ready to chase some children away so He wouldn't have to bother with them, but Christ told His disciples, "Suffer the little children to come unto me, and forbid them not: for of such is the kingdom of God" (Mark 10:14).

Then Christ explained to His disciples that even adults have to accept Him with the simple faith of a little child in order to become a part of God's kingdom. Thus, we can be assured that God desires to be in communion with our children, and that their meditations on God and His Word will help them overcome temptations. Devotions are especially important during those four traumatic years between twelve and sixteen, when your sons and daughters grow from being boys and girls into men and women, with all the associated hormone changes, impulses, cravings, and feelings of guilt and inadequacy.

The Apostle Paul said, "There hath no temptation taken you but such as is *common to man:* but God is faithful, who will not suffer you to be tempted above that ye are able; but will with the temptation also *make a way to escape,* that ye may be able to bear it" (I Cor. 10:13). This verse was a tremendous help to me when I memorized it as a young teenager, and it continues to be. Paul also said, "And my God shall *supply all your needs* according to His riches in glory in Christ Jesus" (Phil. 4:19, NASV). The human body, soul, and spirit have a multitude of needs. Satan will usually tempt us through our natural physical and emotional needs. These needs include the need for air, food, water, stimulation, sex, love, self-worth, power, aggression, comfort, security, and relief from psychic tensions. Many Christians have been erroneously taught that living the Christian life means totally denying many of these natural needs. The Christian may be called upon by God to deny some of his wants, but God has already promised to supply all of our needs. There's a difference. No wonder so many people are afraid to become Christians. They have been told that becoming a Christian means denying many natural needs. What foolishness! God created these needs within us. He can use all of the needs in our lives for His own glory. He promised us in Philippians 4:19 that He would *supply* all our needs, not *deny* them. But He wants to supply them in *His way,* and according to *His principles of love.* Satan wants to supply these same needs in his way, according to his principles of selfishness, greed, and hate. Our needs are not temptations. Satan's ways of meeting them are the temptations. Our natural human tendency is to meet our needs in Satan's ways. It takes the New Birth and spiritual insights to see how we can meet these natural needs in God's ways, with *much greater ultimate joy and satisfaction.*

Take the need for sex, for instance. God made sex and God made the need for sex. God made the male and female sex hormones that influence our sexual drives. In males, they reach their peak in the late teens. In females, they don't reach their peak until the early thirties. I don't know why God made it that way, but I'm sure He had a reason. I imagine the temptations during the late teenage years would be much greater than they already are if male and female reached their peaks at the same time. *But God has provided a way to satisfy those sexual needs—through an intimate marriage.*

God has also provided ways to relieve sexual tensions in single males, such as "wet dreams" during sleep at night. That serotonin really works overtime during the teenage years! I'm sure that God uses these unconscious dreams in disguised symbolic language to release sexual tensions in a way that will not produce guilt feelings in the individual. I personally do not recommend masturbation. The Bible never mentions it specifically, but does warn us to "abstain from fleshly lusts, which war against the soul" (I Peter 2:11). Teenage patients who talk to me about masturbation almost always express guilt feelings about it, and their guilt is usually about their thoughts rather than the action itself. I usually inform them that my medical books say that 99 percent of males masturbate and that the other 1 percent are usually lying about it. Then I tell them my personal opinion, that they would probably feel less guilt if they would stop and allow God to relieve their sexual tensions through wet dreams. Many of them are relieved to find out that they are not the only ones who have ever done this, or that it is not the unpardonable sin. I let them know that some godly men think there is nothing wrong with it, but that my own opinion is that it stirs up fleshly lusts which war against the soul. I highly recommend that you fathers discuss this topic privately with your teenage sons, and you mothers with your daughters, since 60 percent of females practice it regularly also. I recommend that you approach it matter-of-factly, with an accepting attitude. You would probably be surprised how much things like this plague teenagers as well as adults.

Frequent social contacts with spiritually mature members of the opposite sex are also a healthy outlet. I personally will never allow my sons or daughters to date anyone who is not a growing Christian. When they are eighteen years old and go off to college, they'll be on their own. But until then, they'll have my conscience to live with as well as their own. But Christian dating meets the sexual needs of their spirit and soul. I usually recommend group dating at age fourteen, double dating at age fifteen, and single dating at age sixteen, for teenagers of average maturity. Allowing your teenagers to date ahead of this schedule will usually subject them to more temptations than they are able to handle. Their bodies mature more quickly than their emotional levels. Those Christians who say that our sexual needs—spiritual, emotional, or physical—are dirty or sinful are saying that God made a mistake in creating them within us. In fact, a portion of our brain (known as the limbic brain) was specifically designed by God to handle, among other things, the sexual drives in our life.

The conclusion of this discussion about temptations is that we should not deny our natural needs. Nor should we meet them in Satan's ways. Either of these methods of dealing with our needs would only serve to create even more intense temptations. We should meet all our needs in God's ways, including our sexual needs, and thus take away Satan's power to tempt us. The Christian life will be much easier if our needs are being met. God wants them to be. If there are no unsatisfied needs, there will be no temptations. So teach these concepts to your children, and tell them that the next time they are tempted, they should stop to think about which of their needs they have not been meeting lately. Then recommend that they ask God to help them to meet that need in a way that will be pleasing to Him rather than Satan. This will do tremendous things for their self-worth. It will relieve a lot of guilt. It will also constantly remind them that God loves them and is concerned about their everyday needs. And your accepting attitude will show them, at least on a subconscious level, that God is also quite understanding and accepting of the struggles and temptations they go through. Self-worth comes from doing what we know is right, and not doing those things that we believe are wrong. When we do things that we know are selfish and sinful, we lose self-worth. There's no way around it. And emotional problems are sure to follow as our self-worth continues to depreciate in value. It's bad enough to have our money depreciate. So let's invest in something that can appreciate in value—our own self-worth and the self-worth of our children. God admonishes us, "Cast not away therefore your confidence, which hath great recompence of reward" (Heb. 10:35). If our children choose Satan's ways to meet their needs, they will be casting away their confidence in their own good character. Encourage them rather to enter the "Sabbath Rest" described in Hebrews and simply to turn their lives over to God, relying on *His power* to help them live by *His principles,* so they can develop *His way of thinking* and thoroughly enjoy the *abundant life.*

Even the vast complexity of our human bodies teaches us that we are of great worth to the God who created us for His glory. In an average day, the average human being will breathe over 28,000 times, inhaling about 436 cubic feet of air. His heart will beat over 100,000 times and will pump over 250 pounds of blood per hour. He will use over 450 major muscles and 9 billion brain cells. His blood cells will travel thousands of miles. His body is made up of about 60 trillion cells. Dividing them up, he could give 15,000 cells to each man, woman, and child on the planet earth. And each cell contains thousands of enzymes, ribosomes, golgi apparatuses, endoplasmic reticula, DNA, RNA, and hundreds of other minute structures that all work together like a complete factory. The average human has about 20 billion brain cells and nerve cells, and they are arranged with millions of interconnections like a very complex computer. Scientists have estimated that to build a computer with the capabilities and circuitry of the human brain, they would need a building the size of the Pentagon to house it. Surely we are fearfully and wonderfully made, as the Bible tells us (see Ps. 139:14).

If the blood cells of an average human were lined up in single file, they would reach all the way to the moon and halfway back. Christ tells us that a sparrow doesn't fall to the ground without the Father knowing about it—and we are much more important than those sparrows—so much so that even the hairs of our head are numbered (see Matt. 10:29-33). God said of man, "For I have created him for my glory, I have formed him; yea, I have made him" (Isa. 43:7). If any of you ever start believing Satan's lie that you are inferior, or if your children ever express to you the feeling that they are inferior, just turn to Psalm 139. Psalm 139 is God's prescription for feelings of inferiority. I want to conclude this section on how to develop self-worth in your children by again quoting portions of that psalm.

O LORD, YOU have examined my heart and know everything about me. You know when I sit or stand. When far away you know my every thought. You chart the path ahead of me, and tell me where to stop and rest. Every moment, you know where I am. You know what I am going to say before I even say it. You both precede and follow me, and place your hand of blessing on my head.

This is too glorious, too wonderful to believe! I can never be lost to your Spirit! I can never get away from my God! If I go up to heaven, you are there; if I go down to the place of the dead, you are there. If I ride the morning winds to the farthest oceans, even there your hand will guide me, your strength will support me. If I try to hide in the darkness, the night becomes light around me. For even darkness cannot hide from God; to you the night shines as bright as day. Darkness and light are both alike to you.

You made all the delicate, inner parts of my body, and knit them together in my mother's womb. Thank you for making me so wonderfully complex! It is amazing to think about. Your workmanship is marvelous—and how well I know it. You were there while I was being formed in utter seclusion! You saw me before I was born and scheduled each day of my life before I began to breathe. Every day was recorded in your Book!

How precious it is, Lord, to realize that you are thinking about me constantly! I can't even count how many times a day your thoughts turn towards me. And when I waken in the morning, you are still thinking of me!

...Search me, O God, and know my heart; test my thoughts. Point out anything you find in me that makes you sad, and lead me along the path of everlasting life.

—Ps. 139:1-18, 23-24, LB

# PART TWO

## From Conception to Age Six:
### General Principles

# Those First Six Years

Many psychiatrists estimate on the basis of their studies that approximately 85 percent of the adult personality is already formed by the time the individual is *six years old*. Imagine that! A brand new baby, born in America today, will probably live to be seventy-five years old, and with new scientific discoveries, that may end up being extended to eighty-five or ninety. But how that baby's parents train him or her during those crucial first six years will determine how that individual will enjoy and succeed in life during the other seventy or eighty years. God has given us parents a tremendous responsibility! Dr. Gary Collins, Professor of Pastoral Psychology and Counseling at Trinity Evangelical Seminary, states:

> Developmental psychologists have conducted literally thousands of studies, and the results of these investigations have substantially increased our knowledge and understanding of the nature of childhood. A survey of some of these psychological conclusions could be of value to church leaders and Christian parents as they seek to "train up a child in the way he should go" (Proverbs 22:6).[1]

The Communist Party and the Roman Catholic Church have emphasized the importance of those early years. I believe that those of us in the evangelical community must also be aware of the

1. Gary Collins, *Man in Transition,* p. 32.

45

important responsibility God has given those of us who have children, especially if they are under six years of age.

God's concern for children is quite evident throughout Scripture. Mark records, "And they brought young children to him, that he should touch them: and his disciples rebuked those that brought them" (Mark 10:13). The disciples obviously thought Christ was too busy talking to adults to waste His time with children. They must have thought that "children should be seen and not heard." Mark goes on to record that "when Jesus saw it, he was much displeased, and said unto them, Suffer the little children to come unto me, and forbid them not: for of such is the kingdom of God. Verily I say unto you, Whosoever shall not receive the kingdom of God as a little child, he shall not enter therein. And he took them up in his arms, put his hands upon them, and blessed them" (Mark 10:14-16). God's concern for children was also made evident by Matthew:

> At the same time came the disciples unto Jesus, saying, Who is the greatest in the kingdom of heaven? And Jesus called a little child unto him, and set him in the midst of them, and said, Verily I say unto you, Except ye be converted, and become as little children, ye shall not enter into the kingdom of heaven. Whosoever therefore shall humble himself as this little child, the same is greatest in the kingdom of heaven. And whoso shall receive one such little child in my name receiveth me. But whoso shall offend one of these little ones which believe in me, it were better for him that a millstone were hanged about his neck, and that he were drowned in the depth of the sea. *Woe unto the world because of offences!*                          —Matt. 18:1-7

I would like to share with you one more warning God has given us about children. It is a warning that changed my whole outlook on the vast importance of child-rearing. It is a warning that has given me more determination as I carry on my work in family psychotherapy as a Christian psychiatrist. It is also a warning that was influential in stirring up my desire to practice some preventative psychiatry, especially among my fellow Christians. That crucial warning from God is worded as follows: *"For I, the Lord your God, am a jealous God, visiting the iniquity of the fathers on the children, on the third and fourth generations of those who hate me, but showing lovingkindness to thousands of those who love me and keep my commandments"* (Exod. 20:5-6).

This passage troubled me when I first read it. I knew that the Bible is without error, and yet I simply could not understand how a loving God would punish three or four generations of children for the sins of their parents. It didn't seem consistent with those passages about Christ's love for children as recorded in the Gospels. But when I went into psychiatry and extensively studied about healthy and unhealthy parent-child relationships, and saw scores of mentally disturbed children and had to deal with their parents and grandparents, the meaning of this passage became quite obvious to me. It simply means that if we, as parents, live sinful lives—meaning lives that are not in accord with the health-producing principles of God's Word—there will be a profound effect upon our children, and our children's children, to three or four generations. God is not punishing our offspring for our sins, *we are*—by not living according to His precepts.

In my review of the scientific literature on parent-child relationships, and from my own experiences as a psychiatrist, I have learned a great deal about which types of families produce which types of mental illness in their children. During one full year of research at Duke University, I also uncovered much information on which types of religious backgrounds produce which types of mental illness, and which types of religious experiences produce good mental health. I think the best way I can effectively share these findings with you, without using psychiatric jargon and terminology, is to tell you *how to produce* various types of mental illness in your children. It will be a novel, more enjoyable way of learning some important principles. I'll be teaching you how to produce various types of mental illness in your children so you will know what *not* to do if you want them to be emotionally and mentally healthy. I will share with you some easy steps for producing ten common types of mental illness or personality disorder. I will then discuss some of the most recent psychiatric findings on emotionally healthy families as well.

Before I begin, however, I want it understood that there are exceptions to every rule. Some children have been brought up under the most adverse circumstances, only to attain greatness as adults. Others have been reared in relatively normal Christian homes, but developed manic-depression, schizophrenia, or some other mental illness because of a strong inherited predisposition or some other transparent factors. The human brain, with its 20 billion cells, complicated biochemistry, interconnecting circuits, and electrical activity, is far too complex for us to be overly simplistic in our approach to mental illness. But at the same time, there are definite trends that have been observed over and over again in the families of various types of mentally disturbed children. God wants us to know the truth. The Bible is absolute truth. But God didn't print the entire body of truth in the Scriptures. If He had, our Bibles would be bigger than ocean liners, and it would be quite difficult to carry them around! They would also be quite expensive! So I think God would have us, as Christians, take a skeptical but open-minded look at the truth man learns from scientific investigations. If we do, we will have a definite advantage over non-Christians, who know many scientific facts but don't have the absolute standard of authority we have in the Scriptures. With these warnings, I will now proceed to share with you some of these definite trends.

# 5

## How to Develop
## Emotionally Disturbed Children

**A. Ten easy steps for developing your normal, healthy baby into a drug addict or alcoholic.**

These steps are the same for both drug addiction and alcoholism, since a majority of cases of both drug addiction and alcoholism stem from the same type of personality disorder.

1. Spoil him; give him everything he wants if you can afford it.

2. When he does wrong, you may nag him, but never spank him (unless he is showing signs of independence).

3. Foster his dependence on you, so drugs or alcohol can replace you when he is older.

4. Protect him from your husband and from all those mean teachers who threaten to spank him from time to time. Sue them if you wish.

5. Make all of his decisions for him, since you are a lot older and wiser than he is. He might make mistakes and learn from them if you don't.

6. Criticize his father openly, so your son can lose his own self-respect and confidence.

7. Always bail him out of trouble so he will like you. Besides, he

might harm your reputation if he gets a police record. Never let him suffer the consequences of his own behavior.

8. Always step in and solve his problems for him, so he can depend on you and run to you when the going gets tough. Then when he is older and still hasn't learned how to solve his own problems, he can continue to run from them through heroin or alcohol.

9. Just to play it safe, be sure to dominate your husband and drive him to drink too, if you can.

10. Take lots of prescription drugs yourself, so that taking non-prescription drugs won't be a major step for him.[1]

In my opinion—as a psychiatrist who has worked with scores of drug addicts and alcoholics—drug addiction and alcoholism are *not* "drug" or "alcohol" problems, as they are frequently mislabeled. And they are *not* an inherited disorder, even though in some cases there are some inherited tendencies. They are a *choice,* and this choice is usually made by people with severe dependent personality disorders. They generally come from families where there were a weak father and an overcontrolling mother who spoiled them excessively. A disproportionate percentage of the alcoholics and drug addicts I have worked with have been the youngest or only boy in the family, a factor which gave their mothers added temptations to spoil them. Many times, they were the only alcoholic or drug addict in an otherwise normal family, and considered themselves the black sheep of the family.

The only cures I have seen have come about when the addict himself has chosen to mature and work on his dependency problem, preferably switching his dependency to God instead of alcohol or drugs. When I work with them, I never mention drugs or alcohol, and I refuse to listen to their stories about drugs or alcohol. This would only encourage them to continue their habits, so they could brag about them. I also refuse to become their "mother." Most of them try very hard to get me to do things for them that they ought to be doing for themselves. Then they try to make me feel guilty when I refuse to do these favors for them. The best way for me to show them genuine Christian love is to be indifferent as to

---

1. See bibliography references 45, 57, 95, 187, 249, 271, 298, 351, 385, 402.

whether or not they like me, then to proceed to do the things that I know will have the most beneficial effects on them in the long run. Don't give them money. You'll just be supporting their habit. Don't help them get out of trouble with the law. They need desperately to suffer the consequences of their behavior, since they never did when they were growing up.

The best thing you can do for them is to help them to become aware of their severe dependent personality disorder and encourage them to go out of their way to do things for themselves. I think the ideal treatment for an alcoholic or drug addict would be to send him out into a jungle somewhere for a month or two with a Bible, a compass, and a jackknife, and nobody around for several hundred miles—especially his mother. This would produce independence, maturity, and increased self-confidence, and I'm sure would cure many of them. The U.S. government spends billions of dollars treating alcoholics in V.A. hospitals, but about 95 percent never choose to quit drinking. The hospital merely becomes a mother-substitute where they can dry out and avoid responsibilities. The cure-rate for drug addicts is even lower. I have never cured an addict, and I never will. But some of the addicts I have worked with have matured and decided to cure themselves—with God's help.

I never treat an alcoholic without treating his wife as well. The reason for this is that when alcoholics are cured and become responsible husbands and fathers, many of their wives have nervous breakdowns. The wives are nearly always remarkably like the alcoholic's mother—domineering, perfectionistic, and masochistic. So the wives need help accepting their new role as subservient wife instead of substitute-mother. Without such help many of these wives would divorce their cured husbands and marry another practicing alcoholic.

**B.  How to develop your normal child into a homosexual.**

1. Start out by using the ten easy steps followed by the alcoholic's mother, but this won't be enough.

2. Show your love for your son by protecting him very carefully. Don't let him play football or baseball with the other boys— he might get hurt! Don't let him be a newspaper boy or patrol boy; he might catch pneumonia out in the bad weather.

3. Be sure he spends lots of time with you and very little with his father (or any other adult males).

4. Teach him to sew and cook, and how to knit too. After all, sexist attitudes about chores are out of date nowadays.[2]

5. Walk him to and from school so none of the bullies will beat little Johnny up.

6. Let him play consistently with the little neighborhood girls or his sisters and their friends. There just aren't any boys his age in the neighborhood that you would want him to play with.

7. Joke with him about the feminine name you gave him, and tell what a cute girl he would have been. Tell him that you really had wanted a girl and dressed him in his big sister's clothes when he was little. That way, when he reaches puberty and his contemporaries start falling in love with the opposite sex, he can too—with boys, since he thinks of himself basically as a girl.[3]

If your baby is a girl, just follow the same principles in reverse: call her Jack, never make her wear a dress, and don't spend much time with her, since she prefers playing football with her father anyway. Homosexuality is on the rise in today's society. And with the Women's Liberation Movement, more and more weak men are feeling threatened by women and choosing homosexual rather than heterosexual relationships. The practice of homosexuality, just like drug addiction or alcoholism, is a choice, not an inherited disorder. And it is a sinful choice at that. God inspired Moses to write specific commandments about homosexuality, labeling it a sin and calling on the Jewish community to kill anyone caught practicing homosexual acts (see Lev. 18:22; 20:13). Even men dressing as women and women dressing as men are declared to be acting contrary to the will of God (see Deut. 22:5).

---

2. Actually, it is fine for our sons to share in any chores, even feminine chores, from time to time. However, many of the homosexual males I have treated grew up in homes where they did feminine chores almost exclusively, while their brothers did the chores most Americans would consider masculine. Their mothers wanted a girl, so they treated these boys like girls in many ways, including giving them primarily feminine chores.

3. See bibliography references 162, 361, 412.

God's attitudes toward homosexual acts are recorded in the New Testament as well. Paul writes:

> For even though they knew God, they did not honor Him as God, or give thanks; but they became futile in their specula-ations, and their foolish heart was darkened. Professing to be wise, they became fools, and exchanged the glory of the in-corruptible God for an image in the form of corruptible man and of birds and fourfooted animals and crawling creatures. Therefore God gave them over in the lusts of their hearts to impurity, that their bodies might be dis-honored among them. For they exchanged the truth of God for a lie, and worshiped and served the creature [secu-lar humanitarianism] rather than the Creator, who is blessed forever. Amen. For this reason, God gave them over to de-grading passions; for their women exchanged the natural func-tion for that which is unnatural [lesbianism], and in the same way also the men abandoned the natural function of the woman and burned in their desire towards one another, men with men committing indecent acts and receiving in their own persons the due penalty of their error [homosexuality]. And just as they did not see fit to acknowledge God any longer, God gave them over to a depraved mind, to do those things which are not proper, being filled with all unright-eousness, wickedness, greed, malice; full of envy, murder, strife, deceit, malice [the desire to hurt others or get even]; they are gossips, slanderers, haters of God, insolent, arrogant, boastful, inventors of evil, disobedient to parents, without understanding, untrustworthy, unloving, unmerciful; and, although they know the ordinance of God, that those who practice such things are worthy of death, they not only do the same, but also give hearty approval to those who practice them.                                    —Rom. 1:21-32, NASV

I have yet to see any psychiatry book that describes homosexuality in such a unique way.

Paul also records, "Do not be deceived; neither fornicators, nor idolaters, nor adulterers, nor effeminate, nor homosexuals, nor thieves, nor covetous, nor drunkards, nor revilers, nor swindlers, shall inherit the kingdom of God" (I Cor. 6:9-10, NASV). Here God makes it quite plain that even being an effeminate boy is a sin in His sight. Boys become effeminate when they grow up iden-tifying with their mothers instead of with their fathers. At Duke University I had a teenage male patient who was a Christian, but was struggling against strong desires to commit homosexual acts.

When taking his psychiatric history, I noted that his father, also a Christian, spent most of his free time playing with his older son, leaving the younger boy home with his mother. When my patient got to elementary school, he said he found himself naturally wanting to play with the girls instead of with the boys. When he turned thirteen and entered puberty, he started to have crushes on boys, as did the girls with whom he played, and to imagine homosexual acts with the boys he liked. His older brother turned out normal. Fortunately, this boy is doing things for himself to become more masculine and to change his way of thinking, and is not allowing himself to commit such acts or even to dwell on them in his mind. I'm sure he will marry some day, raise a family, and live a relatively normal life—maybe even an exceptional Christian life— but he will always carry around some scars.

Paul taught his spiritual son, Timothy:

> But we know that the Law is good, if one uses it lawfully, realizing the fact that law is not made for a righteous man, but for those who are lawless and rebellious, for the ungodly and sinners, for the unholy and profane, for those who kill their fathers or mothers, for murderers and immoral men and homosexuals and kidnappers and liars and perjurers, and whatever else is contrary to sound teaching.
> —I Tim. 1:8-10, NASV

Homosexuality was rampant in the cities of Sodom and Gomorrah. Lot had to bar the doors of his house to keep the homosexuals from raping his male visitors. The Book of Jude refers to this:

> And the angels that did not keep their own position but left their proper dwelling have been kept by him in eternal chains in the nether gloom until the judgment of the great day; just as Sodom and Gomorrah and the surrounding cities, which likewise acted immorally and indulged in unnatural lust, serve as an example by undergoing a punishment of eternal fire.                    —Jude 6-7, NASV

The United States is rapidly becoming more and more like Sodom and Gomorrah, and I believe some portions of our major cities already are like Sodom and Gomorrah. And the liberals are running around telling everybody that it's all right. I know a godly man who recently served on a steering committee for one of the largest denominations in America. He had to debate some of his more liberal religious peers who argued that their denomination should accept homosexuality as a normal practice and not a sin. Fortunately (and with God's help, I'm sure), the liberals were defeated this time. Moreover, many liberal psychiatrists are asserting that homosexuality should no longer be considered abnormal, although a majority of psychiatrists are probably still against such a motion. But I think the day is coming when both religious denominations and psychiatry will accept homosexuality as normal and not a sin; and I would guess that the religious groups will probably beat psychiatry to it, since psychiatrists understand in greater depth the many other developmental deviations that have occurred in the homosexuals they have had as patients. I may be wrong about who will win this race, however.

When Christians feel homosexual temptations, and some do, they should resist (just as they would resist the temptation to other sins). The temptation itself is not a sin, but dwelling on it or yielding to it is. And in spite of the temptation they can choose to be heterosexuals and to practice heterosexuality rather than to practice homosexuality. Every human being has both male and female sex hormones. Accordingly, homosexuality might be more of a temptation physiologically for those people who have a nearly even balance of those hormones. At any rate it will be more of a temptation for those who have not had a strong parent of the same sex to identify with, especially during the first six to ten years of life.

## C. How to develop your normal child into a sociopathic criminal.

1. As usual, start with the ten easy steps the alcoholic's mother uses, with the following exceptions and additions:

2. *Never spank your child.* Physical punishment is a thing of the past. In fact, spanking is now considered immoral and is even against the law in Sweden (which just happens to have the highest teenage suicide rate in the entire world).[4]

3. Let your child express himself any way he feels like it. He'll learn from your example how to behave—he doesn't need any discipline.

---

4. Sweden, once a Christian stronghold and now a twentieth-century model of permissiveness, is the only nation in the world that I know of where Christians have to spank their children in the privacy of their homes for fear that their neighbors will turn them in to the police.

4. Don't run his life; let him run yours. Let him manipulate you and play on your guilt if he doesn't get his own way.

5. Don't enforce the household rules—if there are any. That way he'll be able to choose which laws of society he will break when he is older, and he won't fear the consequences, since he has never suffered any.

6. Don't bother him with chores. Do all of his chores for him. Then he can be irresponsible when he is older and always blame others when his responsibilities don't get done right.

7. Be sure to give in when he throws a temper tantrum. He might hit you if you don't. Don't ever cross him when he is angry.

8. It will help if you choose to believe his lies. You may even want to tell a few yourself. Cheat on your income taxes too.

9. Criticize others openly and routinely so he will realize that he is better than everyone else. Don't let him associate with those overly religious Jones kids—he's too good for them.

10. Give him a big allowance and don't make him do anything for it. He may get the idea that he'll have to work for a living later on if you make him work for it. If he does do anything worthwhile around the house, be sure to pay him richly for each and every good deed. You wouldn't want him to think that a feeling of responsibility is its own reward.[5]

Most of the sociopaths I have worked with—and I have worked either directly or indirectly with hundreds of them—have come from this type of home background. The first patient that comes to my mind is a teenage boy whose mother followed every one of these steps all his life. His parents both taught at a small Christian college, where the boy's father was dean of men. I remember the boy as being outstandingly handsome. This may have been a contributing factor, since teachers, relatives, and parents tend to especially spoil good-looking children. The mother brought the boy to me because he was getting into so much trouble with the law, and she was running out of ways to bail him out. She probably thought that if I had a few sessions with him, I would write a

---

5. For many extensive case studies of sociopaths, see H. M. Cleckley, *Mask of Sanity*.

letter to the judge asking that he not suffer the consequences of
his illegal acts. Well, she brought him to the wrong psychiatrist
for that! She told me how she had tucked him in when he went
to bed a couple nights before. As she was leaving the room, he
said to her, "I didn't give you permission to leave the room, did
I?" So she apologized to him and sat beside him until he gave
her permission to leave. Actually he never did give her permission
—she stealthily left when he finally fell asleep at 4 a.m. Almost any
child would turn out sociopathic with that kind of mother. His
father, the dean, was weak-kneed and apologetic, saying strong
things occasionally, and threatening the boy occasionally, but never
following through. I recommended to the mother and father that
they set definite limits, discipline the boy every single time he broke
one of the limits without listening to any of his excuses, give him
a few chores, let him earn his own spending money, and let him
suffer the consequences of any of society's laws that he chose to
break. I told them that if they couldn't do this, they should transfer the boy to a youth home or foster home where someone *would*
do this, for the boy's sake; and I told them that I would make
these recommendations to the judge if he wanted my psychiatric
opinion (which is the usual case). I told them that if this program were not enforced immediately, I saw no hope for the boy
other than spending most of his life in prison. The boy's parents
then thanked me politely, told me they would do this, set up another
appointment with me, and never returned. I have a good notion
as to where that boy is today. His parents loved themselves too
much to do what was right for their son, because doing what was
right would make him angry at them, and they weren't willing
to tolerate his anger.

Another comment I would like to make is that although most
of the sociopaths I have worked with come from this type of home,
many sociopaths come from homes where they were severely beaten
over and over, frequently by alcoholic fathers or by mothers prone
to child abuse. These children look down on their parents and
become so bitter toward them that they transfer these feelings
to society in general, hating society and thinking themselves to
be better than society, with a strong desire to "get even." Some
psychiatrists have reviewed prison records and found this to be
quite common. So either extreme is harmful to the healthy development of a child. Another finding is that sociopaths have a

higher incidence of alcoholism and homosexuality.[6] This is easy to understand since in most cases sociopaths are reared by parents similar to those of alcoholics and homosexuals.

### D.  How to develop your normal child into a hysterical daughter.

In reviewing all the cases I have had as a psychiatrist, approximately 25 percent have been hysterical females, meaning that they either had a hysterical personality disorder or a hysterical neurosis, the two of which are related. I have also had a few hysterical males, although this particular type of disorder is more common in females. Here are twelve easy steps for producing one:

1. Use the same ten easy steps the alcoholic's mother used, point by point; but in addition, do the following:

2. Spoil her; always let her get her way, especially if she pouts or cries.

3. Marry an immature husband and never meet his natural sexual needs. For warmth and affection he will become very close (too close, in fact) to his daughter instead.

4. Lie to yourself a lot, so she can learn to use the technique of denial for herself.

5. *Always praise her for her looks, never for her character.* Put a mirror on every wall, so she can continually admire herself. (This is one of the most important rules for producing hysteria.)

6. Whenever she runs away—and she'll probably do this frequently—be sure to run after her and apologize for not letting her have her own way in the first place.

7. Whenever she pretends to be sad and feigns a suicide attempt by swallowing a couple dozen aspirins or sleeping pills, be sure to save her dramatically and show her how guilty you feel for not letting her have her own way in the first place. This will be easy, since she will never overdose unless you or her boyfriend is nearby to rescue her. (Note: In the United States, less than one out of every twenty suicide attempts by females

---

6. In *Psychiatry,* a standard textbook, Merrill T. Eaton and Margaret H. Peterson state that sociopaths usually prefer heterosexual relationships, but that because they want immediate gratification, "most histories include some homosexual relationships and often relationships with animals" (p. 251).

that get recorded end in actual death. In my own experience, I have seen and talked to scores of females in emergency rooms after they have made a suicide gesture, and I have never yet seen one of them die from it, even though they almost all claim they were really trying to die. I even saw one lady from up in the mountains who overdosed on four iron tablets after an argument with her husband! Seven times as many women as men attempt suicide in the United States, but twice as many men die of it. The reason for this is that men usually use guns or other violent means, and half of them die as a result of their attempt.)[7]

8. Encourage her to become a movie star. By now she is so dramatic that acting would be quite natural for her.

9. Get divorced and remarried two or three times, so she can learn what you already know: that all men are good-for-nothings, but you might as well live with one anyway.

10. Encourage her to wear the most seductive clothing. Actually, you won't need to encourage her much, because she will do this naturally to please her father, who keeps on praising her for her good looks rather than for her character. (Note: Over one-third of the hysterical females I have treated have even had sexual intercourse with their fathers or stepfathers. Usually they claim they were raped by their fathers, denying the obvious fact that they also had a strong hand in the situation by seducing them, either consciously or unconsciously. Five percent of American women and 2 percent of American men have experienced incest while growing up.)

11. When she comes home from a date two hours late, you and your husband should scold her for such behavior. Then with a curious smirk on your face ask her for all the titillating details and do enjoy every minute of it. But try not to be aware of how much you are enjoying her adventure, even though she can tell that you are.

---

7. Even though suicide attempts by females rarely end in death, this sort of immature behavior should not be taken lightly. Professional counseling should be sought. Including both men and women in the statistics, 10 percent of Americans who survive a suicide attempt die of suicide within ten years (see Thomas P. Detrie and Henry G. Jarecki, *Modern Psychiatric Treatment*, p. 58).

12. Reward her whenever she plays sick. Then she can somatasize all her future emotional conflicts rather than face up to them, running from physician to physician but never finding out what's wrong, and getting angrier and angrier at those male chauvinist M.D.'s. (She continues to spend hundreds of dollars getting their advice, however.)[8]

According to the Psychiatric Diagnostic Manual, which is the bible of psychiatry throughout the world, individuals with hysterical personality disorders are "characterized by excitability, emotional instability, over-reactivity, and self-dramatizaton. This self-dramatization is always attention-getting and often seductive, whether or not the patient is aware of its purpose. These personalities are also immature, self-centered, often vain, and usually dependent on others."[9] Hysterics also have a higher than normal incidence of what we call passive-aggressive personality traits, which include "obstructionism, pouting, procrastination, intentional inefficiency, or stubbornness."[10] These are ways of getting even with the person they are dependent upon without being openly hostile. Lest we become overly introspective, most of us have behaved in some of these ways some of the time, but individuals with true hysterical personalities behave in almost all of these ways almost all of the time. It's a matter of degrees.

I would like to tell you briefly about one female hysteric I treated for several years, and one male hysteric—a Roman Catholic priest—whom I treated for a couple of months. Since I am sworn to secrecy by my Hippocratic Oath as a physician, and for the good of my patients, I will follow the usual procedure of changing their names for my illustrations. Jane was a fourteen-year-old girl when I inherited her as a patient. She had been admitted to a psychiatric ward of a general hospital after repeatedly running away, some minor drug abuse, and some bizarre behavior patterns. For example, she cut up her back with a razor blade in the school bathroom, then ran into her classroom, telling her female teacher—whom she

---

8. Most hysterics I have treated have also been hypochondriacs. By the mere power of suggestion, I have "cured" hysterics of blindness, paralysis, seizure disorders, multiple sclerosis, and many other illnesses they thought they had. See bibliography references 163, 175, 188, and 286 for research data on hysteria.

9. *Diagnostic and Statistical Manual of Mental Disorders,* p. 43.

10. Ibid., pp. 43-44.

had a crush on—that her sister had cut her. Jane would do almost anything to get attention! When we saw her talking to the juice carts on the ward, we thought she must have been completely out of her mind, but we found out later that even this was a dramatic attention-getting device. After psychotherapy with her for six weeks in the hospital, I followed Jane with weekly outpatient psychotherapy sessions for two years. During that period Jane ran away once more for half a day, overdosed half a dozen times or so in an attempt to manipulate her mother, smoked marijuana occasionally, and had about a hundred temper tantrums. All of this was a dramatic improvement over her previous behavior. By the time she was sixteen, she went to live in a youth home for girls and had matured quite a bit. When I inherited her as a patient at age fourteen, she was operating at about the three-year-old level of psychological maturity, even though her I.Q. was tested out at 135. By the time she was sixteen, she was behaving like a ten to twelve-year-old most of the time.

Parents sometimes bring in a teenager whose rearing they have bungled for fourteen or sixteen years, and expect the psychiatrist—since he has that magical "Master of Deity" degree—to correct all their mistakes in a few weeks of therapy. It doesn't work that way! All we can do is help the parents to find some ways to modify the 5 or 10 percent of that teenager's personality that isn't already formed. In reviewing Jane's first six years of life, I discovered that she was born into an upper-class family in which the mother was extremely Victorian and the father financially successful, but psychologically very weak and immature. The boss of the family was a very domineering maternal grandmother, who was also a business executive. Since Jane's father was immature, and Jane's mother never satisfied him sexually—thinking sex was somewhat vulgar—Jane's father turned all of his attention to Jane. He completely ignored his wife and the other children. He praised Jane over and over again for how cute she was, and wouldn't think of disciplining her for anything. Whatever Jane wanted, Jane got. Her father and mother slept in separate bedrooms, and Jane slept every night with her father. During her preschool years, Jane was molested at least once by her maternal grandfather, who was becoming somewhat senile and had never gotten sexual satisfaction from his domineering wife.

When Jane was five, she and her father were lying in bed

together when, all of a sudden, her father had a heart attack. An ambulance was called, and as he was being carried out of the bedroom, he told his frightened daughter, "Don't worry, Honey, I'll be back." But he died at the hospital, and Jane refused to believe that he was dead. For months she would look for him in closets and behind doors. He was her whole life. With her vivid imagination, she would conjure him up and imagine him walking into her room to talk to her several times a day. She finally quit doing this when she was sixteen, though she may still be doing it on rare occasions. Using her strong denial, she would actually believe he was there sometimes. In her childish way of understanding, she blamed her father for leaving her when she needed him so much. In reality, she probably would have been much worse if he had lived and continued to treat her the way he did—like a substitute wife. So she loved her father and hated him at the same time. She became bitter towards men in general, and more and more seductive as she grew older. She developed a very hysterical personality with all of its characteristics. When I served as her therapist for over two years, she learned to trust and identify with an older male who would not yield to her seduction and manipulation, but who showed her genuine Christian love in a matter-of-fact way. During the course of therapy she did put her faith in Jesus Christ, and she tried off and on to grow in the Lord. But she found herself trying to manipulate God in the same way that she had manipulated her father. As most people do, she thought God must be a lot like her father, and had difficulty accepting His omniscience, omnipotence, omnipresence, and His divine mixture of genuine love and perfect justice. I spent scores of hours trying to teach Jane's mother how to handle her at home. But her mother, who had arthritis and a heart condition, simply could not force herself to discipline Jane in the way she needed to be disciplined, so Jane went to live in a youth home for girls in a nearby city. The last letter I received from Jane let me know that she was doing quite well there, even though she was still trying to play on my guilt for having recommended that she not live at home with her mother any more.

Not all hysterics are women. If you apply the same techniques I have listed to your son, you can just as easily make a male hysteric out of him, and there are quite a few male hysterics around. Some of you may know one. I hope none of you is married to one.

One male hysteric that I treated was a Roman Catholic priest. He came to me complaining about all of his superiors, who were constantly misinterpreting his actions. Whenever his superiors would walk into the church and find him caressing a female parishioner, they would accuse him of being overly seductive. Of course, in his view he was only showing her sympathy for her marital and other problems. He complained that his bishop kept harassing him because of his liberal ideas about women's liberation and other women's rights causes. I ordered complete psychological testing for him, so I could find out what was really going on. I wrote my own predictions down, and when the psychological tests —including the Rorschach ink-blot test—came back, they supported my predictions 100 percent. He was a male hysteric who unconsciously hated women. When he saw a feminine ink blot, he would think it was an atomic bomb. It all stemmed back to his relationship with his neurotic mother, who pampered him all his life and continually praised him for his appearance rather than his character. She also followed most of the other steps listed above.

Hysterics traditionally seduce persons of the opposite sex, either consciously or subconsciously, so they can put them down and prove that they are good-for-nothings like everyone else of the opposite sex. Many prostitutes are hysterics. Many a female hysteric seeks a good man to bring down sexually, so she can tell everyone that he seduced her, thus ruining his reputation. Many of them even make up stories of ministers and physicians who supposedly have seduced them. The Book of Proverbs describes hysterical females and males better than any book on psychiatry I have read. Solomon describes the hysterical male: "A naughty person, a wicked man, walketh with a froward mouth. He winketh with his eyes, he speaketh with his feet, he teacheth with his fingers; Frowardness is in his heart, he deviseth mischief continually; he soweth discord" (Prov. 6:12-14). Solomon calls hysterical females "strange women" and says that they seek out the precious life, to bring him down. He warns godly young men that:

> The lips of a strange woman drop as an honeycomb, and her mouth is smoother than oil: But her end is bitter as wormwood, sharp as a twoedged sword. Her feet go down to death; her steps take hold on hell. Lest thou shouldest ponder the path of life, her ways are moveable [unstable], that thou canst not know them. Hear me now therefore, O ye children,

and depart not from the words of my mouth. Remove thy way far from her, and come not nigh the door of her house: Lest thou give thine honour unto others, and thy years unto the cruel: Lest strangers be filled with thy wealth; and thy labours be in the house of a stranger; And thou mourn at the last, when thy flesh and thy body are consumed [probably referring to the devastating effects of syphilis], And say, How have I hated instruction, and my heart despised reproof; And have not obeyed the voice of my teachers, nor inclined mine ear to them that instructed me! I was almost in all evil in the midst of the congregation and assembly. Drink waters out of thine own cistern, and running waters out of thine own well. Let thy fountains be dispersed abroad, and rivers of waters in the streets. Let them be only thine own, and not strangers' with thee. Let thy fountain be blessed: and rejoice with the wife of thy youth. Let her be as the loving hind and pleasant roe; let her breasts satisfy thee at all times; and be thou ravished always with her love. And why wilt thou, my son, be ravished with a strange woman, and embrace the bosom of a stranger? For the ways of man are before the eyes of the LORD, and he pondereth all his goings.

—Prov. 5:3-21

## E.    How to develop your normal child into an adult schizophrenic.

All of the literature I have reviewed indicates a strong genetic predisposition to schizophrenia, more so than most other mental illnesses. Many childhood schizophrenics come from quite normal homes, as do some adult schizophrenics. And then again, many people have inherited a genetic predisposition for schizophrenia yet never develop the disease, because they were reared in loving healthy homes that were based on principles consistent with what God recommends in Scripture. As a matter of fact, *many of those individuals who would have become schizophrenic under adverse circumstances instead become very creative.* On the other hand, some individuals do not inherit a strong genetic predisposition for schizophrenia, but become schizophrenic anyway because they were reared in schizophrenogenic (schizophrenic-producing) homes. I'm going to give you five easy steps for producing a schizophrenic environmentally. But first, let me tell you what schizophrenia is. Schizophrenia is defined as a

mental disorder of psychotic level characterized by disturbances in thinking, mood, and behavior. The thinking disturbance is manifested by a distortion of reality, especially by delusions and hallucinations, accompanied by fragmentation of associations that results in incoherent speech. The mood disturbance is manifested by inappropriate affective responses. The behavior disturbance is manifested by ambivalence, apathetic withdrawal, and bizarre activity.[11]

Here's how to produce a schizophrenic:

1. Again, use most of the same basic rules as the alcoholic's mother, with the following exceptions:
2. Tell your child you love him, but *never hug him or show any genuine warmth*. When you have to carry him as a baby, put him on your hip, facing away from you, rather than snuggling him up close to you and facing you.
3. Promise him you'll do things with him, but always think of excuses when the time comes; encourage your husband to do the same.
4. Husbands should be seen and not heard, and they should be seen only when they have permission from you. The weaker your husband is, the easier it will be to make a schizophrenic out of your son or daughter, especially if you are cold and impersonal whenever you lie to your child by telling him that you love him.
5. In contrast to the alcoholic's mother, be very weak and ineffectual yourself. If you and your husband are both psychologically weak and ineffectual, it will help a great deal.[12]

I had one patient who was a ten-year-old schizophrenic boy. He was reared by a weak, ineffectual mother who would not discipline him. She was very cold and impersonal. She had divorced her husband many years earlier. He was a chronic paranoid schizophrenic himself, and spent most of his adult life in V.A. hospitals. When the boy was admitted to the hospital, at the insistence of social workers, he had a wild appearance—torn clothes, long claw-like fingernails, a glaring stare—and very little body movement. He hadn't had a bath in several weeks. The mother said she simply could not get him to take a bath. I told the mother that the hospital policy was for the parents not to visit the children on the

11. Alfred M. Freedman, et al., *Modern Synopsis of Psychiatry,* p. 791.
12. See bibliography references 11, 38, 39, 43, 97, 102, 112, 113, 119, 126, 139, 146, 148, 149, 160, 191, 210, 211, 224, 229, 238, 315, 317, 318, 326, 363, 364, 372, 381, 382, 383, 384, 388, 416, 418, 420.

psychiatric ward for the first three days after admission, so they can adjust to being away from home. She accepted this readily, but when I asked her to tell her son that she wouldn't be back for three days, she just stared at him. She was so ineffectual that she couldn't even tell him that, for fear he might not like her. We treated him with major tranquilizers and behavior modification, and he got a lot better. He could laugh again, and play with other children. We recommended to the courts that he be placed in a foster home or a boys home, rather than go back to his schizophrenogenic mother. The last I heard, she was suing the social work service to get him back.

Another schizophrenic patient that I evaluated at Duke University was an eighteen-year-old girl. Her mother was borderline schizophrenic herself, and her father was neurotic. Her parents had used most of the above rules for developing a schizophrenic— they were quite ineffectual, cold, and so on. They were also ultra-charismatic, claiming, for example, to have seen the Holy Spirit in person and to have cast out demons. The schizophrenic girl was especially disappointed to find out I had never spoken in tongues. Her conversation went from one subject to another; she would break off in mid-sentence, not remembering what she had been talking about. Her thoughts constantly went back to sexual things, and her mood changed rapidly back and forth from elation to tearful sadness. She seemed to think the world revolved around her, and she had the answers for any question. I have seen many like her get a great deal better after two or three weeks on the proper medications, but when I recommended that she take medications, she refused and the mother was too ineffectual to insist that she take them. So they never came back, even after several telephone calls asking them to.

One of the saddest things in psychiatry is knowing you could help someone, then having them refuse your help. Solomon, the wisest human counselor, said, "If you rebuke a mocker, you will only get a smart retort; yes, he will snarl at you. So don't bother with him; he will only hate you for trying to help him. But a wise man, when rebuked [or given insights], will love you all the more. Teach a wise man, and he will be the wiser; teach a good man, and he will learn more" (Prov. 9:7-9, LB). And so in my psychiatric practice, I share with my patients observations and insights which are sometimes painful (rebukes). What they do with those insights is their responsibility. I can only hope and pray that they will use them to change their behavior and improve their mental and spiritual condition.

## F.  How to develop an obsessive child.

According to the *Diagnostic and Statistical Manual of Mental Disorders* (DSM-II), obsessive-compulsive personality is the diagnosis for individuals who are "excessively rigid, over-inhibited, over-conscientious, over-dutiful, and unable to relax easily."[13] If this progresses to a neurosis, the condition is characterized by

> the persistent intrusion of unwanted thoughts, urges, or actions that the patient is unable to stop. The thoughts may consist of single words or ideas, ruminations, or trains of thought often perceived by the patient as nonsensical. The actions vary from simple movements to complex rituals such as repeated handwashing. Anxiety and distress are often present either if the patient is prevented from completing his compulsive ritual or if he is concerned about being unable to control it himself.[14]

Here's how to produce an obsessive child:

1. Talk all the time, but don't be very active physically, and never listen to what your child has to say.

2. Expect perfect etiquette and manners from your child from his day of birth on. Don't tolerate any mistakes.

3. Be an introvert. Don't let him see you interacting in a healthy manner with other human beings.

4. Be very critical of the people around you—this includes your minister, your neighbors, your husband, and, most importantly, your child.

5. Be a real snob.

6. Be sure to domineer your husband as well as your children. This is very important.

7. Emphasize instrumental morality as a way of being superior to other children, or of getting to heaven.

---

13. *Manual of Mental Disorders,* p. 43.
14. Ibid., p. 40.

8. Don't make any serious commitments to God yourself, and be critical of the religious convictions of your child's grandparents.

9. Tell your child that his father is the boss, but in reality, allow your husband to be nothing but a figurehead.

10. Expect your child to be completely toilet-trained by the time he is twelve months old. Then, when he grows older, he can get even with you by being constipated much of the time.

11. Be a real miser with your money. Always save for the future, and don't let that future ever come.

12. Emphasize the letter of the law rather than the spirit of the law. Make your rules quite rigid, and never allow any exceptions.

13. Practice the Victorian ethic. Shame your child for being a sexual being.[15]

Research has shown that these are the kinds of principles the parents of obsessive children follow. This is quite consistent with my own findings. Actually, a degree of obsessiveness can be very beneficial in life. It can help a person to be hard-working, conscientious, and genuinely moral. *Almost all of the physicians and medical students that I have given personality tests to have several obsessive-compulsive traits.* If they weren't organized and industrious, they would never make it through the grinding demands of medical school and private practice. Not all doctors have the nice hours and independent wealth of Marcus Welby, M.D. Many seminary students and ministers are quite obsessive-compulsive also. This can help them to accomplish great tasks for God, provided they also know how to relax and enjoy life at the same time. I'm sure the Apostle Paul had some healthy obsessive-compulsive tendencies, and he may have had to overcome some unhealthy ones. But obsessive-compulsiveness can get out of hand if we, as parents, use the thirteen rules listed above. I've seen obsessive children who literally hate themselves for not being perfect, even though most of them are superior in intelligence and in many other ways. If they go to a

---

15. Paul L. Adams, "Family Characteristics of Obsessive Children." See also bibliography references 176, 188, 338.

Christian party and start having a little fun, they feel guilty. They think it's not right to have fun, especially if they could be at home in their room doing their homework over for the third time!

## G.  How to develop an accident-prone child.

1.  Be somewhat neurotic and marry a neurotic husband.

2.  Get into serious hassles with your husband, especially over your child. That way the child can blame himself and react to family stresses by hurting himself to relieve his guilt.

3.  Ignore your child, especially when he shows confidence or good character traits. That way, he will be noticed only when he gets hurt again.

4.  It will help if you and your husband are both gone most of the time. Just leave him at home with his older brothers and sisters. Be too tired and busy to notice him when you do get home, that is, if he's not in bed already.

5.  Overreact with extreme sympathy when he does get a scrape or a bruise, since you feel guilty for ignoring him the rest of the time.[16]

The average age when accident-prone children are seen by a psychiatrist is about seven or eight. Usually they have been accident-prone for several years. The tendency appears to be slightly more common in girls than in boys, and in the youngest child of the family. The accident proneness frequently goes away when the psychiatrist finishes treating the child's parents.

## H.  How to develop an obese child and anorexic teenager.

This syndrome may sound strange to many of you. It's known as *anorexia nervosa,* and used to be quite rare. But there has been a fivefold increase in the incidence of anorexia nervosa in the past generation.[17] Hundreds of research studies have been done on anorexia, but none have been conclusive about the reason for the

---

16. Peter Husband and Pat E. Hinton, "Families of Children with Repeated Accidents."
17. "Epidemiology of Anorexia Nervosa," p. 556; also G. F. M. Russell, "Clinical and Endocrine Features of Anorexia Nervosa," p. 40.

dramatic rise in the incidence of this disease in the past generation. *The mothers of anorexics are frequently women of achievement or career women, frustrated in their aspirations,*[18] *so I think that there is a good chance that some of the philosophies of the Women's Liberation Movement and the rapidly changing roles of women in our society may be partially responsible.*

Over 95 percent of the adolescents who develop anorexia nervosa are females, frequently overly dependent females with pent-up hostilities toward their parents.[19] Most anorexics were somewhat obese in childhood, are above average in intelligence, are from the upper socio-economic class, and are the daughters of professional parents, many of whom are in the nurturing professions.[20] They frequently have fears about growing up, and especially about becoming a woman. Many have sexual guilt, sometimes for unfounded reasons.[21] They frequently get along quite well until they start changing from a little girl into a young woman. Then, all of a sudden, they develop a phobia of food, especially fattening foods. Their menstrual cycles cease.[22] At first, the parents think their daughter is on a typical teenage diet—until she keeps on losing, and losing, and losing. About 15 percent of anorexics become increasingly emaciated until they die of starvation and its effects.[23] I had one twenty-two-year-old anorexic who got down to thirty-eight pounds. She didn't improve very much, and I assume that she has probably died in the past few years. On the other hand, one of my best patients was a sixteen-year-old girl who got down to sixty-six pounds, responded quite well to psychotherapy and spiritual encouragement, recovered completely, and has done excellently ever since. She still sends me occasional postcards. Many anorexics recover, but continue to have sexual maladjustments and *difficulty becoming intimate with a man.*

The results of some research studies (e.g., abnormal EEG's)

---

18. Hilda Bruch, "Family Transactions in Eating Disorders."
19. Ibid.
20. Arthur H. Crisp, "Premorbid Factors in Adult Disorders of Weight, with Particular Reference to Primary Anorexia Nervosa."
21. Arthur H. Crisp, "Reported Birth Weight and Growth Rates in a Group of Patients with Primary Anorexia Nervosa (Weight Phobia)."
22. See bibliography references 172, 334, 404, 408.
23. See bibliography references 79, 230.

indicate a genetic predisposition for this disease.[24] The parents of anorexics are quite similar to the parents of children who become obese and simply stay obese. Perhaps the genetic predisposition may make the difference. Anyway, the rules I am about to give are based on general trends that have been observed in the families of both obese children and anorexic children.

1. Start out by using most of the rules used by the drug addicts' mothers, so you can create a superdependent child. (Note: The thirty-eight-pound patient I told you about was so dependent upon her mother that she used her emaciated condition to manipulate her mother into carrying her around like a baby wherever she wanted to go. The mother did this willingly in spite of our warnings that it was very detrimental to her daughter's condition.)

2. Be a frustrated women's libber.

3. Give your children lots of food instead of lots of love.

4. Fathers should be passive in the home, intelligent, and financially successful, preferably teachers or doctors or members of some other nurturing profession.[25]

5. Mothers should be overweight and neurotically overprotective. They should also wear the pants in the family.[26]

6. Don't show much respect for your husband.[27]

7. Be dominant, restrictive, and oversolicitous. Also be sure your family lives near your own mother, so she can dominate your life a little too.[28]

8. Marry an obsessive-compulsive, Victorian husband who doesn't

---

24. William P. Wilson, ed., *Applications of Electroencephalography in Psychiatry*, p. 268. See also bibliography references 77, 78, 82, 110, 134, 150, 155, 177, 242, 255, 365.
25. See bibliography references 53, 80, 81.
26. Ibid.
27. Bruch, "Eating Disorders."
28. Patricia Wold, "Family Structure in Three Cases of Anorexia Nervosa: The Role of the Father."

like women much because his mother bossed him around quite a bit.[29]

9. Direct your husband's pent-up hostility toward your daughter, so he will be more accepting of you.[30]

One of the world's leading authorities on anorexia and obesity problems is Dr. Hilda Bruch, a prominent woman physician. In her research studies (several of which are listed in my bibliography) she notes that women who feel a conscious or unconscious rejection toward their children frequently compensate for it by excessive feeding and overprotective measures. Food thus has an exaggerated emotional value and becomes a love-substitute. She also notes that these mothers are frequently *frustrated career women who don't respect their husbands.*[31]

I would like to divert our attention here briefly to some of the research findings, and some of my own personal opinions, on the Women's Liberation Movement. First of all, I think many of the complaints of the Women's Libbers are quite legitimate. One of our best friends is a female lab technician who gets a couple hundred a month less than male lab technicians with the same amount of training and experience. I don't think that's right. And I personally believe that God calls many women to make great contributions to society through professional careers. However, I really get angry when I hear Women's Libbers criticize and downgrade other women for choosing to be housewives or for submitting to their husbands' authority. I think being a housewife is a calling from God that is just as worthwhile as any other calling, and frequently a lot more difficult. Take John Wesley's mother, for instance. He was the fifteenth of nineteen children, and his mother didn't have the modern conveniences American mothers have today. And yet, on top of all her other chores, she managed to spend at least one hour each week with each child individually for devotions. No wonder God was able to use John and Charles Wesley to bring about a revival that reached around the world. Look at the godly mother they had. This story has been repeated over and over again

29. Ibid.

30. Ibid. For an award-winning article on the treatment of anorexia nervosa, see Ronald Liebman, et al., "An Integrated Treatment Program for Anorexia Nervosa."

31. Bruch, "Eating Disorders."

in history, but the books are written about the great sons, and their great mothers are frequently neglected. I thank God over and over for the godly mother I had and still have. I also thank Him for the elderly unmarried woman in my home church who prayed for me in her closet every day when I was in high school. What an impact that had on my life! She's in heaven now, and she's one of the first people I'm going to hug at the rapture!

Many people are surprised to find out that the ideal godly woman described in Proverbs 31 had servant girls help her at home so she could have time to invest in a little real estate (v. 16), do a little farming (v. 16), and make girdles to sell commercially (v. 24). But she also "watches carefully all that goes on throughout her household, and is never lazy" (v. 27). Moreover, she is a great help to her husband and richly satisfies his needs (vv. 11-12).

Edith Schaeffer, the wife of author Francis Schaeffer, has written an excellent book for women, entitled *Hidden Art,* in which she shows numerous ways in which godly women can be creative in the home, making good use of their God-given talents. She says that much of the impetus for the Women's Lib movement comes from frustrated housewives who aren't expressing their creativity in the home. I wish every Christian woman would read this book.

I think the Women's Libbers have some legitimate complaints, but I am also aware of some morally corrupt trends within the movement, such as the call by some to make war against God's Word and God Himself. As a psychiatrist, I don't like their denunciation of male authority in the home, since the vast majority of neurotics I see come from homes that are dominated by women. Janet Zollinger Giele, of Radcliffe Institute in Cambridge, Massachusetts, recently published an article in which she stated that our young people "have been steeped in the new morality, the new psychology, the experience of mechanization and the interchangeability of personnel. It took only a small step to extend these principles to sex roles."[32] She states that "recent demographic trends indicate a shift in the parental and marital roles of both men and women.... The nature of the family is being transformed as the worlds of women and men increasingly overlap."[33] This is

---

32. Janet Zollinger Giele, "Changes in the Modern Family: Their Impact on Sex Roles," p. 757.
33. Ibid.

especially true of women born after the great depression. I hope God won't have to bring us through another depression to bring us to our senses. Karl Marx taught that "the patriarchal family must go because it is the chief institution in contemporary society that oppresses and enslaves women."[34] Dr. Henry Greenbaum is a psychiatrist and Freudian analyst who is pro-Women's Lib in general. But even Dr. Greenbaum states that the Women's Lib movement is attacking marriage, family, and parenthood, which are essential human needs. He states that these trends will "lower the quality of life."[35] He also makes the rather astute observation that "whatever form our evolving institutions do take will depend to a great extent on our moral value systems and the quality of people."[36]

Research studies show that over 40 percent of American mothers with children eighteen years of age or under are presently employed.[37] These studies indicate that maternal employment is sometimes beneficial and sometimes harmful to the family, depending on various circumstances. Maternal employment was found to be generally harmful if the mother's job lowered her self-esteem, if she was working against the wishes of other family members, or if her children had to be kept during the day in inadequate facilities.[38]

### I. How to develop an enuretic (bedwetting) or encopretic (soiling) child.

Occasional bedwetting and soiling are quite normal in young children. Research studies show us that, in the case of bedwetting, 88 percent of children quit by about four and one-half years of age, 93 percent by age seven and one-half, and 98 percent by age seventeen.[39] It may surprise you to find out that from 0.5 to 2 percent of our American servicemen continue to wet their beds occasionally.[40] It has been estimated that about 10 percent of bed-

34. Alice S. Rossi, "Family Development in a Changing World," p. 1057.
35. Henry Greenbaum, "Marriage, Family and Parenthood."
36. Ibid.
37. Mary C. Howell, "Employed Mothers and Their Families."
38. Ibid.
39. Alfred M. Freedman and Harold I. Kaplan, eds., *Comprehensive Textbook of Psychiatry*, p. 1380.
40. Ibid.

wetting in late childhood is organic, meaning the child may have a small bladder or some other physical difficulty. If this is the case, teaching him to hold in his urine longer can frequently serve to stretch his bladder and eliminate bedwetting. Ninety percent of bedwetting in children five years or older, however, is felt to be psychologically caused, usually an expression of hostility toward one or both of his parents. So if you, as parents, stay calm and matter-of-fact, and have the child clean and change his own wet bed without scolding him, you'll be doing the right thing. If he's doing it to express hostility and to get you upset, or to give you extra work to do, this reaction on your part will take all the fun out of it—especially since he has to clean his own bed. And if in fact he does have a small bladder, you're still doing the right thing because you're not scolding him, and cleaning up his bed himself will help him to feel more responsible and independent, and less guilty. If it continues to be a problem, there are medications, like low doses of Tofrānil, that will usually eliminate the problem within a week or two. Then the medications can be stopped a month or two later to see if they are still needed.[41]

Occasional soiling is also quite common in young children, but after age five or so, it is generally considered more serious psychiatrically than bedwetting is. It can also be treated with low doses of prescription psychiatric medications, but family counseling is generally recommended as well.

Here are some general rules for increasing the likelihood of producing an enuretic or encopretic child of the psychological variety:

1. Mothers should be divorced or married to husbands who are almost always gone. (Note: In one study of fourteen encopretic children, for instance, eight lived with a divorced mother and the other six had fathers who were gone all [e.g., overseas military assignments] or most of the time [e.g., two jobs].)[42]

2. Be ambivalent toward motherhood (Women's Libbers again).

41. Paul M. Bindelglas, et al., "Medical and Psychosocial Factors in Enuretic Children Treated with Imipramine Hydrochloride."

42. Jules C. Bemporad, et al., "Characteristics of Encopretic Patients and Their Families."

3. Show the rejection you feel for your child by being domineering, overintruding, and overprotective.

4. Openly criticize your husband for being stupid, socially inept, and gone all the time.

5. Isolate your feelings and show a real lack of warmth.

6. Nag a lot.

7. Be preoccupied with your child's intestinal functions.

8. Mother and father should argue openly and frequently about how to raise the child.

9. If and when the fathers are home, they should be weak and ineffectual.

10. It will help if you force toilet-training on your child before he is neurologically ready for it. (Note: Children vary in neurological readiness for toilet-training anywhere from eighteen months to four years of age, with the average being about two and one-half years of age.)[43]

I have treated a number of enuretics and encopretics, but one ten-year-old boy especially sticks out in my mind. He had a divorced, borderline schizophrenic mother who was cold and ineffectual and felt strong rejection toward the boy. His mother would wrap up his stools to show the doctor. She had delusions about their being as big as horse manure and constantly plugging up her sewer system. We hospitalized the boy and he did very well in the child psychiatry unit. Only one time did he put a stool on the floor, and that was out of anger at me for not letting him have his own way about something. When I suggested to the mother that her son might do better at a Christian home for boys, she jumped at the chance to get him out of her home, but pretended that she didn't want to lose him. He did a lot of growing up at that new home, where he felt accepted and loved. In the meantime, I treated the mother with major tranquilizers and arranged for a female therapist to see her regularly, in hopes that in a year or two mother and son might both be ready to live together again, but this time without psychologically damaging the boy for life.

---

43. Ibid. See also Jean Marie Hoag, et al., "The Encopretic Child and His Family."

## J.   How to develop a hyperkinetic (hyperactive) child.

Before giving you some easy steps to follow, I want to say a few words about hyperactive children. I have evaluated and treated a large number of them. During the initial evaluation, I talk to the child, watch him awhile, watch him interact with his parents through a one-way mirror, and do an extensive neurological exam. Here is what I usually find, and the literature will bear me out. The most common finding is that the boy—and I say boy because about nine out of ten hyperactive children are boys—isn't really hyperactive at all. He's just wired at a high normal level of activity. The higher androgen level in boys makes them generally more active than girls. Many of these parents had a girl first and, surprised to find out how active their boy is, just want to know if this is normal.

During the evaluation I also ask the parents quite a few questions about their manner of discipline in the home. The mothers, and sometimes even the fathers, are simply unwilling to give their child a good healthy spanking when he gets out of hand. These mothers are usually quite ineffectual. They have weak egos and are so selfish in wanting the child to like them that they are unwilling to spank him, even when they know in their hearts that it would be best for him. So in effect the child has no real limits. But children can't stand to be without limits. Children with no limits will be constantly misbehaving and running around in order to get limits put on them. When limits are established, children will try these limits. If the parents reinforce these limits with good solid discipline, the children will quit testing, sit back, and relax. It gives them real security. And they know their parents care about them enough to set limits. In my opinion, the lack of physical discipline and limit-setting in Sweden is the reason Sweden has the world's highest teenage suicide rate. Limits bring real security.

There's another group of hyperkinetic children, perhaps 10 to 20 percent of the so-called hyperkinetics that I evaluate. This group stands out because they have some minor abnormalities on their neurological exam. Their intelligence is normal or frequently even better than normal, but in comparison with other children their age they are somewhat clumsy with fine finger movements. They have more trouble skipping, consistently get their letters backward when writing, and do a number of other things that mark them as having a minor neurological problem. They have what we call late maturation of the nervous system. I'll explain it briefly. During the first six years of life or so, a fatty sheath is being formed around a child's nerve cells. This is similar to the insulation we put around electrical wires and is what I mean by neurological maturation. Pathologists who have studied electron-microscope slides of the brains of children who have died have noted that this maturation is completed earlier in girls than in boys —about age five or six in girls, and about age six or seven in boys. That's why neurologically girls are more ready for school at age six than most boys. In some boys, and in a few girls, this neurological maturation does not become complete until the age of twelve or thirteen. Sometimes it never does. Children with late maturation have a number of neurological problems which generally clear up when maturation is complete. They are more restless and definitely hyperactive. Some have specific learning difficulties, especially in reading and writing. These difficulties also frequently clear up at a later age. But in the meantime these children are often misunderstood. They are labeled as having behavior problems or as being retarded (even though they have normal intelligence), and as a result they generally develop a poor self-concept.

Over 90 percent of these children can be treated medically with dramatic results. I have had a number of them come into my office, run around the room, spin around in my chair, even climb up drapes. I give them a low dose of Ritalin, and fifteen or twenty minutes later they're sitting in a chair answering questions with "yes sir." They calmly go to the testing room next door and do well on I.Q. tests. They go home and behave; when they go to school, they can sit still and concentrate better, and their grades usually come up. They're a joy to treat because their parents think I'm a miracle-worker. Of course, it is just the medicine affecting their nervous system to work as though it were myelinated already. Every six months or so, we stop the medications for about a week to see if the child still needs them. When maturation is complete, he will be as calm off medication as he is on medication, so we leave him off it from then on. Actually, Ritalin is a type of amphetamine. Amphetamines speed up adults, making them more active and nervous. They are also habit-forming. That's why I never prescribe amphetamines for adults. But I give hyperkinetic children very low doses. I've never seen a child become addicted to Ritalin, although I'm sure it's possible. Nor have I ever seen adverse reactions to stopping it all at once. If Ritalin doesn't work, there are several other medications which probably will. Some researchers say Ritalin works only in children with late neuronal maturation, but I disagree. I've given it to a number of hyperactive children who had no neurological abnormalities and came from homes that lacked discipline. It worked fine for most of them too. I would have therapy sessions with the parents for several weeks, get them into some parent-training classes on how to discipline, and take the children off Ritalin when the parents were finally ready to give discipline and love a real try. If they did, the children got along fine without any medication. Many parents think their child has hyperkinetic syndrome secondary to late neuronal maturation when actually all the child has is a lack of limits. And the opposite is true sometimes too. I know of some parents who kept beating their child excessively to get him to quiet down, when in reality he had this neurological syndrome.

Most family doctors know very little about this syndrome or how to treat it, so if you suspect it in one of your own children, or a neighbor's child, I would recommend that the child be seen by a child psychiatrist or by trained people at a child study center. It really wouldn't matter, in all probability, whether the child psychiatrist were a Christian or not to evaluate something like this. Listed here are a few easy steps to follow if you want to produce hyperkinesis (hyperactivity) in your normal child.

1. Don't spank him when he needs it.

2. Nag at him occasionally, but don't ever force him to stay within his limits—that is, if there are any limits.

3. It will help if you are divorced, or if your husband is gone much of the time.

There! These three easy rules should be enough to do the trick in your son or daughter![44]

---

44. Roscoe A. Dykman, et al., "Experimental Approaches to the Study of Minimal Brain Dysfunction: A Follow-up Study." See also John E. Peters, et al., *Physicians' Handbook: Screening for MBD.*

# 6

## *Five Factors Found in Mentally Healthy Families*

Now that I have told you what not to do, I would like to pass along to you some *positive* recommendations on *what to do* to develop your children into adults who will be exceptionally happy and mature, both emotionally and spiritually. First I'll list five factors consistently found in mentally healthy families; then I'll discuss each of these five factors briefly.[1]

A.  *Love*. Parents should have genuine love for each other and for their children.

B.  *Discipline*. A concept unpopular before the student activism of the '60s is now coming back in vogue.

C.  *Consistency*. Both parents should stick together, using the same rules and consistently enforcing those rules so that what a child gets away with on some occasions is not the cause for which he is capriciously punished at another time.

D.  *Example*. In healthy families, the parents don't expect the children to live up to standards they themselves don't keep. Parents should expect their children to live up to the standards they themselves observe.

1. These five factors are discussed in the following references in the bibliography: 13, 24, 25, 26, 62, 64, 116, 130, 132, 152, 153, 156, 195, 263, 280, 292. These factors are also discussed in most of the psychiatry textbooks listed in the bibliography.

   *E.  A man at the head of the home.* The vast majority of neurotics, both children and adults, grew up in homes where
   there was no father or the father was absent or weak, and
   the mother was domineering.

## A.  Love.

   First on the above list of factors consistently found in mentally
healthy families is *love*. This is not the counterfeit love of the
overprotective mother. In fact, psychological studies done on smothering, overprotective mothers who never spank their child show
that they have hidden feelings of rejection toward the child. When
they look at certain ink blots, for example, they see atom bombs
exploding—a signal of rejection toward the child. Awareness of
these feelings produces an uncomfortable guilt, so they try to
convince themselves that they love their child by overprotecting
him. The result is an immature, overly dependent child. It's a
defense mechanism to hide their underlying hatred from themselves and others. As I have mentioned before, they have such a
neurotic need for their children to like them that they won't
spank their children, even when they know the children really
need it; they fear that their children will remain angry at them
for several minutes after the spanking. So they ignore or complain
about their children's disobedience, or threaten to tell their father
on them when he gets home, thus dividing the children from their
father.

   Psychiatrists aren't the only ones who can tell if a mother's
love for her children is genuine. God showed this in the Bible
nearly three thousand years ago. Solomon said, "If you refuse to
discipline your child [spare the rod, KJ], *it proves you don't love
him; for if you love him, you will be prompt to punish him"* (Prov.
13:24, LB). Solomon also warned, "Don't fail to correct your children; Discipline won't hurt them. They won't die if you use a
stick on them. Punishment will keep them out of hell" (Prov.
23:13-14, LB). And further, "The rod and reproof give wisdom,
but a child who gets his own way brings shame to his mother"
(Prov. 29:15, NASV).

   When undisciplined children grow up, they are immature and
inadequate. They break laws, become addicted to drugs, are guilty
of improper sexual conduct, and literally bring their mother to
shame, just as God said they would. Not only this, but they learn

to hate their mothers by the time they are teenagers, and frequently much sooner. So one of the best ways to show genuine love for your child is to spank him when he needs it, such as when he rebels against your authority.

Another way of showing genuine love for your child is to give him positive reinforcement. Some children misbehave a lot because that's the only way they can get the attention of their parents. *Children have to have attention and stimulation. If they can't get it by good behavior, they'll get it by bad behavior.* Parents who praise their child frequently for his good behavior—sharing his toys with his siblings, for example—will encourage him to continue his good behavior. Getting praised for it makes him feel good and helps him to like himself. Our older boy was praised early for hugging our daughter, even though half of the time he was probably squeezing her to get even with her; now he's one of the "huggingest" boys around. It really makes parenthood worthwhile when my three children climb up into my lap and whisper into my ear, "Daddy, I want to tell you a secret. I love you a whole bunch." Then I give them a big hug, telling them that I love them a whole bunch too, and we reinforce each other in our loving behavior.

Another thing we can do is to consider each child a significant person, no matter how young that child may be. It's so easy to ignore our children and treat them as though they are not important. I have to work on that myself.

When I get into a deep train of thought (during Monday night football games, for example, my wife has to practically hit me on the head with a baseball bat to get my attention), I tune everything else out. So I have to make a real effort to answer my wife or children when they ask me something. What are some other ways we can show genuine love?

The Apostle Paul tells us,

> Love is very patient and kind, never jealous or envious, never boastful or proud, never haughty or selfish or rude. Love does not demand its own way. It is not irritable or touchy. It does not hold grudges and will hardly even notice when others do wrong. It is never glad about injustice, but rejoices whenever truth wins out. If you love someone you will be loyal to him no matter what the cost. You will always believe in him, always expect the best of him, and always stand your ground in defending him.          —I Cor. 13:4-7, LB

In Deuteronomy 6:5, we are commanded to love God with all our heart, soul, and might. Loving God is a good preparation for loving our children. Christ tells us, "A new commandment I give to you, that you love one another, even as I have loved you, that you also love one another. By this all men will know that you are My disciples, if you have love for one another" (John 13:34-35, NASV). The Apostle John tells us, "And this is His commandment, that we believe in the name of His Son Jesus Christ, and love one another, just as He commanded us" (I John 3:23, NASV). God promises to reward us for having enough love in our hearts to live by His principles. Christ tells us, "He who has My commandments, and keeps them, he it is who loves Me; and he who loves Me shall be loved by My Father, and I will love him, and will disclose Myself to him" (John 14:21, NASV). To think that we can have the God who created this universe love us and share Himself with us intimately. That's fantastic!

Another way to show love for our children is to have genuine love between husbands and wives. A partial cause of most neurotic mother-child relationships is that the mother is not getting emotional and sexual satisfaction from her husband. God inspired the Apostle Paul to instruct us:

> Husbands, love your wives, just as Christ also loved the church and gave himself up for her; that he might sanctify her, having cleansed her by the washing of water, [which is] with the word. . . . So husbands ought also to love their own wives as their own bodies. *He who loves his own wife loves himself;* for no one ever yet hated his own flesh, but nourishes and cherishes it, just as Christ also does the church, because we are members of His body. For this cause a man shall leave his father and mother, and shall cleave to his wife, and the two shall become one flesh. . . . Let each individual among you also love his own wife even as himself; and let the wife see to it that she respect her husband.      —Eph. 5:25-33, NASV

Be sure to notice the part of this passage that says, "He who loves his own wife loves himself" (v. 28b). Loving ourselves in a healthy way is essential for developing intimate love with our wives. So we need to love God, love ourselves in a scriptural way, love our wives, love our children, and then reach out to share our love with others. Too many people start out at the wrong end of this spectrum, trying to be self-sacrificing humanitarians while ignoring their children, their wives, themselves, and God. I'm not saying you should put yourself above others; I'm merely saying that you can't genuinely love others until you love yourself in a healthy way. That's why God commands us to love our neighbors as much as we love ourselves (see Mark 12:31). God's Word tells us, "Husbands, love your wives, and do not be embittered [or hold grudges] against them" (Col. 3:19, NASV). If we carry around pent-up hostility, we will express it in unconscious ways that will affect the entire family. It's all right to get angry. It's what we do with our anger that can become sinful. If a husband and wife tell me they have never had a disagreement, I tell them that one of them isn't necessary! But when we get angry at each other, or at our children, we should talk it out, and then forgive each other. God's Word tells us, "Be ye angry, and sin not: let not the sun go down upon your wrath" (Eph. 4:26). It's not always a sin to be angry, but it is a sin to go to bed without dealing with that anger.

And finally, God commands us husbands: "Grant [your wife] honor as a fellow-heir of the grace of life, so that your prayers may not be hindered" (I Peter 3:7, NASV). No matter what we have been told, we are not better than our wives. We are *equal* in importance in the eyes of the God who created us for each other. God has merely given us different responsibilities. We are made in such a way that our families will be healthiest if the husbands assume the ultimate leadership in the home. And so love in the home implies self-worth, intimacy with our mate, intimacy with our children, and intimacy with God. The kind of love found in mentally healthy families is love that provides emotional, social, and physical security.[2]

## B.  Discipline.

I have already shared with you a number of Scripture verses on discipline in the home. The Bible clearly calls for reproof and spanking as ideal punishments for young children, and as a psychiatrist I agree wholeheartedly, even though some psychiatrists would disagree. Spanking is quick, and then it's over. It's not long and drawn out. It's applying the "board of education to the seat of knowledge"! It occurs immediately after the offense, so the young child knows what he is getting punished for. If you take away a

2.  Clair Isbister, "The Family: Past, Present and Future."

young child's privileges for something he did wrong, within a few minutes he will have forgotten what he did wrong; he won't understand what the punishment is all about, and it will not be effective. God affirms this principle when He tells us, "Because the sentence against an evil deed is not executed quickly, therefore the hearts of the sons of men among them are given fully to do evil" (Eccles. 8:11, NASV). I'll discuss more about discipline for each age group later on. Let me just mention here that discipline in the home also refers to a degree of self-discipline. If you want the disciplining of your children to be effective, try disciplining yourselves a little too. In the words of Solomon, "Like a city that is broken into and without walls, is a man who has no control over his spirit [no self-control]" (Prov. 25:28, NASV).

## C.  Consistency.

Consistency is also vitally important. A child must know his limits in order to feel secure. He can't get away with something, only to find himself getting punished for the very same thing a minute or two later. Be consistent. Many researchers were surprised to find out that emotional illness is not as closely linked to the severity or leniency of discipline as it is to parental inconsistency in discipline. The husband may be a little harsh, and the wife may be a little too lenient, so they use different standards of discipline and the poor children can't please anybody. I say *husbands and wives must provide a united front. If you disagree on discipline, don't do your disagreeing in front of the children.* Talk it out privately and arrive at some compromise, but be consistent as to how you discipline your children. If you are unable to reach a compromise, God has established the husband as the leader in the home, so whatever he says goes. If he is too harsh, the children will live through it. Consistency is the most important thing anyway. Of course, if your husband is physically abusive and hits the children over the head with a chair, call the police first; then talk him into seeing a Christian psychiatrist or counselor to deal with his pent-up hostility. Brutal men are usually very insecure, and try to be tough to prove their manhood. If they can learn to like themselves in a healthy way, they will lose their need to prove their manhood by being brutal. If, on the other hand, your husband is not being abusive, if you think he is being just a little unreasonable, and if you can't reach a compromise, do things his way. If they start to backfire on him, he may decide to change on his own. Most men are willing to change their minds occasionally if they think it is their own idea. There is an old saying that goes, "All women, and a few great men, change their minds!"

In his book, *Man in Transition,* Gary Collins notes that children need to feel accepted by us in order to accept themselves. Dr. Collins states,

> Jesus accepted everyone—even the unlovely—although He didn't always accept their behavior. Christian parents and church members must do the same. This acceptance by others, however, should be consistent. It is hard for a child to feel accepted if he gets favorable treatment at one time and unfavorable treatment at other times. Even when children are being disciplined, parents can show that they accept and love the child, in spite of his undesirable behavior.[3]

David once asked the question, "Oh LORD, who may abide in Thy tent? Who may dwell on Thy holy hill?" (Ps. 15:1, NASV). David answered the question by telling us that if we want to abide in God's tent, that is, to have fellowship with God, we must be the sort of person who "honors those who fear the LORD," and who "swears to his own hurt, and *does not change*" (Ps. 15:4, NASV). I believe David is talking about being consistent even if it hurts sometimes. Peter instructed us, "To sum up, let all be harmonious, sympathetic, brotherly, kind-hearted, and humble in spirit; not returning evil for evil, or insult for insult, but giving a blessing instead; for you were called for the very purpose that you might inherit a blessing" (I Peter 3:8-9, NASV). So let's be harmonious and consistent with each other and with our children.

## D.  Example.

Our children learn their behavior from us. In the end, *they do what we do* much more than what we say they should do. I had an alcoholic patient one time who was bragging to me about the discipline he practiced with his children. He told me that he made them go to church every Sunday morning, every Sunday night, and every Wednesday night. He made them read their Bibles every day. He made them study for at least one hour every night

---

3.  Gary Collins, *Man in Transition,* p. 66.

after school. And he wouldn't let them watch any television, because there were too many beer commercials. I responded, "This is fine, but do you go to church with them?" He said he didn't. Then I asked him if he read his Bible every day, and he said he hardly ever read it. Then I asked him if he studied very much, and he said he didn't. I asked him what he did every night, and he said he watched television and drank a fifth of whiskey. He was somewhat offended at me for making him aware of the fact that he was setting a poor example. His children will probably turn out the very opposite of what he wants, because he is telling them one thing and practicing another.

The Apostle Paul told his converts to follow his example—to do as he did. God said, *"O that there were such an heart in them, that they would fear me, and keep all my commandments always, that it might be well with them, and with their children for ever!"* (Deut. 5:29). Here God shows His tremendous love for us by voicing His desire that we live by His principles so that things will go well for us and for our children, and our children's children. He is saying that if we live by His principles, generations after us will follow our example. Do you want your children to exhibit the fruits of the Spirit? Then practice "love, joy, peace, patience, kindness, goodness, faithfulness, gentleness, self-control" (Gal. 5:22-23, NASV). Do you want your children to be truthful? Then follow God's advice when He tells us to speak the truth in love (see Eph. 4:15). Do you want your children to forgive each other, and to forgive you for mistakes you have made? Then follow God's advice when He tells you to "be kind to one another, tender-hearted, forgiving each other, just as God in Christ also has forgiven you" (Eph. 4:32, NASV).

I think we should extend our example beyond our own families into the community in which we live. God warns us quite strongly that any overseer in a church (pastor, deacon, elder) "must be one who manages his own household well, keeping his children under control with all dignity; but if a man does not know how to manage his own household, how will he take care of the church of God?" (I Tim. 3:4-5, NASV). God's Word is quite blunt here. If you are not managing your own family well, you are setting a poor example and have no right to try to manage God's flock as well. If you do try, in spite of your poor example, you will without a doubt be acting contrary to the will of God. One of my greatest accomplishments as a psychiatrist occurred when I convinced an alcoholic, adulterous, hostile minister to quit the ministry. He became a deputy sheriff instead. He may be just as unsuited to this line of work, but at least he's not misguiding God's precious sheep.

### E. A man at the head of the home.

As I have mentioned previously, a domineering, smothering mother and a weak father lie at the root of the vast majority of mental illnesses in children. Most mentally disturbed adults come from that type of parental heritage also. Solomon tells about two kinds of wives: "A worthy wife is her husband's joy and crown; the other kind tears down everything he has" (Prov. 12:4, LB). In the average American home, a child is with his mother five or six times as much as he is with his father. That's why I addressed my rules for producing neurotic children primarily to mothers. They bear a very heavy responsibility in American society today.

But let's take a good look at what God has to say about who should lead the home. God's Word says, "Wives, be subject to your husbands, as is fitting in the Lord" (Col. 3:18, NASV). God's Word also says, "For the husband is the head of the wife, as Christ also is the head of the church, He Himself being the Savior of the body" (Eph. 5:23, NASV). When God first created Adam, God said, "It is not good for the man to be alone; I will make him a helper suitable for him" (Gen. 2:18, NASV). Then after creating Eve, God told her, "Your desire shall be for your husband, and he shall rule over you" (Gen. 3:16, NASV). If any of you are married to an unsaved husband, here are God's instructions for you:

> In the same way, you wives, be submissive to your own husbands so that even if any of them are disobedient to the word they may be won without a word by the behavior of their wives, as they observe your chaste and respectful behavior. And let not your adornment be external *only*—braiding the hair, and wearing gold jewelry, and putting on dresses; but let it be the hidden person of the heart, with the imperishable quality of a gentle and quiet spirit, which is precious in the sight of God. For in this way in former times the holy women also, who hoped in God, used to adorn them-

selves, being submissive to their own husbands. Thus Sarah obeyed Abraham, calling him lord, and you have become her children if you do what is right without being frightened by any fear.                    —I Peter 3:1-6, NASV

The world will put increasing pressures on Christian women to assume equal authority in the home, or even greater authority than the husbands. But I would urge you, for the sake of your children as well as for the sake of obeying God's commandments, *"Don't copy the behavior and customs of this world"* (Rom. 12:2, LB).

# 7

## Spiritual Development

We are made up of body, soul, and spirit, so if we feed a child well and use healthy psychological principles, but ignore his spiritual development, we will be developing only two-thirds of a person. And since we will all live somewhere—either in heaven or in hell—forever, I believe the development of the child's spirit is the most important of the three. *Psychological development will enable our children to live in society and earn a living, but spiritual development will enable them to understand the meaning of life.* Carl Jung once stated, "The least of things with a meaning is worth more in life than the greatest of things without it." I have had wealthy patients with everything this world has to offer—but they were groping desperately for meaning in life.

At Duke University Medical Center I have done extensive research under Dr. William P. Wilson. Dr. Wilson is the Head of the Neurophysiology Department. He has published over 150 scientific articles and several books; he's the former President of the Southern Electroencephalographic Society, and has also been an officer in the Southern Psychiatric Association. Dr. Wilson was an agnostic not too many years ago. He had acquired everything scholastically and scientifically—but he says he had a gnawing void in his life. He went to a Boy Scout retreat with his son several years ago, and a lay witness told the boy scouts about God's simple plan of salvation. Dr. William P. Wilson, Chairman of the Neurophysi-

ology Department at Duke University, decided then and there to
humble himself and accept Jesus Christ as his personal Savior.
That met his void. He has been a changed man ever since, and
a tremendous witness for our Lord. I'm very thankful that God
gave me the opportunity to study under Dr. Wilson. We have
spent many hours praying together for our patients, and for each
other's needs.

Dr. Wilson's conversion thrills me, but something that thrills
me even more is the salvation of a young child whose parents
have lovingly guided his spiritual development by following God's
commandments to *teach* (Deut. 6:6-7), to *train* (Prov. 22:6), and
to *build* (Eph. 6:4) their child in a way that would enable him
to experience the abundant life (John 10:10). *This is where Chris-*
*tian men have fallen short. They have become so wrapped up in*
*the world that they have neglected their highest calling—the spir-*
*itual development of their children.*

God tells us fathers that He "established a testimony in Jacob,
and appointed a law in Israel, which He commanded our fathers,
that they should teach them to their children; that the generation
to come might know, even the children yet to be born, that they
may arise and tell them to their children, that they should put
their confidence in God, and not forget the works of God, but
keep His commandments" (Ps. 78:5-7, NASV). God has also said,
"And these words, which I command thee this day, shall be in
thine heart; And thou shalt teach them diligently unto thy children, and shalt talk of them when thou sittest in thine house,
and when thou walkest by the way, and when thou liest down,
and when thou risest up" (Deut. 6:6-7). God gave instruction to
"know well the condition of your flocks, and pay attention to your
herds" (Prov. 27:23, NASV). Solomon told us that "in the fear
of the Lord there is strong confidence, and his children will have
refuge" (Prov. 14:26, NASV). Now that we have seen our tremendous responsibility before God, let's look briefly at ways to
encourage spiritual development in each age group.

## A.  Prenatal.

You can't teach your child Bible verses before he is born, but
you can influence the environment in which he develops by enjoying the pregnancy, listening to soothing music, and taking good

care of your physical, emotional, and spiritual needs. Many scientists believe that such measures can influence the developing baby in some ways, although the proofs are not definite.

## B.  Infants (birth to fifteen months).

Some of the foundations for spiritual development are laid during infancy. The infant certainly does not understand our religious beliefs and concepts as such, but our religious beliefs and concepts strongly influence the attitudes we will have toward that infant. The infant can sense the overall home atmosphere, and begins to respond to our behavior and attitudes.

## C.  Toddlers (fifteen to thirty-six months).

The young toddler is rapidly acquiring language skills, grasping for new experiences, and observing everything that happens in the small world around him. How the child and his father relate to each other lays the groundwork for his future conceptions about what God is like. You can start by teaching him to say a memorized prayer to a loving, heavenly Father, though at thirty-six months of age, of course, he will be saying the words but thinking about what his earthly father is like. If you are a harsh, critical father, that will influence his conception of the Father to whom he is praying. If the child is in a loving, secure, and accepting environment during these months, he will develop a basic trust that will enable him later to have a more meaningful faith in God. I think what you let your child watch on television, and the music you play in the home, strongly influence his personality development in ways that will either facilitate or hinder his future spiritual development.

## D.  Preschoolers (three to six years).

During these years, our children pick up thousands of words in their vocabularies, but their knowledge of abstract concepts is still almost nil. They reason concretely, and everything is either black or white. This is known as dichotomous thinking. Without a stimulating environment, and some formal education, many people never outgrow this dichotomous way of thinking. In children this age, words are just that—words. Gary Collins mentions that even during the national anthem, which is supposed to be sung with such meaning, young children frequently substitute words like "the grandpas we watched were so gallantly streaming."[1] And they think that's what the song is about. This is just one example of how children this age reason.

I studied the works of Jean Piaget to some extent in my psychiatric training, especially when I was learning child psychiatry. My wife, who has a master's degree in early childhood development, studied Piaget even more than I did. Piaget did very extensive research on the neurological, social, and moral development of children. He even set up a timetable for the earlier years.[2] From his studies, we know among other things when the average child will say his first word, be neurologically ready for toilet-training, understand concrete concepts, tie his shoes, and understand abstract concepts. I'll be quoting Piaget a number of times in this book. His studies show that three- to six-year-old children reason quite concretely, and that they believe almost everything we tell them. The average child, in a relatively good school system, doesn't begin to reason abstractly until he is about eleven years old.[3] That's why prolonged reasoning with a three- to six-year-old child about his misconduct is such a futile waste of time. I make this mistake occasionally with my younger children; all the time I am reasoning with them about the moral concept they have disobeyed, their little minds are wandering at least a mile away. A quick spanking, hard enough to bring repentance, is so much more effective and useful in dealing with children this age. They can understand that if they do certain bad things, like rebelling, the result will be either a short verbal rebuke or else instant physical pain; and if they do certain good things, like sharing their toys, the result will be parental praise, approval, and maybe even a big hug. This is what psychiatrists call behavior modification—positive reinforcement of the behavior you want to develop, and negative reinforcement of the behavior you want to discourage. Sometimes just ignoring some types of mild bad behavior is in itself negative reinforcement.

By now some of you may be asking yourselves, "What does

---

1. Gary Collins, *Man in Transition,* p. 48.
2. See bibliography references 307-13.
3. John E. Peters, *Lectures on Piaget.*

all of this have to do with the spiritual development of my three-
to six-year-old?" Well, the answer is that we need to understand
his level of reasoning in order to multiply our effectiveness in
teaching him spiritual things. For example, stories about Jesus
and some of the little children in the Bible have a great deal
of meaning to children this age, whereas teaching them about abstract concepts like parable interpretation or "agape" love will
only make them wish you would hurry up and get done so they
can get back to their toys. The more appropriate the spiritual
training the child has during these three years, the more he will
rely on his Christian faith when he is older and has meaningfully
accepted Jesus Christ as his Savior. I believe some children *can*
understand enough during the latter part of their first six years
to know that they are frequently sinful, that they want God to
forgive them, and that they want to live forever in heaven—and
they put their simple faith in Christ, who taught that unless we
as adults put our faith in Him in the manner of a little child,
we will in no wise inherit the kingdom. I was reared in a very
godly home, and I was six years old when I understood enough
to put my faith in Christ. Moreover, I have personally led to
Christ five- and six-year-olds whom I felt to be genuinely ready for
salvation.

As we help our three- to six-year-olds develop spiritually, we
must keep in mind that the main sources of their learning, whether
at church or at home, are their total life experiences rather than
our words. As Gary Collins says, "A 'loving heavenly Father' is
foolishness if the child's earthly father is harsh and unkind.... Even
the child's views of God, Heaven, angels, and Hell are in terms
of pictures he has seen."[4] Children this age frequently pray as
though God were a magician in the sky whose purpose is to grant
their thoughtless and selfish wishes. I have known a great number
of adults who still pray that way. They try to play God and to
use God's magic to accomplish *their will,* instead of asking God
to show them *His will* in the matter, so they can act accordingly.
As we pray with our children, we should show them by our example that prayer is a means of merging our will with the will
of God.

During this stage of development, children pick up their

---

4. Collins, *Man in Transition,* p. 53.

notions of what is right or wrong from what they see us doing, not from what we say is right or wrong. For instance, I know on the basis of Scripture that there is nothing sinful about feeling the emotion of anger, and I encourage my oldest child to let me know when he feels angry (see, e.g., Eph. 4:26). If he inappropriately hits me when he is angry or throws something at me, I spank him; but if he comes up to me and tells me he is feeling angry toward me or someone else, I thank him for telling me and we talk about it for a while. But somewhere or other, probably from my own behavior at some time, he has picked up the concept that it is sinful to feel anger. To my surprise I found this out when we were watching a Walt Disney show on television one afternoon. There was a good man in the show who became quite angry when he discovered that someone had stolen his prize watermelon. Later, the boy who stole it came and apologized. He and the man shook hands and made arrangements for the boy to do some work on the farm to pay for having stolen the watermelon (which is a great idea, by the way, because it will relieve the boy's guilt feelings and at the same time teach him that there are consequences for bad behavior). Anyway, I was glad my older boy and I had watched it together. But about an hour or two later, he came up to me and said, "Daddy, that man was bad!" I didn't know what he was talking about, so I asked him. He told me that the man in the watermelon story was a bad man. So I told him, "No he wasn't! He was a good man! What makes you think he was a bad man?" And to my dismay he replied, "He was a bad man, because he got angry." So I explained to him that it's all right to feel angry. It all depends on what we do with that anger.

Another thing we have to watch out for is lying to our children. This is a terrible thing to do, and yet lying to our children is an American tradition. Before any of you throw this book away, let me explain what I mean. Our child loses a tooth, and what's the traditional thing to do? Why, of course! We tell him that if he'll put his tooth under his pillow, a tooth fairy will sneak in at night and put money there. When Christ's birthday, commonly known as Christmas, comes around, the American tradition is to go to all ends to convince our three- to six-year-olds that there is a man called Santa Claus who is omniscient ("he sees you when you're sleeping, he knows when you're awake"), omnipresent ("he

knows if you've been bad or good," no matter where in the world
you live), and omnipotent (he can carry tons of toys all around
the world in a matter of hours, and fly up and down chimneys)
For many Christian children, Santa Claus is an idol that replaces
Jesus Christ, whose birthday we are supposedly celebrating.[5] But
instead of focusing on His birthday, Christmas becomes a big
materialistic experience that keeps us going from Thanksgiving
until New Year's Day! Do you realize that when your six-year-old
goes to school and finds out you, his Christian parents, have
been lying to him for six years about something that has become
a major part of his religious beliefs, he will subsequently have
doubts about everything else you have taught him—especially about
God? Is this a laughing matter? I don't think so.

I'm not a mean old Scrooge who wants to take all the fun
out of Christmas. When we go to the department store during
the Christmas season, I take my children toward Santa's corner,
telling them on the way: "Ah! There's another man dressed up
in a funny red suit and beard. Go climb on his lap and he'll give
you some candy." My son Dan laughs and says, "There's not really
a Santa Claus, Daddy, is there?" And I'll respond, "No, Santa
Claus is just a funny game that we play." Then Dan will cheer-
fully climb up on Santa's lap, and when Santa asks him what he
wants for Christmas, Dan will point into his bag and say, "I want
some of that candy!" He has just as much fun with Santa Claus
as the boy who prays to him every night. But unlike that other
boy Dan can always trust his parents to tell him the truth about
everything. When we get home from the store, Dan frequently
asks me something like, "Where do that man dressed like Santa
Claus and his mommy live?" (He still calls all wives "mommies.")
So I tell him that the man and his wife probably live somewhere
not too far from the store, and probably have some children just
as we do. And he's satisfied.

I don't think there is any one right way to celebrate Christmas.
It would be dichotomous thinking for me to say so. But I do think
that there are a lot of wrong ways to celebrate the birth of Christ.
Our three children are still quite young, so we have a brief religious ceremony in the home. We tell them a true story about
the birth of Christ, showing them our little manger scene as we

5. Ibid., pp. 55-56.

tell it. Then we all get on our knees and I pray for about a minute or two, thanking God for sending His Son Jesus to become a man, so that when He got big, He could die on that tree to pay for all the bad things that all of us (daddy included) have done. Then we carry on with some of our family traditions. For example, we drive around and look at the Christmas lights. Arriving home, we light a fire in the fireplace, eat some pistachio ice cream, drink a little egg nog, and then go to sleep. This is all on Christmas Eve, by the way. On Christmas morning, we let the children open a few simple presents that have been sitting under the Christmas tree for days, presents they know are from mommy and daddy and not from Santa Claus. We tell them that we give presents to remind us that the wise men brought presents to Jesus, and that Jesus is God's present to us—but at their age that's as deep as we get. When they are older, I'll tell them other facts. I'll tell them that Martin Luther, a great Christian who lived many years ago, was the first man to put an evergreen tree in his home at Christmas, and that he did so because it was shaped like an arrow pointing up to God in heaven. So I'm not a Scrooge who makes his children stay on their knees all day Christmas.

Some Christians don't give any presents at Christmas because of the materialism involved, and I must admit, I don't blame them a bit! They have their fun in other ways, and explain to their children why they don't buy presents for that particular day. I think that's a good idea and may adopt it at some future date, but for the present my conscience is satisfied with giving each other some simple gifts—things that we need anyway.

The same holds true for Easter. We tell our children the Easter story very simply over and over again—how Jesus died and came back to life again, because He is God, that He is still alive and helps us every day, and that some day we will all go up to heaven to live with Him forever and ever. But we also take the children to the local neighborhood Easter egg hunt, and color a few eggs ourselves. We give them a plastic shovel and bucket with some candy in it for a present. This they can use later for digging sand. We even have their picture taken at a store, as they sit on an Easter Bunny's lap—but again they know ahead of time that it is a girl wearing a costume.

Another thing we can do to be truthful with our children

is to be sure to let them know when we are telling them a fairy tale and when we are telling them a true story. It's very difficult for a young child to separate the two. I believe some of the traditional fairy tales American and European mothers tell their young children can have detrimental effects. All the stories of violence and witches and people cutting off other people's heads create tremendous fears in three- to six-year-olds who see mean giants hiding in their closets at night. My wife and I are even somewhat selective as to which Bible stories to tell our children at each stage of their development. I eventually want them to know all the Bible stories, that is, when they are ready to comprehend their significance. We don't read them the Song of Solomon yet, but we will when they are teenagers. I would encourage you to buy your children Christian story books and to use them often, along with some healthy secular story books. Fleming H. Revell publishers even put out Christian comic books. Just remember that your child's brain is much more complex than our best computers, and like a computer, what you feed into your child's brain during those first six years is what's going to come out of his brain the next seventy years. This applies to television and the type of music played in the home too. My approach to raising children might be called a type of Gestalt approach. "Gestalt" means looking at the whole forest instead of just singling out one tree. One single mistake, like one tree in the forest, won't do much harm to our children. In fact, they can tolerate quite a few parental errors and still turn out quite normal. It's only when most of the forest has been raised on Satan's fertilizer instead of God's rain that we produce a depreciated plot of land.[6]

---

6. If you comprehend the meaning of this last sentence, you have what we call abstract reasoning ability. If you think the sentence merely refers to fertilizer and trees, you have only concrete reasoning ability. The average child, according to Piaget, is able to understand these last three sentences at about age eleven if he has had an adequate education.

# PART III THREE

*From Conception to Age Six:*
*Specific Findings*

# 8

## Prenatal Development

In spite of the fact that some geniuses weighed only a few pounds at birth, and that some mentally retarded persons weighed quite a bit at birth, there are indications in pediatric research that there is some relationship between higher birth weight and higher I.Q. If your child didn't weigh much at birth, don't worry about it. There's not that much of a difference if he gains enough weight the first six months of life. The significance of this is that when you are pregnant, you should be sure to eat some protein every day, to drink some milk, to take vitamin tablets with iron, and not to smoke cigarettes. It's the quality of food, not the quantity. The average pregnant woman should gain about eighteen to twenty pounds during the nine months of pregnancy, and most of that will be in the last three or four months.[1] Gaining too much weight during pregnancy will make the baby's delivery more difficult, not to mention what it will do to your own self-worth and your husband's opinion of you. If you are already overweight when you get pregnant, you won't need to gain anything if you eat

---

1. J. Robert Willson, et al., *Obstetrics and Gynecology*, p. 274. According to Willson, the fetus (7-1/2 lbs.), placenta (1 to 1-1/2 lbs.), amniotic fluid (1 to 2 lbs.), increase in the size of the uterus (2 to 2-1/2 lbs.) and breasts (2 to 3 lbs.), and increased blood volume (3 lbs.), as well as increased extravascular fluid, make up the eighteen to twenty pounds the average woman should gain during pregnancy.

the proper foods and take vitamins.[2] But I don't recommend that
you lose weight during pregnancy. God has arranged your body
physiology so that the developing baby gets what it needs first,
and what's left goes to you.

The other major area of concern during pregnancy is the
emotional condition of the mother. Depending on background
and experiences, pregnancy, especially the first pregnancy, can be
quite an anxiety-producing experience. *All women have ambiva-*
*lent feelings about pregnancy when they are pregnant.* That's normal. The worst thing a pregnant woman can do is to feel guilty
about these ambivalent feelings, or to try to convince herself that
she doesn't have them. If she keeps them pent up inside, they
will cause physiological changes in her body chemistry which could
potentially damage her health as well as influence the physical
development and eventual emotional condition of the developing
baby.

I know a military obstetrician who was treating several pregnant women with severe cases of toxemia. A couple of them were
near death, according to the doctor. And they weren't responding
to medical treatment. So he told them he was going to have to
abort their pregnancies. They agreed. He anesthetized them, splat-
tered some blood on them, and sent them back to their rooms
without having done anything at all to them. When they woke up,
they were told their babies had been aborted. They expressed some
brief sorrow, but *they all got over their toxemia of pregnancy.*[3] The
doctor used some faulty medical and legal judgment in doing what
he did, but he wanted to save their lives and the lives of their fetuses.
When the women found out several days later that they were still
pregnant and that the doctor had lied to them, they were quite
angry at him, and he found himself in considerable trouble with
his superior officers.

This experience implies a relationship between the unex-
pressed anxiety conflicts and the autonomic physiological reactions
in the expectant mother. So the best thing a pregnant woman can
do is to be aware of her ambivalent feelings—the positive and

---

2. Ibid.

3. This small (and illegal) research project in no way proves that all toxemias
of pregnancy are the result of psychic conflicts. Many physiological factors are
involved, but this illustration does imply a strong psycho-physiological correla-
tion in these particular women.

negatives aspects of having a baby, the fears of delivery itself, even ambivalent feelings about being a woman—and to talk them out with her husband and other significant people in her life. It's especially good to talk to another woman who has gone through the same experience, so you can share with each other. There is absolutely nothing abnormal or sinful about having these feelings. It would be abnormal if you didn't have them. And they won't do you any harm if you will talk them out and resolve them. Also be sure to meet your other normal emotional and spiritual needs. Have devotions every day, get plenty of rest, have your husband take you out once a week or more, listen to relaxing and preferably Christian music, and keep right on having the usual amount of sexual intercourse with your husband.[4] Some medical books say to have sex until the last month, and others say until delivery. Only very old medical books advise cutting down on sex during pregnancy. The average married couple has sex two or three times a week, and this a fairly good indicator of their overall emotional stability and relationship with each other.

---

4. Willson, *Obstetrics and Gynecology,* p. 277.

9

# The Newborn

I enjoyed delivering babies more than any other experience during my medical school training. It can also be quite an experience for the delivering mother—a good experience or a bad experience. It will be whatever you make of it. I don't think it really matters whether you opt for natural childbirth, caudal anesthesia, or "twilight sleep." Just do whatever is right for you without yielding to pressures from anyone else. I know that labor is quite painful—God said it would be (see Gen. 3:16). Nonetheless, the general feeling of obstetricians who have delivered babies in various parts of the world is that American women are the most immature about childbirth. And as a psychiatrist, I know that expectations greatly influence the actual experience. There are tribes in Africa that migrate from place to place to find food. When they are marching from one area to another, and one of their women goes into labor, she goes to the side of the road, squats down and has her baby, and then catches up to the rest of the tribe. I have also heard that most European women have natural childbirth, simply gritting their teeth during labor pains, whereas many American women scream for several hours before they find out they are only having false labor. My wife tells me, however, that if men had to go through labor, very few families would have more than one child! She may be right.

I do think breast-feeding is far superior to bottle-feeding, especially during the first few months of life. Modern hospitals today bring the mothers and babies together for breast-feeding if the mothers request it. During the first few days, the baby doesn't get much milk from the mother—he doesn't need it. What he does get is some fluid containing millions of maternal antibodies that will help protect him against infections. Mother's milk is far superior to cows' milk in many ways: it contains all needed proteins, including a higher quality of protein, and it's sterile and inexpensive.[1] And there is something about breast-feeding that brings not only physical but emotional warmth to both mother and baby. Breast-feeding also causes hormones to be released in the mother that actually cause the hips to pull back together, restoring her normal figure.[2] These hormones (especially the hormone prolactin) also serve as a natural tranquilizer for the mother, causing feelings of acceptance toward the child and contentment.[3] And although some women do have smaller breasts after breast-feeding, the average mother often permanently increases her breast size.

There are both rewarding and unrewarding ways to breast-feed. One study was made of fifteen male and fifteen female newborn babies breast-feeding. Notes were taken on the newborns' responses as their mothers took them off the nipple. The study was continued until they were eight months old. Those babies that didn't have a satisfactory time at the breast as a newborn, as measured by crying and thrashing, were also more tense at eight months, as measured by withdrawal from strange adults and strange situations. Those babies that were satisfied at the breast-feeding as newborns, as measured by high but unstressful activity after nipple withdrawal, were also more active, happier, and less tense at eight months.[4] I don't think nature has any more beautiful sight than a loving mother breast-feeding her totally dependent baby, and there is nothing more touching in the psychological realm than the relationship between a mother and her baby.

Another interesting study was done in which tape recordings

---

1. Mohsen Ziai, ed., *Pediatrics,* p. 193.
2. J. Robert Willson, et al., *Obstetrics and Gynecology,* p. 613.
3. Theodore Lidz, *The Person,* p. 130.
4. B. J. McGrade, "Newborn Activity and Emotional Response at Eight Months."

of thirty-one newborns were played to eight new mothers, forty-eight hours after delivery. All eight were able to select the cry of their own infant from the thirty-one recorded.[5] A second group of ten mothers in multi-bed hospital wards following delivery was observed to see if they woke up at night on hearing their own baby cry, or for that matter on hearing any baby cry. During the first three nights, fifteen out of twenty-six waking episodes were caused by their own baby's cry. After the third night, twenty-two out of twenty-three were for their own baby.[6] I think that's really a beautiful illustration of the mother-baby relationship. I know when our children cry at night, I seldom wake up at all!

Another study was done to analyze the development of feelings of attachment in fifty-four mothers during the first three months of their first child's life. The study showed that in the first month to six weeks, "the model mother experienced impersonal feelings of affection toward her infant, whom she tended to perceive as an anonymous nonsocial object."[7] In the second month, when the infants began to smile and look at things longer, "maternal feelings intensified and the infant was now viewed as a person with unique characteristics who recognized his mother."[8] After three months had passed, "maternal attachments were sufficiently strong to make the infant's absence unpleasant and his imagined loss an intolerable prospect."[9] It is significant that this investigation revealed that "mothers who developed an attachment late in time or not at all either did not want infants or had babies with deviant behavior."[10] Thus, significant things are happening even in the first three months of life which will affect the eventual adult emotional condition and personality.

My advice on having a baby is that you would be much better off if you wait until you are psychologically ready for one. Don't have babies because of pressure from parents or friends. Have them if and when you are emotionally ready to have them. Studies have shown an increased divorce rate in couples who have a baby dur-

---

5. D. Formby, "Maternal Recognition of Infant's Cry."
6. Ibid.
7. K. S. Robson, et al., "Patterns and Determinants of Maternal Attachments," p. 976.
8. Ibid.
9. Ibid.
10. Ibid.

ing the first two years of marriage, and a somewhat decreased divorce rate in couples who have their first baby after at least two years of marriage. I think it takes a couple of years merely to adjust to living with each other. So if you've been married less than a year and your marriage is already floundering, don't have a baby, hoping that the baby will bring you closer together. It will probably drive you farther apart. Work out your marital hang-ups first; think about a family later.

One of the most common problems psychiatrists are called upon to handle is postpartum depression. This is a rather serious depression starting soon after delivery and lasting for months, sometimes reaching psychotic proportions. Women who suffer from it need antidepressant medications initially, followed by long-term counseling sessions to help them accept motherhood.[11] Most women feel somewhat let down after delivery. This is to be expected; after all you have lost some blood and are anemic, and are now faced with getting up all hours of the night to change and feed the baby. But that usually takes care of itself if the mother gets some help, eats right, and catches up on her sleep. Also, the baby usually settles down to a more regular schedule within a few weeks. If the baby doesn't settle down to a regular schedule at one or two months, I think you should do yourself a favor and settle him down to one. A little crying won't hurt him. Check with your pediatrician about specific problems in this area though.

One more topic I would like to discuss in this chapter is babies born with birth defects and how to accept them. Fortunately, God has arranged a mother's physiology in such a way that most fetuses with birth defects end up as miscarriages within three or four months of pregnancy. The average mother will have about one miscarriage for every four or five pregnancies. But God allows some of these defective babies, including Mongoloids, to be born. I'm not going to debate the theological issue of whether this is God's directive or permissive will, but I do know that God allows it. And I know that Psalm 139 says that we were designed by God in our mother's womb and that the blueprint for this design was made thousands of years before we were even conceived. If my wife and I ever have a Mongoloid child or a child with other

---

11. Alfred M. Freedman and Harold I. Kaplan, eds., *Comprehensive Textbook of Psychiatry*, pp. 1161-63.

birth defects, I'm sure we will probably think it is God's directive will, but I don't claim to know the mind of God (see Deut. 29:29). I do know that God is love, and that "all things work together for good to them that love God, to them who are the called according to his purpose" (Rom. 8:28). I don't think being a psychiatrist would help me much either, if it happened to me. I would probably go through the usual stages of disbelief, followed by anger toward God, followed by anger toward myself, followed by some degree of grief, and hopefully followed by a resolution of the conflict, with much greater maturity and understanding than I had before. It can go the other way, though, and end up in excessive denial and social isolation. Then there is the problem later on of deciding whether to put a severely retarded youngster in a special home, or to keep him in his own home where he is disrupting the entire family's life. There are no clear-cut answers. I know godly people who have put their mentally handicapped youngsters in homes and are glad they did, and I know godly people who have kept them in their own homes and are glad they did. I personally believe that sometimes it is better for the severely retarded child to live in a home where he can get special training, with his parents visiting him as needed, but that in other cases it may be better to keep him in your own home.[12]

---

12. See bibliography references 114, 268, 279, and 380 for discussions of the mentally handicapped, and references 27, 39, and 285 for discussions of physically handicapped children.

# 10

## Infants
## (Birth to Fifteen Months)

### A. The importance of infancy.

Dr. Theodore Lidz, Chairman of the Department of Psychiatry at Yale University School of Medicine, states quite emphatically that "during no other period of life is the person so transformed both physically and developmentally" as during infancy.[1] He further states that "no part of his life experience will be as solidly incorporated in the individual, become so irrevocably a part of him, as his infancy."[2] Lack of physical care can result in ill health, wasting away, and death. Lack of social nurturing will result in distortions of emotional development and stunting of intellectual growth.

Even an improper diet can influence the infant's ultimate intellectual capacity, since *all of the nerve and brain cells a person will ever have are produced by six months of age.*[3] After six months of age, brain cells may continue to enlarge, but no more new cells will ever be formed. That's why the infant needs plenty of protein, which he gets primarily from milk, during those first six months of life. Many mothers in the ghetto bottle-feed their babies; since they can't afford much milk, they put things like Kool-Aid

---

1. Theodore Lidz, *The Person,* p. 117.
2. Ibid.
3. Mohsen Ziai, ed., *Pediatrics,* p. 48.

into their babies' bottles, and the result is fewer brain cells for their children for the rest of their lives. Programs like Head Start are usually too late. During those first six months the infant's physical needs predominate. During the remainder of his infancy, socialization and affection are just as important as his physical needs.

Another reason why infancy is so important is that during the fifteen months of infancy, the child's ultimate potential for developing *basic trust* is established, depending primarily on how trustworthy his mother is in meeting his basic needs. What makes things difficult is that a mother can give her infant too little or too much support. The human infant is among the most helpless and dependent of all of God's creatures. Too little support can leave the infant struggling for emotional survival, whereas too much support can lead the infant to become overly dependent. Dr. Gary Collins notes that development during infancy is "characterized by rapid physical growth, initial perceptual and intellectual development, a learning to cope with new experiences, early social and emotional development, and the beginnings of personality formation."[4] I think you can understand from these facts the tremendous importance of infancy.

## B.  The importance of stimulation and experience in infancy.

*1. The four basic drives.*

Human beings have four basic drives: (1) tissue drives, such as the need for oxygen, water, and food; (2) sexual drives; (3) defensive drives—primarily fear and aggression, which Walter B. Cannon labeled the "fight or flight" mechanism; and (4) drives for stimulation and activity.

*2. Spitz's study on marasmus.*

During World War II, a number of infants were placed in a European foundling home. Their mothers were allowed to stay with them during the first three months of life, during which time the infants developed normally. Then, apart from their mothers, they were cared for by nurses at a ratio of one nurse per eight to twelve infants. The infants were fed well, and got good medical attention, but received very little stimulation in the way of being handled by the busy nurses. As a result of this lack of stimulation,

---

4. Gary Collins, *Man in Transition,* p. 39.

30 percent of them died of malnutrition within the first year. Most of the survivors could not stand, walk, or talk by the age of four, and had become permanently and severely mentally retarded.[5] This condition, in which an infant refuses to eat and becomes more and more emaciated, is known as *marasmus* (pronounced ma-raz'-mus). It is also called failure to thrive, and occurs frequently, even in America. Research studies show that many of the parents of infants suffering from marasmus are physically abusive, with a high incidence of alcoholic fathers. Many of these infants have to be legally taken out of their homes, to be reared in foster homes instead. If caught in time, and if given a lot of physical stimulation, some of these infants recover and may even live relatively normal lives thereafter.[6]

### 3. Duke's "TV Kid."

I know of a very small, emaciated six-year-old boy whose mother worked long hours and left him every day with his maternal grandmother. Unfortunately, the grandmother couldn't tolerate children, so she put him in a crib every day from infancy, and put the crib in front of a TV set in a small room with nothing else and nobody else in it. The child's only company was that TV set, except when the grandmother brought in his food and laid it in his crib. By the age of six, the boy was very poorly developed, emaciated, and the size of an average three-year-old. He could not talk, except for repeating TV commercials, which he did over and over again. When his child psychiatrist at Duke Hospital asked him questions, he would spout off another TV commercial quite accurately. Various people worked with the lad extensively, but he was permanently handicapped both physically and mentally. The mother was rehabilitated and the child was eventually returned to her custody. He'll probably be nicknamed "The TV Kid." Unfortunately, this is not a rarity in America today. I have seen numerous unmarried mothers on welfare with as many as sixteen or eighteen children. They were drawing large welfare checks, while their children were out roaming the streets. I remember

---

5. René A. Spitz, "Hospitalism: An Inquiry into the Genesis of Psychiatric Conditions in Early Childhood."

6. Sue L. Evans, et al., "Failure to Thrive. A Study of 45 Children and Their Families." See also P. S. Goldman, "The Relationship Between the Amount of Stimulation in Infancy and Subsequent Emotionality."

driving through downtown Memphis close to midnight one time and seeing groups of very young children playing kick the can. I wept for them.

### 4. Animal studies.

The importance of stimulation, and of the *right kinds* of stimulation, has also been demonstrated in various animals. Dogs, for instance, that were restricted as pups by being raised in cages, developed striking abnormalities of behavior by the time they reached maturity.[7] When these same dogs were allowed to leave their cages as young adults, they exhibited excessive behavioral arousal—meaning that they became overly excited by anything new in their environment. They went into whirling fits so violent that they frequently would break the skin on their heads against the walls. They also exhibited impairment of selective perceptual processes—meaning that they ran around the room from one object to another, rarely showing sustained attention to any single object. They also had considerable difficulty getting along with normally reared dogs that were placed in their area. Another interesting study showed that rats which were handled daily, early in life, had a much more vigorous antibody response to infections than did rats deprived of physical handling early in life.[8] And so in the animal kingdom, as well as in man, the adult's emotional condition and personality are strongly influenced by the amount and type of stimulation received during infancy.[9]

### C.  Mother substitutes.

### 1. Mothers in the American labor force.

With 40 percent of American mothers currently in the labor force, either part-time or full-time, "mother substitutes" becomes an even more important subject than it already was. One research study showed that "the loss of mother is disturbing to an infant and produces a searching, agitated response. Substitute mothering serves to relieve the distress, the extent depending in part on the degree of mothering provided and in part on the specific nature

---

7. R. Melzack, "The Role of Early Experience in Emotional Arousal," p. 721.
8. G. F. Solomon, "Emotions, Stress, the Central Nervous System, and Immunity."
9. Goldman, "Stimulation in Infancy," p. 649.

of the tie to mother."[10] Further, if the loss of the infant's mother is not relieved, "the infant soon lapses into a state of severe depression and withdrawal that appears to conserve his resources and minimize the danger of injury."[11]

### 2. Piaget's findings.

Some of Jean Piaget's studies indicate that adequate mother substitutes are all right the first six months of life or so, but that on the social level the mother is very specifically needed by about seven months of age.[12] The infant then needs his own mother for security and socialization, or there will be a variable extent of permanent emotional and intellectual damage. Before the child is seven or eight months of age, another competent person can be substituted for the mother without any serious consequences, but not very readily after that age.

### 3. Unconditional acceptance.

Dr. Eugene McDanald states that "the mother's unconditional acceptance of the infant is the precursor to healthy self-acceptance which enables him to make the most of himself within the framework of his personal strengths and limitations, both physical and mental."[13] He adds further that "the child who has been unconditionally loved has a good conscience, experiences normal anxiety, and is relatively free in his choice of action."[14] On the other hand, the infant who has been conditionally loved, as he grows older, "has a restrictive or a 'bad' conscience and experiences undue quantities of anxiety, hostility, and guilt which engender various forms of compulsive behavior of a social or antisocial character."[15] By the time a child is old enough to go to school, most of his character structure has already been established. An emotionally healthy, reflective child will be greatly enriched by this new contact with peers, teachers, and information. However, the anxiety-laden child who fears the unknown will feel threatened by his new interpersonal and environmental relationships. Dr. McDanald

---

10. I. C. Kaufman, et al., "Effects of Separation from Mother on the Emotional Behavior of Infant Monkeys," p. 695.

11. Ibid.

12. John E. Peters, *Lectures on Piaget.*

13. Eugene McDanald, "Emotional Growth of the Child," p. 74.

14. Ibid.

15. Ibid.

has wisely remarked, "The person who reaches adulthood with the feeling that life has been kind to him wants to give something of himself back to life."[16] I would strongly advise those of you who are working mothers, especially if your children are still infants, to quit your jobs. Don't be afraid to deprive your infants of material things if you can give them yourselves instead. I have a special place in my heart for handicapped and retarded children, and I believe they, even more than non-handicapped children, need their mother's unconditional love and acceptance to prepare them for what they will have to face when they become old enough to go to school.

### 4. Hospitalized infants.

Another group of children who especially need their mothers are children who have to be hospitalized. Studies have shown that young children whose mothers don't come and spend a lot of time with them in the hospital have a significantly higher mortality rate.[17]

### 5. Over-indulgence versus deprivation.

I want to remind you once again that meeting the infant's desires can be overdone or underdone. Overly-indulged infants become inappropriately optimistic and expect the world to look out for them when they reach adulthood. Deprived infants have a deep-seated pessimism, become hostile and resentful when their needs are not met, and tend to give up easily.[18]

### 6. Harlow's monkeys!

I want to end this section on mother substitutes by telling you about Harlow's monkeys. Harry and Margaret Harlow are a husband and wife research team who conducted an interesting and by now fairly well-known study on mother substitution in monkeys. They took a group of young monkeys away from their mothers, and put them in areas where they could choose between two imitation mothers. One "mother" was made out of wire, and had a baby bottle attached which was kept full of milk. The other "mother" was a soft, terry cloth mother, but with no feeding device attached. Interestingly, the monkeys would go get milk from

---

16. Ibid., p. 79.
17. Lidz, *The Person*, p. 150. See also M. Lynch, et al., "Family Unit in Children's Psychiatric Hospital."
18. Lidz, *The Person*, p. 151.

the wire mother, but run to the soft terry cloth mother whenever they were frightened.[19] So be a soft terry cloth mother, not a wire mother.

## D. Developmental adaptation in infancy.

*1. Six major tasks to which infants must adapt.*

  a. Developing responses to environmental stimuli.

  b. Controlling normal body functions, such as feeding, elimination, and sleeping.

  c. Adapting to physical illnesses.

  d. Adapting to major behavioral changes, such as weaning.

  e. Adapting to more and more social expectations imposed by parents.

  f. Adapting to rapidly developing modes of mobility (crawling, standing, walking, falling).

*2. Problems of family mobility.*

Gary Collins notes that the typical problem areas of infants and their mothers center around "feeding, weaning, sleeping, thumb-sucking, excessive crying and, later, toilet training."[20] He mentions that

> in years gone by, the mother gained support, encouragement and advice on these matters from experienced and sympathetic relatives, but this has all changed with the current mobility of families. In the United States approximately one family in every four moves each year. Relatives are now often far away, and the young parents who reside in relatively unfamiliar communities must depend more on books and articles —some of which give conflicting and confusing advice.[21]

*3. Mountains or molehills?*

Parents frequently make mountains out of molehills, worrying about things that are absolutely normal—especially with the first child. For instance, thumb-sucking, genital play and "security blan-

---

19. Harry F. Harlow and Margaret K. Harlow, *The Affectional Systems in Behavior of Non-Human Primates.*
20. Collins, *Man in Transition,* p. 4.
21. **Ibid.**

kets" should all be expected as normal ways in which infants gain
comfort. Depriving the infant of such gratification may result in
frustration and increased insecurity. It's best to ignore these things,
especially in infancy.

*4. Stress is good for you (and your child too)!*

Parents are also frequently overly concerned about various
minor stresses injuring the mental health of their infants, when
in reality a degree of stress is beneficial to the infant.[22] Dr. Theodore Lidz states that "overprotection or development in an extremely stable and homogeneous setting is likely to produce color-
less individuals. As everyday experience often shows, difficulty can
strengthen one; trauma can produce defenses that can serve well
in later emergencies; deprivations can harden."[23] So it's all a matter
of degrees again. On telling me some of the stresses they have
been through, some patients are surprised when I respond, "Great!
Stress is good for you! It will help you to mature!"

*5. Sensory-motor stage of development.*

The neurological stages of development in infancy are best
described by Jean Piaget, the Swiss psychologist. Piaget calls infancy the sensory-motor stage of development, since it is primarily
a preverbal stage during which the infant gains sensory and motor
skills. During the first month of life, the infant learns by repetition of his innate reflexes, such as sucking, crying, blinking, and
breathing. During the second month, the infant learns that he has
voluntary control over some of these automatic responses. He can
stick his thumb in his mouth, stare, suck, and make noises at will
now. During the next six or seven months he will learn to play,
show emotion, imitate, and spend longer periods of time investi-
gating various objects by sticking them in his mouth and rubbing
them. Toward the end of the first year, he is able to crawl around
and may even be starting to walk. He tries to experience everything
available. This means his parents must make the house child-
proof. The average American home contains about seventeen poi-
sonous substances or medications that an exploring infant could
get into, such as furniture polish, aspirins, insecticides, and pre-

22. William Reese, Lecture to medical students, University of Arkansas Medical
Center.
23. Lidz, *The Person*, p. 88.

scription medications in mothers' purses. The major cause of death in infancy is accidents, including household accidents and overdosing. A friend of mine treated a mother for depression after her infant son died from drinking furniture polish while he was supposed to be napping. It can happen to anyone. Yet parents should be aware that infants who grow up in homes where they are constantly getting their hands slapped for getting into things tend to become adults who are rigid in their thinking and fearful of exploring new ideas.

The average one-year-old can say about one or two words, like dada and mama, although some can say quite a few more and others don't start speaking until the end of infancy. The rate of development is no prediction of ultimate I.Q., unless it is extremely slow. Albert Einstein was said to be a late developer, for instance. So don't rush your infant—just accept him, enjoy him, and give him a wide variety of experiences. He'll move on to each stage when he is neurologically ready to do so. A fear of strangers also develops toward the end of the first year, and at about a year, children also show a fear of animals. Some children may also fear an expanse of water, like the ocean, when they see it for the first time. They learn a fear of heights by experience—after falling off the couch a couple of times![24]

### 6. Characteristics of development.

In summary, note that development is (1) orderly and in sequences, (2) uneven—meaning that it occurs in spurts, (3) unique —meaning that no two children develop at exactly the same rate, and (4) the result of both maturation and learning.[25]

## E.  Environment versus heredity.

### 1. The pendulum swings!

Debates have gone on for years over the roles of environment versus heredity. Two generations ago, there was an overemphasis on heredity—a person was a criminal because he inherited a criminal mind and had a criminally-shaped head, and similar foolishness. This foolish thinking continues today in the form of astrology. The past generation generally blamed nearly everything on environment

---

24. Peters, *Lectures on Piaget*. See also bibliography references 307-13.
25. Collins, *Man in Transition*, pp. 26-28.

and ignored hereditary aspects. But with the volumes of research data that are pouring in every day, scientists are now taking a good look at both heredity and environment, because most aspects of the human body and mind, such as eventual personality, are influenced by both hereditary and environmental factors.

*2. Are children really born princes and princesses?*

I was once particularly amused by a guest speaker at Duke University Medical Center. He was a liberal theologian who had graduated from Harvard. He was active in civil rights in the late '60s, and was a teaching member of the transactional analysis movement. He told us that he agreed with Eric Berne, who taught that "children are born princes and princesses, and environment makes frogs out of them."[26] He said that children are born with a good nature, rather than a sinful nature, and that their parents make frogs out of them. If children are born good, my children must have received unfair treatment when the genes were passed around, because they could lie before they could talk.

*3. What the Bible says about your child's nature.*

Children are *not* born with good natures. They are born with sinful natures, and we parents have to work hard to set good examples if we are to teach them to be good, which is against their nature. God's Word tells us that "foolishness is bound in the heart of a child; but the rod of correction shall drive it far from him" (Prov. 22:15). God is saying here that we inherit a sinful (foolish) nature, and that by discipline we learn to be good. Freedman and Kaplan's psychiatry textbook notes that "typically the child learns to say no before he learns to say yes. He knows what he doesn't want long before he is able to formulate what he does want."[27] Jean Piaget's studies also show that moral behavior is learned, and that children are not born with good morals.[28] Young children try to imitate and please their parents to avoid punishment for being bad, and to gain approval for being good. Solomon said, "The rod and reproof give wisdom, but a child who gets his own way brings shame to his mother" (Prov. 29:15, NASV).

---

26. Grant Barnes, Notes from his grand rounds at Duke University.
27. Alfred M. Freedman and Harold I. Kaplan, eds., *Comprehensive Textbook of Psychiatry*, p. 580.
28. See Jean Piaget, *The Moral Judgment of the Child.*

# 11

## Toddlers
## (Fifteen to Thirty-Six Months)

### A. Developmental adaptations.

*1. Seven proverbs on discipline.*

These scriptural principles take on special meaning during the toddler stage of development.

Proverbs 13:24. "He who spares his rod hates his son, but he who loves him disciplines him diligently."

Proverbs 19:18. "Discipline your son while there is hope."

Proverbs 22:6. "Train up a child in the way he should go, and when he is old, he will not depart from it."

Proverbs 22:15. "Foolishness is bound in the heart of a child; but the rod of correction shall drive it far from him."

Proverbs 23:13. "Do not hold back discipline from the child. When you beat him with the rod, he won't die."

Proverbs 29:15. "The rod and reproof give wisdom, but a child who gets his own way brings shame to his mother."

Proverbs 29:17. "Correct your son, and he will give you
comfort; he will also delight your soul."

*2. Parental limit-setting.*

The reason these passages of Scripture take on such meaning
is that this is the stage when the need for discipline really blossoms.
It is one of the most trying stages for the patience of both parents.
The main reason is that the toddler has acquired fantastic, new-
found motor skills, yet has meager mental capacities. His chief
mental capacity seems to be the capacity to be curious about everything that you call a "no-no." By removing many of these "no-no's,"
the toddler can still be allowed and even encouraged to follow his
natural bent toward exploration. During the first fifteen months
of life, known as infancy, the mother is encouraged to develop in
her child as much independence as possible. But during the next
twenty-one months or so, known as the toddler stage, she must teach
the child to respect limits and renounce immediate gratifications,
while still encouraging a healthy degree of independence.

*3. How to drive the "terrible threes" out of a two-year-old.*

My wife and I are both very loving and nurturing parents, and
yet we remember spanking our older son or slapping his hand for
open rebellion many times during those crucial twenty-one months
(15th to 36th months). Since we trained him well during the
toddler stage by encouraging independence and exploration, yet
spanking him for willful disobedience, he came out of it very well
behaved for his age, and he *continued* to have a healthy degree of
independence at the same time. I've heard a lot about the terrible
threes, but I think we drove a lot of the terrible threes out of
him when he was still two, because his third birthday brought on
a new era of relative peace, although he still needed an occasional
spanking. Now that he is older, he loves us so much that he really
strives to please us, doing his chores and going to bed when we ask
him to without complaining, and he rarely needs more than a sad or
scornful look to correct his behavior. We keep the paddle handy
though. Also, the younger children are easier to discipline than
he was, because they follow his good example.

*4. Basic self-trust and a sense of initiative.*

This is a crucial stage in the development of basic self-trust
and a sense of initiative. A domineering, overly demanding, and

overly protective mother, at this stage, will develop in her toddler a lack of self-trust, self-worth, and initiative. A sense of worthlessness results from constantly not living up to parental expectations. One excellent research study showed that many of the mothers of male schizophrenics could not differentiate between their own needs and feelings and those of their sons![1] The schizophrenic's mother, then, would treat him as a symbiotic extension of herself. She expected her son to complete her life by living out the life she couldn't live, limiting the child's autonomy and fostering dependence rather than independence. The husband was either absent or quite passive, and the mother encouraged her son to be different from his father. She played on her son's guilt, making him feel that if he left her it would destroy her. These mothers were basically overprotective and intrusive, but at the same time cold and aloof. The fathers of schizophrenic daughters were frequently seductive but suspicious and paranoid.[2]

5. *Realistic expectations.*

In disciplining the child and setting firm limits, which is absolutely necessary, parents must also *be realistic* as to what is to be expected in a child this age. That's one reason why the first-born child frequently bears the brunt of going through this stage with inexperienced parents who don't know what can realistically be expected of him. We'll discuss some studies on first-born children later on. Let me say here that many of them become quite perfectionistic, as can be seen from the fact that fifteen out of America's first sixteen astronauts were first-born sons. They had to be perfectionistic for the type of work they did. Their lives depended on it.

Take the neurological readiness for toilet-training, for instance. I know mothers who try to toilet-train their infants by the time they reach their first birthday, when in reality, neurological readiness does not come to the average child until anywhere from eighteen months to more than four years of age. And also, we as parents are frequently very disappointed when we have just spanked our child for getting into something he shouldn't, only to find him doing it again five minutes later. The right thing to do, in my opinion, is to patiently spank him again, rather than to throw

1. Theodore Lidz, "The Nature and Origins of Schizophrenic Disorders."
2. Ibid.

up our hands and scream. Children at the toddler stage have very short attention spans and short memories. Parents should be aware of these age characteristics and realize that instructional do's and don't's need to be repeated many times before a toddler understands them. Although the behavior of the toddler may become somewhat exasperating, especially when it results in the destruction of some precious object, or in a mess that is hard to clean up, what the child really needs at this stage of life is calm parents. Such a requirement almost demands a supernatural act of God in many cases.

### 6. How's your child wired?

I mentioned before that every child is wired differently. Boys are generally more active than girls, since they have more androgen in their blood. I know some parents whose children are very well behaved, and require relatively few spankings. A lot of that has to do with the inherited activity level of the children. Some parents warn their child three times every time he does something he knows he shouldn't, then spank him when he does it a fourth time. I don't recommend this, because these children go through life doing all the wrong things three times before fearing any punishment, and in real life, you might get caught after the first, second, or third time.

### 7. Socialization.

At about two years of age, the toddler should have enough basic trust to develop relationships with other children, including the freedom to express and assert himself, even in his crude ways. The presence of other children after the second birthday is very important, because this is the time in his life when he is neurologically and emotionally ready for learning social skills.

### 8. Food refusal.

Food refusal is common during the late toddler stage. This is frequently a manipulative gesture to express hostility toward the parent. But sometimes toddlers simply don't like certain foods. My older son went through a stage of not liking meat when he was about two years old. He would eat everything else on his plate and leave the meat. We knew it was important for him to eat protein, so I asked a nutritionist at the medical center where I worked what she would recommend. She gave me such a simple solution I was almost embarrassed for asking her. She told me to put protein and nothing else on his plate for a few days. If he didn't eat protein, he wouldn't eat. When he got hungry enough, he would get used to eating protein. It worked like a charm and took only one or two meals to break him in. So don't let your toddler succeed in getting you angry by refusing to eat—just remove his food if he becomes too negativistic or dawdles unduly with it. It won't hurt him to miss a meal or two occasionally—in fact, it will help him in the long run. And don't give him any between meal snacks unless he has earned that right by eating a reasonable amount at the previous mealtime. We allow our own children to eat as much as they choose to, but if they don't eat a reasonable amount, they get nothing until the next meal. This way, we have no squabbles at mealtime. Mealtime should be a time for developing social skills, especially between mother and toddler, as well as a time for eating. Be sure you don't substitute food for love or social interaction.

*9. What about pacifiers?*

Mothers frequently ask me my opinion about pacifiers too, so I'll make a few comments on them here. Basically, I think pacifiers are fine, although they can be potentially dangerous. Many mothers tie a pacifier around the neck of their toddler so the pacifier won't get lost, not realizing that this is quite dangerous— the child could fall, catching the string on something, and thus choke. Also, worn-out pacifiers should be thrown away and replaced, because the rubber end of the pacifier has been known to break loose and choke a toddler who bites through it. However, a child at the infant and toddler stages needs a good deal of oral gratification, and I have found that children who get to suck on a pacifier as much as they want to during infancy and the first half of the toddler stage generally do not suck their thumbs so much when they leave these stages. Our two oldest children made heavy use of pacifiers at first. When they were about a year and a half, we tried not giving them a pacifier to see how they would respond, and neither of them missed it. And neither of them sucks his thumb. Our third child refused a pacifier in infancy and never used one at all. If your children do suck their thumbs, the best advice I can give is not to worry about it—it's quite normal. Just ignore it. If they are over five years of age and getting ready to go to school, you will probably want to put a stop to it, but before that time there's nothing to worry about. Some psychiatrists feel that thumb-sucking beyond age four may indicate that that particular child did not receive enough maternal warmth and affection during feeding periods in infancy.[3] Some parents are afraid that thumb-sucking will result in buck teeth, but research studies indicate that buck teeth are seldom the result of thumb-sucking.[4]

### 10. Genital play.

I would also recommend that you ignore genital play during the toddler stage, unless your child is doing so in public. It's part of his natural exploration in discovering his body. If you choose not to ignore it, handle the situation tactfully by merely putting his underwear back on and telling him he should leave it on. But don't ever shame him for it, or threaten him in any way, or he will think his genitals are evil and develop poor sexual concepts later in life. It could even result in neurotic fears in adult life, and sometimes even impotence.

When your children ask questions about their anatomy, and believe me they will, the best thing you can do is to give them truthful, matter-of-fact answers. It is generally felt best to go ahead and use words like urination, vagina, urethra, and penis, rather than the childish words we frequently substitute.[5]

### 11. The concept of sharing.

Another important development during the toddler stage is the willingness to share. If you want your child to understand such concepts as unselfishness, sharing, and the results of stealing, the foundation for these concepts must be laid in the toddler stage. Our children have lots of sibling rivalry just like other children, but they also share quite a bit, because we praise them whenever they do share with each other or with us. And we set the example by sharing many of our things with them. When one takes a toy out of another's hands, we slap his hand or spank him. This is stealing, in a primitive sort of way. It's coveting your neighbor's possession.

---

3. Alfred M. Freedman and Harold I. Kaplan, eds., *Comprehensive Textbook of Psychiatry,* p. 1143.

4. Mohsen Ziai, ed., *Pediatrics,* pp. 725-26.

5. Clyde M. Narramore, *How to Tell Your Children About Sex.*

*12. Piaget's four periods of development.*

We mentioned earlier that infancy falls roughly into Jean Piaget's sensory-motor period of development. This is an appropriate time to list his four periods of development. We will refer to them from time to time:

    a. *Sensory-motor period:* Birth until about eighteen months.

    b. *Preoperational period:* From about eighteen months until the child starts school at about age six.

    c. *Period of concrete operations:* Roughly from ages six through eleven.

    d. *Period of formal operations:* From age eleven or twelve, if the child has been properly educated. At this point the child can begin to be reasoned with abstractly, if he is mature. Many adults never reach this stage of reasoning ability. They can't understand the hidden meanings of various proverbs, for instance. They think that the proverb, "People who live in glass houses shouldn't throw stones," means just that—if your house is made out of glass you shouldn't throw stones because the glass might break. They do not understand the various other implications, such as that people who have faults (which means all of us) shouldn't be criticizing others.[6]

*13. To spank or to reason?*

Since the toddler stage is approximately from fifteen months to thirty-six months of age, any complex reasoning attempts would be a waste of time. Verbal reproofs are sometimes adequate, but if the child is openly rebelling, spanking is the most effective form of discipline.[7]

*14. Language development.*

At the beginning of the toddler stage, at about fifteen months of age, most children are using single words to name some familiar persons or things, like "mama," "dada," "dog," and "eat." They

---

6. John E. Peters, *Lectures on Piaget.*
7. I highly recommend James Dobson's book, *Dare to Discipline.*

also start using a lot of nonsensical gibberish, until they finally start putting two or more words together. The average child can talk in sentences fairly well by three years of age, which marks the end of the toddler stage and the beginning of the preschool years—ages three to six. Language development depends a good deal on how much the parents talk to the child, as well as whether he has older brothers and sisters to learn from. Toddlers also learn to think out loud and talk to themselves, which is perfectly normal.

   *15. Imaginary friends.*

Toddlers also have imaginary friends that they talk to. This is normal. This fantasy life helps them practice talking and also helps them deal with developmental conflicts they are experiencing in ways that are less threatening than real life.

   *16. Play therapy.*

Sit back and watch your children play house. It's quite revealing to see how our children interpret our family interactions and communications. In fact, many child psychiatrists do just that— it's called play therapy—to analyze what is going on in the family that is causing the child's conflicts, and to use the information to help the child—and his parents—resolve those conflicts.

## B.   A toddler's perception of the universe around him.

   *1. The logic of the eighteen-month-old.*

Let's take an imaginary trip back to our own early childhood, most of which we have repressed from our memories. It may be a painful trip, or it may be a pleasant trip, depending on your past experiences, but let's try to see the universe through the eyes of the little child within each of us.

An eighteen-month-old toddler's logic consists primarily of his impulses to carry out his selfish desires, which allow him to release his tensions. He has no foresight and thinks primarily in terms of the present, frequently forgetting the many lessons he has learned from past experiences. Many adults in today's society still appear to be operating with the logic of the eighteen-month-old!

   *2. Man's mind: a telescope or a microscope?*

The mind of man sees the universe as though he were viewing it through a microscope rather than a telescope.[8] It magnifies

_____

8.  Edmund Jacobson, *Biology of Emotions,* p. 72.

only within the short range of his highly selective experience, his select views of reality. Whether an eighteen-month-old toddler or a thirty-eight-year-old man in the prime of his career, or even an eighty-eight-year-old man with years of experience—man does not make decisions and act totally on the basis of true facts and reality, but rather on his impressions of what is factual and real. His decisions are based on past experiences, conscious perception, prejudices, conscious and unconscious drives, emotions, social pressures, mental capability to interpret reality, and many other factors.

### 3. Ways that we lie to ourselves.

Since no man, woman, or child is perfect, no one can see things as they really are 100 percent of the time. Most people, in fact, don't want to—that's where man's approximately twenty-two defense mechanisms (denial, projection, etc.) come in.[9] I personally hope to perceive and understand as much of reality as I can handle psychologically, and pray that my human capacity to grasp reality emotionally and intellectually will be extended as far as possible within my finite capabilities. The Apostle Paul said, "When I was a child, I spake as a child, I understood as a child, I thought as a child: but when I became a man, I put away childish things. For now we see through a glass, darkly; but then face to face: now I know in part; but then shall I know even as also I am known" (I Cor. 13:11-12). I can hardly wait to enroll in the University of Heaven, to learn all of the reality that remains a secret to me now. Moses wrote, "The secret things belong unto the LORD our God: but those things which are revealed belong unto us and to our children for ever, that we may do all the words of this law" (Deut. 29:29).

But in this life we continue to lie to ourselves through some of our twenty-two or so defense mechanisms, which are closely tied to our emotions. A child who has experienced the unpleasant feelings of anxiety or depression will look for ways to prevent those unpleasant feelings from recurring. An anxious feeling will cause physiological changes—such as speeding of the heart and tightening of the muscles—which in turn signal the unconscious to turn on one or more defense mechanisms, so that the child will not see things as they really are. If he sees reality at that moment, his feelings will

9. If the reader desires a thorough understanding of these defense mechanisms, I would refer him to bibliography references 87, 101, 123, 124, 125, 261, 401.

be hurt—literally. Our most basic defense mechanism is repression, which Lidz defines as "the barring or banishment of memories, perceptions, or feelings that would arouse the forbidden."[10] Lidz adds that "in order to prevent rearousal of some childhood sexual experiences or the discomfort of remembering sexual desires for a parent, the entire period of early childhood may be repressed."[11] This is theoretical, of course, but worthy of consideration.

Another defense mechanism which presents itself in early childhood is regression. If a child encounters something that makes him somewhat less secure, such as the birth of a younger child, he may regress to an earlier stage of development at which he did feel secure. He may even go back to wetting his bed or sucking his thumb months after he quit doing those things. Fantasy formation is a defense mechanism that is usually considered healthy at the toddler stage, helping him to dull the pain of reality. Denial is one of the most common defense mechanisms at all ages. Denial refers to "the ability to deny the existence of something disturbing, such as one's own anger or sexual feelings."[12]

### 4.   What is projection?

There are many other defense mechanisms which develop in early childhood. We don't have the time to discuss all of them, but I want you to be aware that they exist in all of us. One more that I will mention is projection, which is attributing one's own impulses or wishes to someone else. Thus, the toddler who feels hostile toward his brother, but does not want the uncomfortable feelings that accompany hostile wishes, will convince himself that it is really his brother who is angry at him. Adults who don't have much self-worth often use projection: they become very critical of others who have hang-ups that unconsciously remind them of their own. This is the mechanism referred to by Christ when He said,

> Don't criticize, and then you won't be criticized. For others
> will treat you as you treat them. And why worry about a
> speck in the eye of a brother when you have a board in
> your own? Should you say, "Friend, let me help you get that
> speck out of your eye," when you can't even see because of

10.  Theodore Lidz, *The Person*, p. 256.
11.  Ibid.
12.  Ibid., p. 258.

the board in your own? Hypocrite! First get rid of the board.
Then you can see to help your brother.

—Matt. 7:1-5, LB

I once had as a patient a depressed minister who couldn't
figure out why he wanted to kill himself, but was aware of the fact
that he felt very hostile toward other people who were hypocritical
and loudmouthed. After getting into therapy with him for a
while, I discovered that he was drinking a fifth of whiskey every day,
quitting only on Sundays so he could preach his sermons. He even
went into a withdrawal seizure one Sunday night. He traveled
on week-ends to be a guest speaker at various places, and when
he did, he always found some lonely woman to spend the night
with in his motel. He also was very verbose. Yet he couldn't tolerate others who were loudmouthed and hypocritical, and didn't
understand what he was doing that made him so depressed. This
was a good example of projection and helped me to understand
the problem better.

5. *Does the universe really revolve around your child?*

In spite of all these ways that the toddler learns to lie to
himself, he matures if he is in a healthy environment, and gradually
learns that the universe does not revolve around him. According
to Piaget, "the elaboration of the universe by sensory-motor intelligence constitutes the transition from a state in which objects
are centered about a self which believes it directs them, although
completely unaware of itself as subject, to a state in which the
self is placed, at least practically, in a stable world conceived as
independent of personal activity."[13]

6. *Psalm 8: We are insignificant but important!*

The psalmist David expressed his awe when he took a good
look at his position in the universe, and then realized that God
loved him dearly in spite of his relative insignificance. In Psalm 8,
David exclaimed:

> O LORD, our Lord,
> How majestic is Thy name in all the earth,
> Who hast displayed Thy splendor above the heavens!
> From the mouth of infants and nursing babes Thou
>     hast established strength,
> Because of Thine adversaries,

---

13. Jean Piaget, *The Construction of Reality in the Child*, p. 350.

To make the enemy and the revengeful cease.

When I consider Thy heavens, the work of Thy fingers,
The moon and the stars, which Thou hast ordained;
What is man, that Thou dost take thought of him?
And the son of man, that Thou dost care for him?
Yet Thou hast made him a little lower than God,
And dost crown him with glory and majesty!

—Ps. 8:1-5, NASV

## C. Mother Substitutes.

### 1. What about Day-care Centers?

Even more so than during infancy, mother substitutes during
the toddler years present a serious problem. Any prolonged separation from the mother during this stage can result in a loss of
initiative or even the determination for survival. Many children
in America today are being farmed out to Day-care Centers, many
of which are very detrimental to the child's ultimate mental health
and outlook on life. Those Day-care Centers that are worthwhile,
have adequate staff and programming, and are somewhat beneficial
to the child, are usually so expensive that it doesn't pay for the
mother to work. An adequate Day-care Center should have at least
one well-adjusted, warm, loving staff member for every four or
five toddlers. This is the minimum.[14]

### 2. The childhood of 714 prisoners.

In 1965, the backgrounds of 546 female prisoners and 168
male prisoners were studied by distinguished London psychiatrists.
They concluded from their studies that the main factors contributing to the eventual delinquency of the prisoners were "multiplicity
of care and lack of stable parent figures in childhood."[15] Many of
these prisoners had also experienced the death of one or both
parents during early childhood.

### 3. Where are America's fathers?

Another study showed that "boys whose fathers have been
away for extended periods during their runabout-preschool years

---

14. For a more detailed understanding of the effects of Day-care Centers and
related topics, see bibliography references 50, 149, 194, 213, 228, 329.

15. F. Brown, et al., "Childhood Bereavement and Subsequent Crime," p. 1048.

report more antisocial behavior than those whose fathers have been consistently present."[16]

### 4. Parent substitutes.

Ideally, toddlers should have their mothers home with them during the day, and both parents home to interact with on evenings and weekends. They should also have opportunity to interact under parental supervision with other children their own age, such as in Sunday School and at the neighbors'. The climbing divorce rate in America is separating children from their fathers, and in most cases the mothers are forced by economics to go to work, so the children are also deprived of a stable relationship with their mothers. God's Word says, "What therefore God has joined together, let *no man* separate" (Mark 10:9, NASV). If there is a death in the family, if the young toddler loses one or both of his parents, then it's time for grandparents, other close relatives, or close friends to step in and help the toddler re-establish a close maternal- or paternal-child relationship as soon as possible, even if the close relative or friend involved doesn't live in the same house. Children need two parents—that's all there is to it! If I die while my children are still growing up, I certainly hope that my wife will get married again to a stable, Christian man—and the sooner the better. The Apostle Paul said, "Therefore, I want younger widows to get married, bear children, keep house, and give the enemy no occasion for reproach" (I Tim. 5:14, NASV).

16. Boyd R. McCandless, *Children: Behavior and Development,* p. 173.

# 12

# Preschoolers
## (Ages Three to Six)

## A. Developmental adaptations during the preschool years.

During the preschool years, rapid development takes place in the emotional life of the child, his socialization, language, and reasoning ability, independence, and sexual identity.

### 1. Emotions.

Emotions play a very important part in the life of preschoolers. In fact emotions frequently find expression more freely in the preschooler than in many adults who have learned to suppress them. At about three years of age, children have many fears—fears of animals, fears of monsters, and even fears of "the big bad wolf." They have trouble differentiating between fact and fantasy, and need to be reassured over and over by their parents. Between three and four years of age, they may express their anger in the form of temper tantrums. If you give them what they want after a temper tantrum, they will continue to have tantrums all their lives. But if you grab them firmly by the shoulders and tell them to stop it, or even spank them if needed, their temper tantrums will cease, since they will serve no useful function. Preschoolers also experience anxiety, jealousy, curiosity, joy, and primitive forms of love.

### 2. Socialization.

Again, remember that people need people, and that adults

who don't have genuine love relationships with other adults do not have good mental health—they have loneliness, emptiness, purposelessness, and emotional pain. So teach your child to be a social creature by exposing him to other children his own age, especially of the same sex. Toward the beginning of the preschool years (age three), the child will not interact much with other children playing in the same area. This is known as parallel playing. But soon they will be running around together and talking to each other more. They eventually become less self-centered, and learn to feel empathy with others. Nursery schools, if adequately staffed, can help speed up social development. And two or three mornings a week away from mother, at this age, will not only do the child some good but will give the mother a little break. Gary Collins states that childhood playing serves at least four useful functions: (1) it permits discharge of energy; (2) it provides needed stimulation; (3) it helps children develop motor skills; and (4) it enables the child to act out and learn to understand adult roles.[1]

*3. Language and reasoning ability.*

Language and reasoning ability are areas of very rapid growth between the ages of three and six. During these years, the child adds thousands of words to his vocabulary, and begins to be able to reason things out concretely. However, he continues to live in a small world in the sense that he still thinks most events center in some way around him, and that almost all people see things the same way he sees them.

*4. Increasing independence.*

During these crucial years, the child takes great strides in becoming more self-sufficient. He learns to feed himself and even cut most of his own food. He learns to dress himself, with perhaps some parental guidance on what to wear, rather than how to put it on. He becomes completely toilet-trained, using the bathroom when he needs and wants to, and cleaning himself afterwards. He becomes less dependent upon the mother socially, as he begins to make friends. In any Christian home, a boy's best friend, especially during these three years, should be his father. Christian fathers should spend much time with their sons and daughters, but especially with their sons, and mothers with their daughters. I have heard many

---

1. Gary Collins, *Man in Transition,* p. 50.

fathers say that they think the quality of time is important—not the quantity. And all I can say to that is "nonsense." A large quantity of time is essential, and if you can improve the quality of time during that large quantity of time, that will be even better.

5. *Solidification of sexual identity.*

The main reason fathers should spend quantities of time with their sons and mothers with their daughters during the preschool years is that these are the years in which sexual identities become solidified. Children need a parent of the same sex to identify with and to model themselves after. Today, it's hard to tell a boy from a girl, and that's not right. Boys should dress like boys and girls like girls, and that applies to their hair styles too.[2] Although no chores are exclusively masculine or feminine, encourage your boys to help daddy with his chores and your girls to help mommy with hers. This will facilitate the sexual identification process. And remember to praise your child primarily for the quality of his behavior and character, not for his looks.

It is also during these years that most children go through a stage in which they think that somehow they will grow up, the parent of the opposite sex will stay the same age, and they will somehow replace the parent of the same sex by marrying the parent of the opposite sex. This is known as the oedipal stage, and even though I think it was greatly overdone by Freud and others, it has been documented over and over again in probably a majority of children. That's why children this age should no longer sleep with a parent of the opposite sex, a practice that is more common than you would think, especially in one-parent homes. Continue to give your children of both sexes warmth and affection, but try not to be overly stimulating to them. When they were younger, they could follow you around when you dressed, used the restroom, and took baths, but now politely yet matter-of-factly wean them off these activities. The children usually won't object a great deal, and will react by demanding privacy themselves when they do these things. They'll understand that it is just part of growing up.

I have seen *many* sons who were suffering from anxiety and other problems because their mothers were unhappily married, or

---

2. This does not mean, however, that girls should not play in bluejeans, and things of that nature.

no longer married, and had unconsciously made little husbands out of them. I have also seen cases where this occurred between father and daughter, such as in the case of hysteria I told you about earlier. Children should also have friends who are of the same sex. And when our children ask us questions about sex-related things, the healthy thing to do is to answer them truthfully and matter-of-factly without showing embarrassment. Don't go on and tell them things they didn't ask for, but answer their questions accurately and specifically.[3] Teach them that some things are talked about privately and done privately, but don't become overly agitated about it. For instance, we shouldn't allow our children at this age to run around in the yard without any clothes on, but if our child is examining his genitals in bed at night when we happen to walk in on him, the best thing to do is ignore it, or politely ask him to leave his pajamas on.

## B.   The preschooler's role in the family.

### 1. Effect of birth order.

The role a child has within his own family structure will greatly influence the development of his personality. While there are definitely exceptions to every rule, especially in psychiatry, there are also general trends which have been observed in children who have different positions in the family. This includes their order of birth. There are advantages and disadvantages to being the oldest, a middle, or the youngest child, and there are special disadvantages to being the only child. Usually, more demands are placed on the oldest child, so he becomes more of a perfectionist. As an adult, he is more likely to achieve success in life, but will probably enjoy it less, and always wish he had achieved even more. I have already mentioned that fifteen of the first sixteen American astronauts were first-born. Second-born children, especially if teased by the first-born, are sometimes more shy and polite, and try to please everybody. From the third child on, children are frequently less inhibited, more outgoing and extroverted, and generally enjoy life more than the first-born, even though they may be less successful. And the youngest child has a greater chance of being spoiled, more dependent, and less mature, depending a

---

3. See Clyde M. Narramore, *How to Tell Your Children About Sex.*

great deal on the maturity of his parents.[4] Children of older parents tend to be more serious-minded than children of young parents. But again, there are exceptions to every rule.

Alfred Adler wrote extensively about positions within the family and their importance. The Chinese have special terms of address for persons of each position within a family, with special status and roles for each position. A study of nineteen-year-old men in the Netherlands revealed that the first-born had the highest I.Q. scores, and that I.Q. scores went very slowly but definitely down as birth order progressed.[5] The difference was not very great, however. Another study showed that menarch occurs later in girls from large families than in girls from small families.[6]

### 2. Scapegoats.

Children also have various special roles within the family, regardless of position, such as scapegoat, baby, pet, miniature husband, and peacemaker.[7] Unfortunately, handicapped children sometimes become the scapegoat who is made fun of and rejected by the other children of his family, especially if the other children feel particularly inadequate themselves.

### 3. Roles parents play.

The different roles parents play in the family also greatly influence the personality of each child growing up within that family. One research study, including personality testing, was done over a seventeen-year period on sixty-four young adults. The project was carried out by Charles H. Rousell and Carl N. Edwards of Harvard University.[8] Their study indicated that permissive home atmospheres tend to produce neurotic (including hypochondriacal) and psychotic disturbances, especially in female children. Cold, permissive home atmospheres tend to result in sociopathic personality disorders in young adult males. Cold, punitive homes tend

---

4. The youngest child is therefore more likely, as a teenager, to abuse drugs and alcohol, since he was frequently more dependent upon his mother and spoiled during those crucial first six years.
5. Lillian Belmont and Francis A. Marolla, "Birth Order, Family Size, and Intelligence," p. 1096.
6. William H. James, "Age at Menarch, Family Size and Birth Order," p. 292.
7. Nancy Rollins, et al., "Some Roles Children Play in Their Families," p. 511.
8. Charles H. Rousell and Carl N. Edwards, "Some Developmental Antecedents of Psychopathology."

to result in the production of phobic and psychotic males. Excessively warm, permissive homes tend to produce strong anxiety and psychotic reactions in males.[9]

### 4. General trends.

Other studies have shown that, in general, a weak father and a weak mother, especially if physically and emotionally quite cold, will develop children with schizophrenic tendencies.[10] A domineering mother and weak father will generally result in various types of neurotic offspring. A strong-willed mother and a strong-willed father will tend to develop overly rebellious children. A weak mother and tyrannical father will tend to produce insecure daughters and tyrannical sons. But a mother with self-worth, character, and genuine love, who is a co-leader in the home, and a father who has self-worth, character, genuine love, and makes the ultimate decisions in the home, will produce mentally healthy children with self-worth, character, and genuine love for others.[11]

### 5. Single-parent families: six million fatherless.

Another very serious problem in American society today is the increasing number of single-parent families. They have problems all their own, such as separation anxiety, grief, anger, depression, loneliness, and sexual identity problems in the children.[12] Unfortunately, there are presently more than six million children in the United States who are living in fatherless homes. An extensive study on 120 children from fatherless homes was carried out by the Psychiatry Department of the University of Florida.[13] They found out that the parent-child relationships are most impaired among "hard-core" fatherless children, meaning those who have been without a father for two or more years. These children are often psychotic or retarded, with severe pathology and a fatalistic view of life. Children who have been without a father for less than two years have fewer severe impairments than the "hard-core"

---

9. Ibid.

10. See J. Block, "Parents of Schizophrenic, Neurotic, Asthmatic, and Congenitally Ill Children: A Comparative Study." See also bibliography references 102, 139, 148, 160, 224, 229, 238, 315, 326, 372, 420.

11. For research on and advice for healthy homes, see bibliography references 13, 24, 25, 26, 62, 64, 90, 116, 130, 132, 152, 153, 156, 195, 263, 280, 292.

12. Robert Krell, "Problems of the Single-Parent Family Unit."

13. Joan L. Kogelschatz, et al., "Family Styles of Fatherless Households."

fatherless, but more problems than children who have fathers.[14] There are so many Christian fathers who are failing in their responsibilities before God that it makes me grieve. I can't repeat enough the fact that a father's first responsibility from God is his own family. All else comes in a distant second. Paul said that if anyone does not provide for the needs of his own household, he is "worse than an infidel" (I Tim. 5:8).

### 6. Children of drug addicts.

Another rising problem in American society today is the problem of drug addicts and the offspring they are producing. One study showed that many babies born to drug addicts have withdrawal symptoms at birth.[15] Many need to be placed in foster homes. Almost all of the children of drug addicts are reared in fatherless homes, since most of the addicted fathers have abandoned the mother and child. Multi-child families which fall into this category are usually fathered by different men. Most of the children neglected by their addicted mothers develop a limited capacity for human relationships and have many other permanent psychological problems.[16]

## C.  Typical areas of concern regarding preschoolers.

Let's turn our attention to typical areas of concern regarding preschoolers. These are everyday problems that we are likely to face in our own preschoolers. I would like to discuss both my own experiences and some research findings regarding fourteen common problem areas for parents of preschoolers.

### 1. TV violence.

Psychiatric researchers at the University of Georgia recently conducted a much-needed study on emotional reactions of young children to TV violence.[17] They showed three brief, violent TV episodes to four- and five-year-old children while continuously measuring the amount of emotional perspiration. The children were also shown two non-violent films. As measured by their skin resistance, the children responded more emotionally to the violent

---

14. Ibid.
15. Sol Nichtern, "The Children of Drug-users," p. 24.
16. Ibid., pp. 24-31.
17. D. K. Osborn and M. Endsley, "Emotional Reactions of Young Children to T.V. Violence."

episodes and remembered them better one week later. When asked which of the five episodes (three violent and two non-violent) they liked the best, they chose one of the violent and one of the non-violent episodes, which happened to be the two cartoons they were shown. The emotion involved with the violent scenes appeared to be primarily fear. Violent scenes with human characters aroused more fear than did violent scenes with cartoon characters. The children were able to recall twice as many details about the human violence than about anything else they saw. This implies a possible relationship between emotionality and the storage and retrieval of information. I think the main lesson we can learn from this and other similar studies is that our children's minds, like our own, are in reality quite complex computers, and what we feed into them is what will come out for years to come. Television can be a useful thing, or it can be a great hindrance to the emotional and spiritual maturation of our children.

### 2. Handicapped children.

A recent study appearing in the *British Medical Journal* showed that "problems which children have with particular handicaps may well in their turn specifically affect aspects of their development and their parents' attitude towards them."[18] Other studies have shown that handicapped children frequently become overly dependent, passive, and somewhat withdrawn. They also frequently learn to get strong secondary gains from illness—which means that their parents and others let them have their own way because they feel sorry for them.[19] If you have a handicapped child, don't deny the handicap, but encourage his independence. And don't pity him—love him and trust his ability to overcome the handicap and to become a responsible individual.

### 3. How to treat twins.

About one out of eighty-six births produces twins, and about one-third of these are identical twins.[20] I think twins are a special blessing from the Lord. But having twins also gives the parents

---

18. Arnon Bentovim, "Handicapped Pre-school Children and Their Families—Effects on the Child's Early Emotional Development," p. 634.

19. Klaus K. Minde, et al., "How They Grow Up: 41 Physically Handicapped Children and Their Families."

20. Alfred M. Freedman and Harold I. Kaplan, eds., *Comprehensive Textbook of Psychiatry*, p. 1493.

added responsibility. The American tradition is to dress twins alike and to have them do everything alike, so they'll be treated fairly. But studies have shown that this is not the best thing for them psychologically. It's best to deal with them in terms of separate individuality. Respect differences in their tastes and opinions. Don't reward, praise, or punish them at the same time, but do so individually. It is better if they wear different styles of clothing, depending on their own tastes. It is even recommended that they attend different classes in school.[21]

### 4. More on bedwetting.

Bedwetting is a very common problem during the preschool years. Statistics show that about 88 percent quit wetting their beds by the time they reach four and one-half years of age, but about 8 to 10 percent will still be wetting their beds from time to time when they reach six years of age, and about 1 to 2 percent even after high school graduation.[22] As I mentioned before, the best thing to do is have the child clean up his own bed, as much as is possible, without unnecessarily shaming him. Treatment methods have already been discussed.

### 5. More on encopresis (soiling).

Soiling, like bedwetting, can be expected in the preschool years. I would encourage you to remember that the normal range for neurological readiness for toilet-training is anywhere between one and one-half and four years of age. It's not considered abnormal, therefore, unless the child is more than four years old. If your child is over four and still soiling from time to time, it would be best to get treatment for him, preferably from a child psychiatrist, who will be best equipped to handle such a problem.

### 6. Thumb-sucking.

Thumb-sucking has also been discussed to some extent. Let me say here that it is considered normal, and that about 20 percent still suck their thumbs even after their sixth birthday.[23] However, if your child is over six, and still sucking his or her thumb regularly, it is usually considered to be a sign that the child is experiencing some anxiety; family counseling would probably be advisable.

---

21. Ibid., p. 1494.
22. Ibid., p. 1380.
23. Ibid., p. 1383.

7. *Nail-biting, nervous tics, and stuttering.*

Don't worry about moderate nail-biting. About 20 percent of college students still bite their nails.[24] Nervous tics, however, such as constant squinting of the eyes, various inappropriate jerky motions, and constant clearing of the throat, are signs of emotional conflicts requiring counseling, preferably by a trained psychiatrist. Tics usually go away as the conflicts are resolved.[25] We also have medications, such as low doses of Haldol, that will eliminate them within twenty-four hours. Haldol has worked on my patients 100 percent of the time so far, but unless the conflicts are resolved, the tics will return when the medication is discontinued. Even lifelong stuttering in an adult can be eliminated 60 percent of the time within about forty-eight hours after taking low doses of Haldol. Stuttering in preschool children is considered normal and should just be ignored. It nearly always goes away by age six. The reason it is so common is that during the preschool years, the child's knowledge and vocabulary are increasing much more rapidly than his neurological ability to get all those words and thoughts expressed verbally.[26] Becoming unduly excited about it only makes it worse, so just ignore stuttering unless the child is over six years old.

8. *Animal fears.*

Animal fears are most common between the ages of three and five. Again, they are nothing to worry about, but they do require patience on the part of the parents who have to explain over and over again to the child that the big bad wolf won't get him!

9. *Obesity.*

I've already said quite a bit about this subject. I would advise strongly that you avoid obesity in your child at any cost. It will greatly hamper his self-worth, and limit the kind of respect he will get from his peers. Elementary school children are very tactless and will keep on broadcasting any defect they see in other children. It's not right, but that's the way it is, so let's deal with the problem realistically.

10. *Warning: Day-care Centers may be hazardous to your child's health!*

---

24. Ibid.
25. Ibid., pp. 1398-99.
26. Ibid., pp. 1378-79.

I think I have already said enough for you to know my position on Day-care Centers. Basically, it is that some are all right for short periods of time, but most of them are psychologically damaging to a child who stays there five days a week, eight or nine hours a day. If you do put your child in a Day-care Center, be sure it has warm, loving, well-trained, multiple mother substitutes. Freedman, Kaplan, and Sadock's Modern Synopsis of Psychiatry states that "inadequate facilities or personnel may be destructive to the proper psychological growth and development of children."[27] I think Day-care Centers should be required by the government to have that message printed over their doors, just like the warning on cigarettes.

### 11. Nightmares and night terrors.

Nightmares and night terrors are also quite common in preschoolers. Because there are many things that a three-to six-year-old doesn't yet understand, he spends a large portion of his sleep-time in dreaming. Therefore, most children will have some nightmares or night terrors. Night terrors involve thrashing around in bed and crying out some, but unlike nightmares the children don't wake up. In fact, you may have a hard time waking them up during a night terror even if you shake them hard. Most children have them for only a short period of time; they go away as the conflicts become resolved. Medications can be given to eliminate night terrors during this period of time, but usually aren't necessary. I would recommend that you keep a nightlight in your preschooler's room, so he can see that there aren't any animals or bogeymen. If your child comes to your bed at night after a nightmare, he should be taken back to his own bed and calmly spoken to a few moments. Sleepwalking is also common in young children, and is nothing to worry about if they stay in the house! Medications can stop this also.

### 12. The housing problem.

It might seem strange that I would list the type of housing a person lives in as a preschool problem, but it is just that. We lived in an apartment during college, graduate school, medical school, and psychiatric training, but I don't recommend apartment living for preschoolers or older children either for that matter, and I have statistics to back up my personal prejudices. Douglas Hooper found that apartment dwellers are more transient in their occupations

---

27. Alfred M. Freedman, et al., Modern Synopsis of Psychiatry, p. 668.

and life-styles and that adults and children who live in private homes have much less mental illness than adults and children living in apartment complexes.[28] As I said, though our family lived in an apartment, we moved into a house as soon as my schooling was completed.

### 13. Childhood depression.

I have seen a number of cases of childhood depression. Frequently it follows the loss of a loved object, a divorce, the death of a parent, or the transfer of a father overseas. Weekly counseling sessions usually meet with success. I also like to facilitate counseling by using low doses of Tofranil, an antidepressant medication, if the depression seems very serious. Childhood depression is usually manifested by social withdrawal, prolonged sadness, and either a marked increase or decrease in activity level.

### 14. How to reduce stress in preschoolers.

Stress is something people have at every age. Some of it is good for us, and necessary for our psychological development. Preschoolers have many adjustments to make, and are developing rapidly between the dependent toddler stage and the independent school-age stage. Simple events like going to Sunday School, to the pediatrician or to the dentist, moving into a new home, having a new baby brother or sister, can all be very stressful for a preschool child. As a matter of fact, going to the dentist is usually quite stressful for me! The best way we, as parents, can reduce these stresses for our children is to prepare them for these events by talking about them ahead of time in words that children will understand.[29] Always be truthful. It can even be distressing for children to go to sleep at night, only to wake up to find a strange babysitter there and their parents gone. We always tell our children when we are going out, even if they will be asleep before the babysitter comes, so they won't be surprised.

---

28. Douglas Hooper, et al., "The Health of Young Families in New Housing."
29. Collins, *Man in Transition,* p. 56.

# PART | | | FOUR

*From Age Six to Eighteen:*
*General Principles*

# Spiritual Development

**13**

Michelangelo, the famous Italian sculptor, painter, architect, and poet of over four hundred years ago, is reported to have made the statement: "As the marble wastes, the sculpture grows." This statement not only applies literally to the development of a piece of sculpture, but also abstractly to the psychological and spiritual development of our children. Nearly three thousand years ago, King Solomon, under the inspiration of God, wrote the statement, "Train up a child in the way he should go: and when he is old, he will not depart from it" (Prov. 22:6).

It has already been stated in this book that approximately 85 percent of the adult personality is already formed by the time the individual reaches his sixth birthday. After the sixth birthday, all we can do is chip away at the last 15 percent of unchipped marble in an attempt to sculpt our children into ideal Christian young adults. By age eighteen, they should be ready to move out of the house, just as a young robin is shoved out of its nest by its mother, trusting as she does in her offspring's God-given ability to make its way in the world on its own two wings. But during those twelve years from the sixth to the eighteenth birthdays, a lot of psychological and spiritual struggles can take place in the family—and most of them are totally unnecessary. The best way to make it easy on ourselves as parents during this twelve-year period (six to eighteen) is to love and discipline our children effectively during those crucial first six years of life.

What I intend to do in this section is to discuss ways that we, as parents, can mold that other 15 percent of our children's personalities. We will discuss the problems older children face, and the most effective ways we, as parents, can help our children through these problems. But as I just stated, by age six we should be knocking away at those final chips of inappropriate marble in an attempt to complete a beautiful work of art. Our primary concern must remain the ultimate inner beauty of character rather than the outward appearances. If your six-year-old isn't 85 percent completed yet, you had better get busy!

## A.  The elementary school years.

### 1. Identification.

Most children are quite cooperative during these years. They want to please their parents and teachers and adopt the morals of their parents. They continue to identify with the parent of the same sex, learning both his good and bad habits. *Healthy and unhealthy communications between the parents themselves greatly affect the child's own self-worth.*[1] A father who is critical of his wife unknowingly is also tearing down the self-worth and self-confidence of his daughters, and the same applies to mothers who criticize their husbands.

### 2. The budding conscience.

The conscience continues to grow during these years, and the identification with the parent of the same sex strengthens the child's self-control because he has a model to copy. He continues to reason concretely until about the age of eleven, when, if properly educated, he can begin to reason out abstract concepts.[2] I believe it is definitely possible for many six-year-olds to have enough of a conscience to experience a genuine repentance for their sins and acceptance of Jesus Christ as Lord and Savior. I have led a number of six-year-olds to the Lord, and I myself was six years old when I put my faith in Christ. As they grow older, their salvation experience will take on new meaning as they learn many of the abstract concepts involved, but all a person needs for salvation is expressed

1. See bibliography references 5, 138, 272, 302, 322, 326.
2. John E. Peters, *Lectures on Piaget.*

in the simple exhortation: "Believe on the Lord Jesus Christ and thou shalt be saved" (Acts 16:31).

### 3. The total devotional atmosphere.

I would encourage you as parents to create a total devotional atmosphere in your home. By this, I do *not* mean having your family sit in a corner praying all day. I mean loving, communicating, playing with your children, exhibiting the fruits of the Spirit, and having some good sacred music on from time to time, geared to the age of your children. This should not be to the exclusion of good secular music as well. I don't believe we can separate our lives into secular and sacred. I believe every part of our lives is sacred—even going to the baseball game and eating hot dogs! Some people are so heavenly-minded that they are no earthly good!

Have family devotions together. This is a must. And make it quite brief for children in this age group or it will become a torture to endure rather than a happy time of sharing Christ with each other. Mealtimes are good times for family devotions, but be creative. Buy your children Christian story books to supplement some good secular books. Reward them for memorizing Bible verses, but select verses which are short and understandable to the child. I decided on my own to start having daily Bible reading when I was ten years old, and I've been doing so ever since. There was no pressure on me from my parents to read my Bible every day, since we had family devotions together every day. But they had prepared me during the first ten years of my life to such a point that when the Spirit of God moved me to begin personal devotions, I was willing and eager to obey. Fathers, take your sons hiking and fishing, and discuss godly children in the Bible, like little Samuel, Hannah's son. Mothers, go shopping with your daughters and discuss the shopping techniques of the godly woman in Proverbs 31. Buy something together for someone else in the household, or for someone in need. Don't sit around at home watching soap operas. I believe soap operas are a contributing factor to mental illness in American housewives today.

### 4. Christian camps.

Christian camps are a good outside influence on the spiritual development of our children. I worked at Pine Cove Camp in

Tyler, Texas, one summer while I was still in medical school. It was a marvelous experience. My wife and I didn't have any children of our own as yet, so we were able to devote ourselves to the children at the camp during the week, and to each other on week-ends. Pine Cove has the philosophy that if you wear a child out all day by letting him have some good old-fashioned fun, then he will listen to a brief but effective gospel message late in the evening around a campfire. That was really effective. Hundreds are saved each summer and many more rededicate their lives to the Lord. I prefer this type of camp to those in which the children are forced to study the Bible all day and wish they were at home playing baseball.

5. *Your choice of a church environment for your children: A major factor.*

The church you take your family to is even more important. I have already mentioned some of the characteristics of a psychologically and spiritually healthy local church. I would refer you to the writings of Getz, Stedman, and Watchman Nee for what I consider a psychologically and spiritually sound church (see bibliography). Allow me to mention a newspaper article I once read.[3] It was about a man in Memphis, Tennessee, who was suing a local church because his son had been terrified by the preacher's assertion that any boy with hair below the ears was definitely going to hell to burn forever. So the boy went forward when the invitation was given and a lady at the front of the church hacked his hair off with a scissors. The poor boy was so frightened that his nose bled most of that afternoon. When asked about the incident, the minister replied, "But I didn't start it, the Lord did—and it works." Well it may work for him, but it doesn't work for me! The Lord told us to go into all the world and spread the gospel, not our own personal hang-ups! The Bible has to be our firm foundation and practical Christianity our way of life. A healthy church can be one of the most useful influences in the emotional and spiritual development of our children, and a healthy church stands on three legs, like a tripod: (1) a sound doctrinal leg; (2) an evangelistic leg; and (3) a relational leg, with genuine sharing and intimate love among the members of that local body of believers.[4]

---

3. *Durham Morning Herald,* Durham, N.C., July 7, 1974, p. 9A.
4. These concepts about a healthy church are discussed in Gene Getz's excellent book, *Sharpening the Focus of the Church.*

## 6. Right and wrong.

Hartshorne and May have conducted a series of experiments on the moral development of children.[5] Their experiments revealed that even though children learn more and more about what is right and wrong as they grow older, they also grow increasingly deceptive. They found that children who were honest in certain situations were dishonest in others. Children with lower intelligence, with emotional instability, or from lower socio-economic environments also lagged behind in moral development. One of their most significant findings was that children who were enrolled in Sunday Schools showed significantly better conduct in the areas of honesty, cooperation, persistence, and inhibition of undesirable behavior.[6]

## 7. Piaget's findings on moral development.

Jean Piaget's studies of moral development in children showed that moral behavior is learned.[7] It makes me angry when I hear liberal psychiatrists and theologians saying that children are born good and society teaches them how to be bad. It's the other way around. They are born with a sinful nature and we have to teach them to deny their selfish impulses and to be good, using both rewards and punishments. Child psychiatrists do this and call it "behavior modification," or the use of "positive and negative reinforcements." These are just big words for what healthy parents do when they praise their children for being good and spank them or warn them for being bad. Solomon tells us that "foolishness is bound in the heart of a child; but the rod of correction shall drive it far from him" (Prov. 22:15). Solomon knew about behavior modification three thousand years ago, and he learned it from Moses, who wrote about it five hundred years before that!

The six-year-old child continues to adopt the conscience of his parents as his own, primarily to gain parental approval and partially out of fear of punishment. At age twelve or thirteen, the morals of his peers will take over in the areas where parental example left off. He will choose the peers who most closely resemble him in character development. Train your child adequately in the first six years of life and you need not fear whom he will choose for his

---

5. H. Hartshorne and M. A. May, "A Summary of the Work of the Character Education Inquiry."

6. Ibid.

7. See Jean Piaget, *The Moral Judgment of the Child.*

friends when he becomes a teenager. Parents like to blame their teenager's behavior on his peers, but this is nearly always an excuse to relieve their own personal guilt.

## B. Those teenage years.

### 1. Are our teen-agers really going to ruin?

Many adults think America's teenagers are going to ruin! Well, many of them are. But many of them *aren't!* In May of 1974, a Gallup Poll came out noting that "seldom in history have the American people so craved moral and spiritual leadership as they do today. All signs point to the fact that religion is gaining a new intellectual respectability in this country."[8] Pollster George Gallup Jr. went on to say, "The assumption that the educated person 'needs' religion less, and is more ready to discard religion as a product of ignorance and superstition, is not borne out by survey findings." Referring to America's young people, Gallup stated that "survey evidence strongly suggests that these groups could well be in the vanguard of religious renewal in this country." He added that "church attendance is as high—if not higher—among persons with a college background than among persons with less formal education." Many educated Christian young people are at the same time hostile to organized religion in general, and I have to admit that I feel the same way about many of the failures of organized religion in this generation. I think that most of Satan's biggest projects are being carried out by various sections of organized religion.

Gallup compared his poll to polls carried out in other nations, and concluded that "the religious character of American youth stands out in bold relief when our young people are compared with the youth of other nations of the world." The United States had the lowest percentage of atheists among its youths—less than 1 percent, compared to 10 percent in France and 12 percent in Sweden. Only 12 percent of American youth say they have "no interest" in religion, compared to 32 percent in Great Britain, 41 percent in Sweden, and 74 percent in Japan.[9] It's not surprising to me that Sweden and Japan are neck-and-neck in a race for the highest

---

8. Gallup Poll, as reported in the *Durham Morning Herald,* Durham, N.C., May 1974.
9. Ibid.

suicide rate among teenagers. I think the only reason Sweden is beating Japan is Sweden's atmosphere of total permissiveness and lack of discipline, whereas Japan's youth still have relatively good discipline, though almost no Christian influence. Gallup concluded that "American youth are not only exceptionally religious when compared to the youth of other nations but also put a higher premium on 'love and sincerity' as a goal in life and less on 'money and position.'"[10]

### 2. The search for identity.

Teenagers naturally develop strong interests in ideals and ideologies as they search for personal identity. While in this stage of development, they are extremely ripe for spiritual commitments, even though Christianity may have bored them previously. They have a powerful need to strengthen their consciences, and begin to look for reasons and meanings in life. I was only sixteen years old when I made one of the biggest decisions of my life. I was already a Christian from a godly home, but was still struggling with what I wanted out of life. I had feelings of guilt, and feelings of confusion about what career to prepare myself for. I felt like a ship trying to go somewhere without a rudder; and even if I had had a rudder, I still wouldn't have known where to head the ship. I asked a man in our local church for some help. He seemed so confident— so sure of himself. And he was for real! That man was Dr. Bob Schindler, who later became a missionary surgeon to Africa. Dr. Schindler offered me a very simple answer that gave new direction to my life. He simply encouraged me to learn Proverbs 3:5-6, then meditate on it awhile. I was ripe for that passage of Scripture: "Trust in the Lord with all thine heart; and lean not unto thine own understanding. In all thy ways acknowledge him, and he shall direct thy paths." I was a Christian, but I hadn't been acknowledging Him in all my ways, and I was certainly leaning on my own understanding. Alone in my bed that night, about midnight, with tears in my eyes, I committed my entire life to Jesus Christ—a decision I still stand on and have never regretted. When I quit struggling and finally rested in Christ, He started showing me the answers I was looking for—and He gave me a real peace. And so I know from experience that the teenage years are ripe for spiritual development.

---

10. Ibid.

*3. The spiritual climate of the home: some Jewish traditions.*

I would again encourage you to create a total spiritual atmosphere in the family, with emphasis on positive communications between parents and teenagers. If you have the right kind of discipline in the home, nagging will be totally unnecessary. After you have read this book, talk with others about some creative ways in which to develop a healthy spiritual climate in your home.

There is one possibility I would like all of you at least to consider. Jewish people have a religious and family tradition that I think has great potential for emotional and spiritual development. I think we should consider using a similar custom in Christian homes. When a Jewish child reaches his thirteenth birthday, entering the teenage years, Jewish families have a big ceremony known as "Bar Mitzvah" for boys, and "Bät Mitzvah" for girls (meaning "son" or "daughter of the commandments"). They invite all the relatives and close friends to this ceremony, and declare the child a young adult, with increased responsibilities as well as increased freedoms. The parents make a verbal contract with the child, which varies with the creativity of the parents.

I plan to have a similar ceremony for my own children when they reach age thirteen. I probably won't give it any special name, but if I did, I would probably call it something like "Son of Responsibility" or "Daughter of Responsibility." I'll write out a contract with my child, giving him some new freedoms along with some new chores and family responsibilities. I will probably agree not to spank him any more, because I think spanking is fine for younger children, but somewhat degrading for teenagers. I personally prefer punishing teenagers with consequences related to the offense. I will remind my child of his or her responsibilities before the Lord also, and encourage him to make some personal commitments to the Lord, perhaps in the form of personal devotions. But I'll trust him to make these decisions on his own, so they will be his commitments rather than mine. I will invite some relatives and close friends of the family, as well as some of his own friends—whomever he wants to come. But I won't allow anyone to bring gifts to this birthday party. It has too many emotional and spiritual implications to get them all confused with materialistic gain. I have a Jewish friend who hated his Bar Mitzvah because everybody brought expensive gifts and had a wild time, almost totally ignoring him and the significance of the event.

Anyway, this is merely a suggestion that I would like you to consider. I think it would have the additional value of reminding the parents that their child is growing up. Parents frequently forget this fact, and continue treating their teenagers as though they were little children. Teenagers can reason like adults, even though they are less mature; our communications with them should show not only our love but also our respect for them as young adults.

### 4. Finally! A faith of their own.

I would like to mention some spiritual developments that typically take place either in the latter teenage years, or early twenties. Before the teenage years, children generally accept everything the parents say as truth, and their religious beliefs are largely the religious beliefs of their parents. But during the late teens or early twenties, the individual's greatest need is to feel independent of his parents. Paul Tournier, in his book entitled *The Whole Person in a Broken World,* describes this stage in the life of a young person as taking off the "coat" of his parents' morality and "knitting" a coat of his own—at a time when he is basically insecure about his own ability to do so. Tournier states that

> this crisis is necessary and normal. Before he attains adult maturity the young man must go through this time of storm and stress when he has to subject everything to question. The day will come when he will discover again many of the treasures of his childhood, when he will return to the faith in which he grew up and the principles which were inculcated in him. For they were true, and life sees to it that he re-discovers them. But then he will give them a quite personal turn; he will profess them as his own convictions, based upon his innermost experience. In psychology, this is called integration.[11]

I think this observation helps me to understand what Solomon was saying when he was inspired to write, "Train up a child in the way he should go, and when he is *old,* he will not depart from it" (Prov. 22:6). Solomon doesn't say the individual won't go through some doubts somewhere in the middle years, but simply that "when he is old, he will not depart from it."

I didn't have any significant doubts about Christianity until I was in graduate school at Michigan State University at the age of

---

11. Paul Tournier, *The Whole Person in a Broken World,* p. 5.

twenty-two. Then I began to wonder whether I believed Christianity simply because I was reared in a Christian home. That's a logical question to ask. So I studied other religions, Bible prophecy, and archaeology, and came to the conclusion that Christ really is God, and the Bible really is God's Word to mankind. I renewed my vows to God, and my faith was eventually strengthened because it had become my own faith, not merely the faith of my parents. I believe I was genuinely converted when I was six years old and put my simple faith in Christ. But when I was sixteen, I had more mature ways of looking at things, so my faith took on new and exciting meanings when I committed my life to Christ. And then, by the time I got to graduate school, I had exercised the scientific method of approaching things to such an extent that I needed a revamping and revitalizing of my faith. By the time I got through medical school and into psychiatric training, my faith was so well-founded that I felt confident in discarding any psychiatric principle that in any way disagreed with Scripture.

I'm secure in the Lord, and I'm glad I went through those maturations at ages sixteen and twenty-two, even though they were somewhat painful at the time. It's somewhat amazing that after each struggle, my doctrinal beliefs were almost exactly the same as what they were when I accepted the Lord at age six. That's what Solomon is talking about in Proverbs 22:6. In his book, *The God Who Is There,* Francis Schaeffer emphasizes the need to ground our children in the Word of God and teach them why we believe what we believe. He says we must "communicate Christianity in a way that any given generation can understand."[12] If we as parents, as well as the youth leaders of our local churches, communicate a living Christianity to our teenagers, along with proofs for why we believe the Bible, we will greatly ease this normal maturing process for our teenagers when they go through it—and they will go through it, I promise you.

### 5. The area of temptations.

There are many other topics we could discuss concerning the spiritual development of teenagers, but I would like to discuss just one more briefly. That is the area of temptations. We have already discussed temptations in some detail earlier in this book, but this is such an important struggle, especially in the teenage years, that

---

12. Francis A. Schaeffer, *The God Who Is There,* p. 139.

I would like to share with you a few additional passages of Scripture on the subject. God inspired John to write, "I have no greater joy than to hear that my children walk in truth" (III John 4). He also wrote, "Sanctify them through thy truth: thy word is truth" (John 17:17). John promises our teenagers that they can overcome the world, stating, "For whatsoever is born of God overcometh the world: and this is the victory that overcometh the world, even our faith" (I John 5:4). But how will our teenagers get that kind of faith? Paul says, "So then faith cometh by hearing, and hearing by the word of God" (Rom. 10:17). In other words, our teenagers need a vital exposure to the Word of God. In his second letter to Timothy, who was probably a teenager when Paul converted him in the city of Lystra, Paul wrote,

> But continue thou in the things which thou hast learned and hast been assured of, knowing of whom thou hast learned them; and that *from a child* thou hast known the holy scriptures, which are able to make thee wise unto salvation through *faith* which is in Christ Jesus. All scripture is given by inspiration of God, and is profitable for doctrine, for reproof, for correction, for instruction in righteousness: That the man of God may be *perfect* [Greek word "artios," implying emotional and spiritual maturity or completeness], thoroughly furnished unto all good works.
> —II Tim. 3:14-17

The psalmist David writes,

> Wherewithal shall a young man cleanse his way? by taking heed thereto according to thy word. With my whole heart have I sought thee: O let me not wander from thy commandments. Thy word have I hid in mine heart, that I might not sin against thee.                                                        —Ps. 119:9-11

Our teenagers are not fighting the battle alone, though! God promises to fight the battle for them if they will yield themselves totally to Him. James, Christ's brother, wrote, "Submit yourselves therefore to God. Resist the devil, and he will flee from you" (James 4:7). And we are also promised, "Greater is he [Christ] that is in you, than he [Satan] that is in the world" (I John 4:4). If the teenager isn't sure if something is right or wrong, he is instructed, "Beloved, believe not every spirit, but try the spirits, whether they are of God" (I John 4:1). A good rule of thumb I followed when I was a teenager is, "When in doubt, don't!" And teenagers should also realize that God never tempts them to sin. This is a popular misconception. James told us, "Let no man say when he is tempted, I am tempted of God: for God cannot be tempted with evil, neither tempteth he any man: But every man is tempted, when he is drawn away of his *own* lust, and enticed" (James 1:13-14). So God doesn't tempt us, He delivers us. And Peter told us, "The Lord knoweth how to deliver the godly out of temptations" (II Peter 2:9).

If our teenagers can make it through these rough years, and continue to mature in the Lord, they will have accomplished much. Or rather, I should say that they have allowed God to accomplish much in their lives. They will reap tremendous rewards in the form of self-worth and self-confidence. The Apostle John tells us, "Beloved, if our heart condemn us not, then have we confidence toward God. And whatsoever we ask, we receive of him, because we keep his commandments, and do those things that are pleasing in his sight" (I John 3:21-22).

# 14

## Those Elementary School Years (Ages Six to Twelve)

### A. Developmental adaptations during the elementary school years.

*1. Adjusting to school.*

If a child has been adequately prepared, and has developed sufficient independence from his mother, going to school for the first time will be more of a fulfillment than a fear. Parents can make first grade easier by giving their four-year-old some part-time nursery school experience, then giving their five-year-old half-days in kindergarten before placing their six-year-old in a full-time first grade. Unfortunately, some elementary school children have to be bussed across town, frequently spending an extra hour or more in a hot or cold bus traveling to and from school. I would avoid this if at all possible. The ideal situation would be to send elementary school children to a good, nearby Christian elementary school, where effective discipline is more likely to be upheld and where students learn Christian character as well as how to read and write. I would not send my children to a Christian school that has poor teachers, however. I would take special pains to check out my child's first-grade teachers, Christian or non-Christian, since they will affect the way he initially looks at the education process in general.

Many children, especially boys, are somewhat late in the maturation of their nervous systems, particularly in the areas of the brain responsible for reading and writing. Many boys, and some girls, will have some minor learning disabilities, like seeing or writing letters backwards, until the nerves associated with such activities are completely myelinated—that is, until they are covered with a fatty sheath, like the insulation around electrical wires. A hostile teacher can be critical of these children and make them feel stupid, in spite of the fact that most of them have average or better than average intelligence.[1] In fact, Albert Einstein was one of these late developers. Once a child is labeled stupid, it's hard to live it down. So it's important that the first-grade teacher be a loving, understanding teacher and at the same time a firm disciplinarian. Once I get to know the teacher, I won't hesitate in the least to give her permission to spank my child if he disobeys. If he complains about it when he gets home, he's likely to get another one from me, depending on the circumstances. It's important for the child to see the teacher and parents as a united front.

### 2. Sexual development.

During the elementary school years, the child identifies strongly with significant persons in his environment. He identifies strongly with the parent of the same sex—if that parent makes himself available. This is essential for normal sexual development. He also identifies with other persons of the same sex. Hero worship is to be expected at this age, so it's important to provide the child with appropriate heroes. Parents can do this indirectly by praising certain individuals, such as athletes, ministers, and Bible heroes, with whom they would like the child to identify. Tell him whom he was named after and why, and tell him the meaning of his name.

Dr. Eugene McDanald states that for a child, "there is no such thing as an irrelevant encounter with persons. His identification with persons is a vital process that determines what he becomes, and the quality of this becoming is dependent on the qualities of the persons he encounters."[2] McDanald adds further that "if the attitudes of others that become part of [the child] reflect tendencies toward self-affirmation and self-renunciation compatible with self-respect and respect for others, they become an arch to new experience."[3]

---

1. See bibliography references 99 and 306.
2. Eugene McDanald, "Emotional Growth of the Child," p. 73.
3. Ibid.

It is vitally important for boys to identify with males and for girls to identify with females. Without such identificaton the child may become a homosexual or a lesbian, if the problem is severe, or have sexual maladjustments in marriage if the problem is less severe. It's unfortunate that we don't have more male elementary school teachers. So many boys go through life with either no father or an absent father, female school teachers, female Sunday School teachers, female babysitters, and so forth. It's no wonder that homosexuality is far more common in males than in females. I would strongly recommend that church leaders provide male Sunday School teachers for elementary boys and female Sunday School teachers for elementary school girls.[4] This will provide both groups someone positive to identify with both sexually and spiritually. During the elementary school years, boys develop a contemptuous attitude toward girls and girlish things. Nearly all boys and girls have some wishes at times of being the opposite sex, so they develop this healthy contempt to repress those wishes during these years. Both sexes need to see the advantages of being what they are, and that each sex has its own distinct advantages.

Sex education is also important for elementary school children, and the best place for sex education is in the home. It should be done little by little, over the years, by answering questions that the child asks, and nothing more. But be sure to answer his questions truthfully, using adult terms, and matter-of-factly. A child of average maturity should know all the facts of life by the time he is ten or eleven years of age.[5] Menstruation should also be explained quite early to elementary school girls because the normal range for the onset of menses is anywhere from nine to sixteen years old, with the average being about thirteen years of age in the United States.[6] Onset of puberty in boys is generally a little later—usually around thirteen to fifteen years of age.[7] That's why seventh-grade girls are frequently bigger than boys.

*3. Social development.*

During the elementary school years, the child develops a real

---

4. In some instances, it would be better to have male Sunday School teachers for the girls also, since identification with healthy father figures is necessary for normal marital adjustment later in life.

5. See Clyde M. Narramore, *How to Tell Your Children About Sex.*

6. J. Robert Willson, et al., *Obstetrics and Gynecology,* p. 69.

7. Mohsen Ziai, ed., *Pediatrics,* p. 38.

sense of belonging. Group participation, especially with Christian children, should be encouraged. He also develops a real sense of responsibility as he shares the chores with his older brothers and sisters. The sense of belonging and responsibility are prerequisites to the development of leadership potential in the child. He must learn to obey before he can learn to lead effectively. His self-concept continues to develop as he sees himself through the eyes of his peers, and also through the eyes of his parents and other authority figures.

Play among children of this age group—be it football, basketball, or baseball—is characterized by poor organization, heated disputes over the rules, lopsided scores, and accusations of cheating. They like to win, but must also learn teamwork—the precious ability to work together in a common cause with fellow human beings. They also like to play marbles for keeps and exchange comic books. I would encourage you to buy your elementary school children some Christian comic books, which are available from the Fleming H. Revell Publishing Company and can be ordered at your local Christian book store. This will give your children a good opportunity to witness to other children about Christ. They're not too young to learn witnessing.

### B. Disciplining your elementary school child.

I have been amazed in the past at how many Christians do not know what the Bible says about disciplining children. When I ask them what they think the correct way of disciplining is, many of them directly contradict God's recommendations in Scripture. I could quote many verses on discipline, but I think Solomon's wise recommendations in Proverbs 13:24, 22:15, 23:13, and 29:15 are adequate to give the general idea. I do think we should analyze Solomon's instructions in light of what the Apostle Paul says in Ephesians, where he writes, "And fathers, do not provoke your children to anger; but bring them up in the discipline and instruction of the Lord" (Eph. 6:4, NASV). The only means of discipline for young children mentioned in the Bible, to the best of my knowledge, are the rod and reproof (e.g., Proverbs 29:15). That doesn't mean that other forms of discipline shouldn't also be exercised, but I think it does mean that spanking with a stick and giving verbal reproofs should be the primary disciplinary tools with young children. Not only that, but according to Ecclesiastes

8:11 the sentence against an evil deed should be executed quickly. For a mother to tell her child that when his father gets home, his father will spank him for what he just did is definitely wrong, both scripturally and psychiatrically. It's wrong scripturally because this is not executing the discipline quickly—it's postponing it. It's wrong psychiatrically for two reasons.

First, the average attention span of an elementary school child is about five to fifteen minutes, and by the time his father gets home and spanks him, he will have forgotten what it was that he did wrong. Even if the father reminds him of what it was, the spanking will have lost its effectiveness. Among the many studies confirming this, Ivan Pavlov's studies on dogs merit special attention. Pavlov rang a bell whenever he brought his dogs food. Soon, instead of waiting until they smelled the food, they learned to salivate as soon as they heard the bell. And whenever Pavlov punished the dogs for doing certain things, they soon learned not to do those things in order to avoid the pain.[8] If your pet dog wets on your carpet, do you tell him that he is going to be punished several hours later when your husband gets home? Of course not! You hit him with your hand or newspaper, and put him outside the door. Well, it's just as useless to tell a child his father will spank him several hours later for something he just did.

Second, delaying punishment until the father comes home is wrong because it separates the child from his father. Many women, in fact, unconsciously or even consciously use this technique exactly for this purpose—to separate the son or daughter from the father in order to win the child's undivided affection, thus setting up a neurotic relationship. This also makes the child think of his father as the sole disciplinarian, and will influence him as an adult to have a very legalistic view of what God is really like. This is so because no matter how much we read the Bible, our overall view of what God is like is to a large degree colored by how we viewed our own father during our childhood. If you grew up without any male authority figures, you will tend to think there isn't any God. If you have become a women's liberationist, you might even think of God as a woman. The father and mother must stand together in the disciplining of their children, and the task of disciplining

8. Alfred M. Freedman and Harold I. Kaplan, eds., *Comprehensive Textbook of Psychiatry,* p. 167.

should be carried out by whoever saw the child disobey and can most quickly reprove or spank him.

A verbal reproof is frequently all that is necessary, especially if the child is committing a particular offense for the first time. Sometimes a verbal reproof followed by sending the child to his room to think it over for five minutes will be effective. But I think isolating a child for long periods of time eventually falls into the category of provoking the child to anger, because after about fifteen minutes, he will either forget or misunderstand what it is that he is being punished for. Spanking is short and immediate, and ten or fifteen minutes later the child will get over any anger he might have felt toward the parent who spanked him. When I spank my own child, he sometimes will be angry with me initially, but within five or ten minutes he almost always comes back to me and says, "I'm sorry, daddy. I love you."

I allow my child to tell me that he is angry, but if he hits me, throws something at me, or shows any disrespect, I spank him again. *If you don't demand respect when a child is young, you won't get any respect—or deserve any, for that matter—when your child gets into his teens.* And you certainly don't want your son to hit you back when he's bigger than you are! My father is 5'6" tall, and I'm 6'4½". I was bigger than my dad by the time I was thirteen or fourteen years old. But I never dared speak impudently to my father in any way—I wouldn't even think of it, then or now. I still shudder if I think about saying something disrespectful to my dad, and I'm certain it is because he "shuddered" me a few times with a stick when I said something disrespectful at the age of two or three. And I can't imagine any father and son being closer to each other than my father and I are right now. I have thanked him a number of times for every spanking he gave me—except for one I didn't deserve, and I forgave him for that one.

An excellent book to read on disciplining children, in my opinion, is *Dare to Discipline* by James Dobson. He emphasizes demanding respect, spanking for willful acts of disobedience, and the fact that every child is different. Some children want parental approval so much that a look of scorn brings repentance. A child like that requires very few spankings. But others are born with more spirit and less concern for parental approval. For a child like this, many spankings for the same offense may be necessary before he finally decides that that particular type of behavior isn't profitable for him. And when you spank him, spank him hard enough so he'll feel it. It used to take quite a hard spanking to get my older son to cry, but after he turned three he cried whenever he saw me go after the stick. He's the spirited type, and required quite a few spankings when he was two years old; but after he turned three, he seldom needed one. I am very pleased with his overall attitude of love, respect and obedience.

Parents frequently tell me that spanking simply doesn't work for their child, but I say it will work for any child unless he is severely mentally retarded. But you have to be consistent, the parents have to stick together, and the spanking has to hurt; and it may need to be repeated a number of times for the same offense. I am not advocating bruising the child; in fact I consider slapping his face or hitting him with a fist to be child abuse and provoking him to wrath (see Eph. 6:4). But remember the words of Solomon: "Do not hold back discipline from the child. When you beat him with the rod, he will not die" (Prov. 23:13, NASV). God is almost mocking us here for being afraid to spank.

God also tells us that "he who spares his rod *hates* his son" (Prov. 13:24). I have found that one way I, as a psychiatrist, can tell if parents really have genuine love for their children is to ask them how they discipline their children. Parents whose love is selfish and immature will either be weak disciplinarians, "sparing the rod," or they will physically abuse their children, beating them with their fists, thus "provoking them to wrath." But as Proverbs 13:24 says, "He who loves him disciplines him diligently."

If your child has average or better than average intelligence, and if his education has been adequate, he will begin to reason abstractly at about the age of ten or eleven.[9] This was proven by the studies of Jean Piaget. Reasoning with a younger child about abstract concepts like the morality of certain behavior patterns is a relative waste of time, although simple, concrete reasoning can sometimes be quite effective in this age group. Some children are exceptionally bright, and may learn to reason abstractly sooner than age ten or eleven, but most children don't. When my children are eleven or twelve years old, I plan to do away with spankings and give them punishments that are related to the offense. I'll reason with them more, and try to communicate with them on an adult-to-

9. John E. Peters, *Lectures on Piaget.*

adult level. But I'll probably hang the paddle somewhere they can see it occasionally so they'll know it's available for special occasions. However, when they reach their teens, I will use other forms of discipline exclusively, punishments related to the offense. For minor things, reasoning with teenagers is frequently all that is needed.

### C.  Social problems some elementary school children face.

*1. Divorce or separation of the parents.*

Divorce is one of the most heartbreaking things in American society today, and it's nearly always the result of one or both parents being too selfish and proud to admit that their conflicts are resolvable. I have *never* yet seen any marital conflicts that were unresolvable, if both partners were willing to work at it. The argument about having incompatible personalities with unresolvable conflicts and differences is pure garbage! Any two people with normal intelligence can learn to enjoy life together if they are willing to humble themselves before Almighty God, swallowing their pride, and work out their conflicts.[10] The easy way out is for a couple with marital and psychological conflicts to divorce each other and remarry. Then there are two couples with marital and psychological conflicts instead of one. Christ listed adultery as permissible grounds for a Christian to divorce (Matthew 5:32 and 19:9), but He didn't encourage divorce even under those circumstances.

As already noted, more than six million children right now are living in fatherless homes in the United States. One extensive study of fatherless children showed that "hard core" fatherless children—meaning those who have had to live two or more years without a father in the home—have significantly more psychiatric difficulties than do normal children who have fathers. Moreover, they have a much more fatalistic view of life.[11] And the number of fatherless families is continuing to rise rapidly in America. These families have a significantly higher incidence of psychological depression, separation anxiety, grief, anger, sexual identity problems, and loneliness. In most cases, the divorce and resultant fatherless home cause more psychological damage to the children than would continued marital maladjustments. One study of 105 families that

---

11. Joan L. Kogelschatz, et al., "Family Styles of Fatherless Households."

10. Paul D. Meier, "Divorce Is Never Necessary," and "Self-Acceptance Leads to Mate-Acceptance."

experienced divorce, for instance, showed that 52 percent continued to have hostile interactions even after the divorce, and 31 percent required from two to ten court interventions during a two-year follow-up period.[12] This study showed that alliances between one parent and child against the other parent were especially common. Whenever a married couple have conflicts—and all married couples will have some conflicts if they are human beings—they have three choices: one mature choice and two immature choices. The mature choice is to resolve the conflicts, even if outside help is needed to do so. The two immature choices are to continue to live together unhappily or to get a divorce and live apart unhappily. Of the two immature choices, getting a divorce is definitely worse. In America today, nearly 40 percent of first marriages end in divorce, and the divorce rate for second marriages is 50 percent higher than the divorce rate for first marriages! Divorcées have more psychiatric problems than any other group of Americans.[13]

### 2. Death in the family.

A death in the family, either of a parent or of a child, is another serious problem. But unlike divorce, which is a willful separation, a death in the family—if handled properly—can be a maturing experience for everyone involved, even though it is tragic.[14]

When I was a senior in high school, I had my first experience teaching Sunday School—it was a group of eight- and nine-year-old boys. After I had taught the class several months, and had come to know the boys fairly well, one of them developed a very serious form of cancer. I wept bitterly when I found out about it. The boy had already accepted Christ as his Savior, and was a rapidly developing young Christian. His doctors were honest with his parents, and the parents were honest with their son, explaining to him the best they knew how that he wouldn't have very much longer on this earth, and that they would miss him a great deal, but Jesus would take care of him in heaven, and they would join him again some day soon and spend the rest of eternity with him. He

---

12. David W. Cline and Jack C. Westman, "The Impact of Divorce on the Family."
13. I highly recommend the excellent article by George Gilder, "In Defense of Monogamy."
14. See bibliography references 7, 35, 50, 86, 100, 169, 221, 343.

was only eight years old, but he understood. He was allowed to grieve over his eventual separation from his parents, but soon brightened up and accepted it. I visited him frequently in the hospital. When his leg was amputated, he became the favorite of many of the doctors and nurses. He witnessed to them routinely, telling them about Jesus and His love, and how he was looking forward to living with Jesus. He had an obvious impact on the lives of those doctors and nurses. He had an obvious impact on my own life too. When he died, we all grieved; but as a result of his young life and death, his father finally accepted Christ as Savior and developed into a pillar of the church. His older brother, a teenager, also accepted Christ. We are told that "all things work together for good to them that love God, to them who are the called according to his purpose" (Rom. 8:28).

Here are the usual steps people go through, whether children or adults, when they first find out about a death or impending death in the family. First, they will deny it. They won't believe it. When they are finally convinced that it is true, they generally go through a period of anger. They will be bitterly angry at God, or the doctor, or someone else. A young child who can't yet comprehend what death is all about may even become bitter at the dying or dead parent, because to his way of understanding, the parent has chosen to die and leave him. Thirdly, there will follow a guilt reaction, which is anger at the self—attempts to blame oneself for the other family member's death, or for not treating him right when he was still alive, or for not saying good-bye before the death occurred. It is to be hoped that the individual will then go through a period of genuine grief over the loss of the loved one. I say "it is to be hoped" because if he holds his feelings in, and pretends he isn't sad, he may carry around unresolved psychological conflicts the rest of his life.

I have seen a number of psychological conflicts resolved by using various psychotherapeutic techniques to allow the patient to go ahead and grieve over the loss of a loved one who may have died many years earlier. After two or three weeks of grieving—sometimes less, and sometimes more—a healthy person who has gone through these stages will resolve his grief, and feel better toward God, himself, the deceased loved one, and the remaining family members. It's something we will all have to go through, and many of us will have to go through it several times in our lives. The most important thing is to be completely honest about it with everyone—and this includes a dying child—and to allow everyone involved to grieve. Holding back the tears is not bravery. It's a mistake.[15]

### 3. Childhood depression.

If a child is seriously depressed for several weeks, he will probably either become very withdrawn and frequently tearful, or else he may show his depression by becoming much more irritable and hard to get along with. I would encourage you as parents to try to get to the root of the problem and find out what it is that's bothering him, so something can be done about it. If serious enough, and if he doesn't get over it, he may need to see a child psychiatrist for a number of sessions, and may even need a short course of antidepressant medications.

### 4. Grandparents in the home.

It is generally recommended that you *not* have your parents living in your home on a permanent basis, whether you have children or not. It's hard enough to keep normal marital conflicts resolved without having someone there to hear the arguments or even enter into some of them. The same goes for brothers or sisters or any other boarders. If you're married, it is best for you to live by yourselves, even though you may develop the urge to lend a helping hand from time to time by letting someone move in with you. But don't do it, especially if you have children. You'll be doing them a real disservice. They deserve your undivided attention, and so does your mate. The best thing a newly married couple can do for the sake of their marriage is to make the break from both sets of parents. This will force you to resolve conflicts instead of running to mother. In some cases, the mother would run to you, whether you ran to her or not! Later on, when you have children, I think it's fine for them to be able to live within driving range of their grandparents. Children have a very special relationship with their grandparents, and it's usually a very healthy one, involving a lot of identification with the grandparent of the same sex. But the grandparents shouldn't live in the same home, and preferably not next door.

Grandparents are also better off living separately from their children, either in their own home or apartment, or else in an

---

15. See Elisabeth Kübler-Ross, *On Death and Dying.*

apartment-type home with other older people to whom they can relate. As Christians, it is our responsibility to take care of elderly parents who are no longer able to take care of themselves. In fact, it's a real opportunity for our children to watch us take care of our parents, teaching them to do the same for us when we are too old to take care of ourselves. The Apostle Paul said, "But if any provide not for his own, and specially for those of his own house, he hath denied the faith, and is worse than an infidel" (I Tim. 5:8). Those are strong words, inspired by a God who loves people of all ages. But my personal opinion is that usually this does not have to mean moving parents into your house, although that does become a viable option in some circumstances. I have seen too many families regret making that decision, and it's hard to back out once you have made it.

### 5. Raising children in foreign lands.

This is another sensitive subject, especially in the evangelical community where many of us have relatives or friends who are missionaries. If any parents feel called by God to go to a foreign mission field, they should go. But they should make their calling sure. A need does not constitute a call. There are needs everywhere. Remember the very old story about the farmer who while out in his field looked up at the clouds and noticed that they formed the letters "P.C." He quit farming and went into the ministry because he thought God was calling him to Preach Christ. His ministry wasn't very effective, because in reality God was calling him to get busy and Plow Corn. Now I would guess by the relative lack of evangelical witnesses in foreign lands that there are probably many more Christians who have disobeyed God's call to be foreign missionaries by staying home, than there are Christians who have misinterpreted God's call by going to foreign lands when God really wanted them to stay home. I think God calls all of us to be missionaries somewhere in some capacity. That's what the great commission is all about (see Matt. 28:19-20).

What I want to emphasize here is that if you have children, make your calling sure, because children who grow up in foreign lands have extra problems to face up to in addition to the usual ones. Many of these extra problems, however, can be avoided, minimized, or resolved, according to a research study by Sidney

Werkman.[16] His study showed that the additional problems involve (1) unusual child-rearing practices and customs, (2) problems with the caretakers of the children, (3) aberrant sexuality, (4) special fears, and (5) a sense of alienation. Dr. Werkman encourages parents to anticipate these potential problems, to discuss them openly, to make plans to avoid or minimize them, and to act decisively on their children's behalf. I believe our children are our first calling from God, no matter what occupation God may call us into. If God called me to go to some foreign mission field, I would assuredly go, but I would choose a mission board and a mission field where I wouldn't have to send my elementary school children five hundred miles away nine months a year. I might be wrong, but in light of Scripture, I really cannot see how I could possibly be following God's will if I did that. I have a good friend, however, whose parents felt called to do that, and he turned out to be an excellent Christian physician. He disagrees with me on this point, but I have counseled a number of patients whose missionary parents "farmed them out" and who have suffered severely as a result of this separation from their parents. Some have even become devout atheists as a reaction to parental rejection. Our family has to be our first and utmost calling from God!

### 6. Handicapped children.

Handicapped children frequently become overdependent, passive, and somewhat withdrawn. Parents may even unconsciously reward them for being weak. Parents should not deny the handicap, but they should make every effort to encourage their handicapped child's independence. He doesn't need their pity. He needs their genuine love, and he needs for them to trust his ability to overcome the handicap psychologically and to become responsible for himself. Elementary school children are very blunt and also tease a lot, a problem the handicapped child will almost certainly face. But being overprotective will only make matters worse.

Sometimes a handicap will strengthen someone to a point that he never would have attained without it. God gave the Apostle Paul a handicap so Paul's pride wouldn't hold him back from accomplishing greatness for the Lord. John Milton wrote his best poetry after going blind. I know of a farm boy from a small southern town

---

16. Sidney L. Werkman, "Hazards of Raising Children in Foreign Countries."

who made average grades in elementary school until he was afflicted with a handicap. That handicap gave him a real determination to prove himself and succeed in life. He was the valedictorian of his high school class, attained nearly straight A's in college, and has become an extraordinarily dedicated Christian physician. He probably never would have achieved what he has without that handicap. So don't pity your handicapped child. Try to figure out how God can use the handicap as a blessing to produce greatness in him.

Dr. Klaus Minde carried out a valuable research study on forty-one physically handicapped children of elementary school age.[17] This study showed that handicapped children have two main hurdles to cross between the ages of five and nine: (1) the conscious recognition that the handicap is not going to disappear suddenly, and (2) the psychological depression that usually follows this awareness. It is to be hoped that at this point the child can be brought to emotional readiness to accept his condition and incorporate it in his life plans.

### 7. School phobias.

A school-phobic child is one who is afraid to go to school and stay there all day. He can't bear to be away from his mother that long. These children are almost always overly dependent on their mothers, who never allowed them to exercise much independence prior to entering school. They are frequently the youngest of several children, a factor which gives the mothers added temptations to spoil them and to resist their growing up and leaving.[18] These children become quite manipulative, since their mothers have usually let them have their own way and given them very little discipline. The best way to handle this problem is to refuse to allow them to stay home under any circumstances, even if they play sick. And the mothers should not go to school with them to keep an eye on them, as many of these mothers do. If the child runs away from school and comes home, give him a spanking he will never forget and take him back immediately. This may need to be repeated a number of times before his will is broken. Then both parents should sit down to re-evaluate their roles as parents, deciding what they can do to love and discipline their child more

17. Klaus K. Minde, et al., "How They Grow Up: 41 Physically Handicapped Children and Their Families."
18. Ian Berg, et al., "Birth Order and Family Size of School-phobic Adolescents."

effectively so he will become more independent and learn to respect himself in a healthy way.

### 8. Miscellaneous problems.

It will probably surprise many of you to find out that about 10 percent of first graders still wet their beds, and 20 percent still suck their thumbs.[19] Bedwetting at this age can be due either to a small bladder or to psychological conflicts. About 90 percent of bedwetting after age six is considered to be psychological rather than a physical problem, usually representing overdependence coupled with pent-up anger toward the parent the child is overly dependent upon.[20] If the bladder is too small, have the child hold in his urine for several hours at a time to stretch the bladder. If his bladder is normal, it would be wise to evaluate whether you are doing things for the child that he should be doing for himself, like dressing him or cutting his foods for him. Don't shame a child for wetting the bed. He probably didn't do it on purpose. Don't become overly excited about it. Just calmly have him clean up his bed and change his sheets. But be sure that *he* does it, even if you think he has a small bladder. He won't feel so guilty about it if he cleans it up himself; and also, if it is a subconscious way to get you upset, making him clean it up will take all the fun out of it, so he'll probably quit doing it. Medications are also available that will usually stop bedwetting promptly, but should be used only as a last resort.[21] Most family doctors don't know about these medications, so a child psychiatrist should be consulted. Besides, the family might benefit by a few sessions to provide insight into what the problem is.

Thumb-sucking after age six is common, but it is considered a sign of anxiety and a sign that the child and parents may need some counseling.[22] Children of perfectionistic parents frequently develop nervous tics, like eye squints or other involuntary habits. This also indicates a need for family counseling and possibly a temporary course of tranquilizer medication for the child.[23] Parents

---

19. Freedman and Kaplan, eds., *Comprehensive Textbook of Psychiatry*, pp. 1380-84.
20. Ibid.
21. Ibid.
22. Ibid.
23. Ibid.

of obese children should also get some counseling. In many cases, food has become a substitute for genuine, intimate love.[24] Frequent soiling of the pants is also a fairly serious symptom after age six, and parents should take their child to a child psychiatrist for evaluation if this is a frequent occurrence.[25] Some pediatricians are also equipped to handle this problem.

---

24. See Hilda Bruch, "Family Transactions in Eating Disorders."
25. Alfred M. Freedman, et al., *Modern Synopsis of Psychiatry,* pp. 610-11.

# 15

## Early Adolescence

### A. Entering adolescence.

Dr. Theodore Lidz, Chairman of the Yale University Department of Psychiatry, defines adolescence as "the period between pubescence and physical maturity...the transition from childhood, initiated by the prepubertal spurt of growth and impelled by the hormonal changes of puberty, to the attainment of adult prerogatives, responsibilities, and self-sufficiency."[1] That's a long definition, but I think you'll get the picture that many big changes take place during adolescence. Take those first four years or so, between the ages of twelve and sixteen. At age twelve, your son or daughter is still considered a child. How often have you heard the expression, "Quit acting like a twelve-year-old"? Four short years later, at the age of sixteen, your son or daughter has become a young man or a young woman, with an adult body, reproductive ability, and a desire to run his or her own life as much as possible. The four years between childhood and young adulthood, from twelve to sixteen years of age, are probably the roughest four years of most people's lives, because there are so many major adjustments to make. Encouraging independent decision-making and spiritual maturity during the first twelve years of life will greatly facilitate the major adjustments during the early adolescent years.

1. Theodore Lidz, *The Person,* p. 299.

I have already discussed the Jewish Bar Mitzvah ceremony on the thirteenth birthday, so I won't discuss it here except to say that I think a new commitment between parents and child on the thirteenth birthday can help them to be aware of the major changes that are about to take place. The child has new privileges and responsibilities, which help prepare him for the self-sufficiency of adulthood. Of course, parental guidance and discipline will continue to be needed until the son or daughter goes out on his own at age eighteen.

## B.  Developmental adaptations during early adolescence.

What are some of the major developmental changes an early adolescent goes through? Well, initially there is a major growth spurt. This growth rather than a particular birthday initiates adolescence, since it occurs at different ages in different individuals. I was about average height on my thirteenth birthday. Some of my friends that were once shorter than I started their growth spurts before I did, and passed me. Then my growth hormone started pouring out of my pituitary gland like water out of Niagara Falls, and I grew ten inches in about fifteen or sixteen months. I was so awkward for a while that relatives quit inviting our family over for dinner—among other things I broke glasses, a camera, and my uncle's pool cue, mostly because I misjudged how long my arms and legs were. And I bumped my head so many times on low overheads that I'm surprised I don't have any residual brain damage!

At age twelve, a child likes other children of the same sex and hates those of the opposite sex, except for maybe a favorite or two. But by age fourteen, most boys have decided that girls aren't so bad after all! In fact, it's hard to think about anything else. When boys spend more time with girls at school and church, it breaks up some of their old friendships—especially with boys that aren't interested in girls yet. Peer groups are rearranged, and there are marked feelings of ambivalence toward individuals of both sexes. Boys who were once friends are now competitors and even bitter enemies for a while. The same applies to girls, of course.

Young adolescents ask themselves the question, "Who am I?" Then they spend the next ten or fifteen years finding out. During this time, a healthy local church can be a positive influence on the impressionable adolescent as he begins his struggle for identity

and guidelines to live by. Sweden was once a Christian stronghold, but Sweden now has the highest adolescent suicide rate in
the entire world because adolescents are offered very few moral
guidelines, and many of the youth give up in their struggle to
find meaning in life. As their abstract reasoning ability continues
to develop rapidly, many adolescents develop fantasies of changing
the world or solving the world's problems. And for some unex-
plained reason, some of us adults never give up those fantasies! A
small group of dedicated Christian men once had an all-night prayer
meeting to pray that God would call someone out of their city
to help evangelize the world and provide new leadership for God's
people. These men had a vision, and so did the teenage son of
one of them. This teenage son was allowed to go with his father
to the prayer meeting, and he made some real commitments to the
Lord as he listened to the prayers of his father and the other men.
The city in which this prayer meeting took place was Charlotte,
North Carolina, and the teenager's name was Billy Graham. When
I watched Billy Graham's Korean crusade on television, I wept
for joy. Here, in a country that was totally pagan one generation
ago, I saw over a million Christians gathered at one meeting to
sing praises to God, and to hear God's Word preached by a humble
man who had a vision as a teenager. D. L. Moody once made the
statement that "the world has yet to see what God can do through
a man who is totally committed to Him." By God's grace, maybe
one of our sons or daughters will be the Billy Graham or the Corrie
TenBoom of the next generation.

## C.  Special problems of early adolescence.

### 1.  Communications breakdown.

Unless parents are especially careful, what used to be a family
home will rapidly develop into a pit stop, used briefly by teenage
sons and daughters for refueling their stomachs and sleeping! One
of the biggest problems during this stage is keeping the lines of
communication open, but this is really important. When a child
reaches adolescence, many families temporarily regress to earlier
modes of experience and behavior. If this is a creative regression,
it can be quite healthy, enabling other family members to empathize with the adolescent's feelings and development.[2] Then they

---

2. Kent Ravenscroft, Jr., "Normal Family Regression at Adolescence."

can grow together again as a family unit. The idea is to avoid being overly rigid. Try to adjust some yourselves while still maintaining overall family stability. You may want to establish a weekly family meeting in order to open lines of communication and to discuss constructive criticisms and suggestions. Solomon said, "A reliable communication permits progress" (Prov. 13:17, LB). He also said, "Through presumption comes nothing but strife, but with those who receive counsel is wisdom" (Prov. 13:10, NASV). And the prophet Amos asked, "Can two walk together, except they be agreed?" (Amos 3:3).

If you want to walk together with your teenagers, you'll have to make a real effort to communicate. A number of research studies have been done on communication patterns in the families of adolescents.[3] One study showed that in the families of aggressive, antisocial adolescents, the predominant pattern was for the father to pretend to be in authority if both parents were in public, but for the mother to be very directive and to disregard the husband on other occasions.[4] The antisocial adolescent tended to "tune out" whenever both parents were present. With passive, negativistic teenagers, the usual communication pattern was for the father to give the teenager wordy lectures, but to disregard whatever the teenager had to say. The mothers also ignored their teenagers, but at least asked them an occasional question. The passive teenagers tended to "close up" most of the time.[5] With introverted, withdrawn teenagers, the usual communication pattern was for the mother to ignore the teenager's presence and to interrupt whenever the teenager spoke. The father generally let the mother dominate, and was very attentive to his wife while frequently interrupting his son or daughter. These introverted teenagers paid close attention to both parents, in spite of the fact that their parents ignored them.[6]

Another interesting family communication study was carried out by Linda Odom and others. They had a number of families enter a room, one family at a time, to do individual and group

---

3. See bibliography references 5, 138, 272, 302, 322, 326, 436.
4. Sigrid R. McPherson, "Who Listens? Who Communicates? How? Styles of Interaction Among Parents and Their Disturbed Adolescent Children."
5. Ibid.
6. Ibid.

interpretations of Rorschach Ink-Blot cards.[7] The families had already been divided into two groups—those whose teenagers had good personality integration, and those whose teenagers had made poor psychological adjustments. The purpose was to see if the family communication patterns had made any difference in the psychological development of the teenagers. It was found that "families of children high in personality integration displayed more direct person-to-person communication, more efficient task orientation, more role clarity on the part of the parents, and less psychological distance than was true for families with lower adjustment children."[8]

Since family communication patterns are so important, I would like to tell you about one more study. This was carried out at the University of Utah by James Alexander, who studied the families of twenty-two normal adolescents and twenty delinquent adolescents.[9] He videotaped all of these families separately during "resolution-of-differences" tasks, and found that the families of the juvenile delinquents were defensive in their communications and did not work at the tasks as a unified group. The families of the normal adolescents, on the other hand, were very supportive of each other and were able to work together as a unit instead of as defensive individuals.

One more communication problem that needs to be mentioned at least briefly is the father-daughter communication problem. When daughters are young, it's quite normal for the little girl to climb on daddy's lap. But all of a sudden in early adolescence, that little girl has developed physically into a beautiful young woman. This results in some uncomfortable feelings in practically all fathers, and there are three major ways in which most fathers communicate with their daughters from that time on. (1) Some fathers feel very uncomfortable about the physical attractiveness of the teenage daughter, not realizing that these feelings are quite normal, and consequently withdraw from their daughters almost altogether. They may even take on an extra job to avoid confronting her. She

---

7. Linda Odom, et al., "A Study of Family Communication Patterns and Personality Integration in Childhood."

8. Ibid., p. 285.

9. James F. Alexander, "Defensive and Supportive Communications in Normal and Deviant Families."

feels rejected by her father, whom she loves very much, and this can result in a variety of psychological problems, such as feelings of unworthiness. As a Christian woman, later in life, she may even have a hard time feeling accepted by God or by her husband.

(2) Some immature fathers continue to rock their daughters on their lap, so to speak, and are overly friendly with their daughters. Some even become quite seductive, with or without being aware of it. I have had a number of female patients who have engaged in a great deal of sexual promiscuity without knowing why. But it was obvious to me that it was because they had been overly stimulated by their fathers. Many even had had sexual relations with their fathers (or in some cases stepfathers), followed by guilt feelings and hostility toward them. These are the hysterical females I described in Chapter Five, who subconsciously hate men and are out to prove that all men are good-for-nothings like their fathers. These girls will seduce anybody they can to prove this, and especially good men, since good men disprove their theory that all men are worthless. Some of them become prostitutes, some become lesbians, but most go from marriage to marriage, always finding out after being married a while that their new husband is worthless too, just like their father. Men frequently marry these women because they are usually quite physically attractive, and these men want a good sexual partner. But once they get married, these women seldom want sex because they don't really enjoy it as a normal woman does.[10]

(3) The third (and obviously the healthy) way for a father to communicate with his teenage daughter is to continue to show genuine love and concern for her, including a healthy hug now and then, but without being seductive. He will also openly display affection for his wife, and the two of them together will show genuine affection for their daughter. The healthy father will also realize that it is perfectly normal to feel physically attracted to his daughter—after all, half of her genes came from the woman he chose to marry. And he can enjoy her good looks without entertaining lustful thoughts. This will provide a basis for a healthy

_____

10. About one-third of American women never experience orgasm, but any woman, with psychotherapy, can learn to overcome this problem once father-daughter conflicts (and whatever other conflicts there may be) are resolved. Most hysterical females are anorgasmic, but many anorgasmic females are *not* hysterical and may have much simpler conflicts.

father-daughter communication pattern, and some day she will find a young man much like her father and have a very happy marriage. The same general principles hold true for sons with their mothers. A healthy mother-son relationship will lead the maturing son eventually to marry a girl "just like the girl that married dear old dad," as the old barbershop song goes. But note that the "other woman" in most divorce cases is not the husband's secretary, but rather the husband's mother, who spoiled him and over-indulged him.

### 2. *Other special problems during early adolescence.*

The communication problems are definitely the biggest problems in early adolescence. After they are taken care of, there is a host of less important special problems faced by teenagers, like the acne and body odor that accompany the hormonal changes.[11] Encouraging teenagers to improve their grooming habits usually takes care of the pimples and body odor, but sometimes medications may be needed for the acne, and these can be obtained from any dermatologist. Most girls begin having periods during early adolescence, and should be warned about this far ahead of time by their mothers so it won't come as a traumatic shock. I already discussed the problem of masturbation and wet dreams in teenage boys in Part One of this book.

One more special problem of early adolescence is adolescent depression. In teenagers, psychological depression is frequently disguised. It's easy to see in adults, because a depressed adult will lose his appetite, lose his sex drive, wake up frequently at night, develop frequent headaches, have feelings of despair. But the teenager often manifests his depression in different ways. If I get a teenage patient who has never been a problem, and then all of a sudden—over a period of a few weeks or months—he becomes increasingly irritable, rebellious, and hostile, with intermittent guilt feelings, I assume that he is probably depressed. If the teenager has been a problem all his life, with poor conduct ratings in school from the first grade on, I do not suspect depression—he was raised wrong and has become a young sociopath. But the depressed, previously good teenagers are quite easy to treat. Sometimes putting them on antidepressant medications alone will dramatically

---

11. Irwin I. Lubowe, "The Pathogenesis of Acne."

lessen the problem in about ten to twenty days.[12] Counseling sessions with the entire family are then necessary, re-establishing broken-down communication patterns.

I once had as a patient a teenage boy who came from a Christian home. The boy had been quite reasonable all his life, but in his early teens the lines of communication broke down and he started getting into all sorts of trouble; and he was even expelled from school. I started him on antidepressant medication, which I only with great difficulty convinced him to take. In fact, he walked angrily out of my office three different times when we discussed subjects he didn't want to talk about. Within ten days he rededicated his life to the Lord, and went to his family doctor and handed him some money. The family doctor asked him what the money was for, and the boy told him that he had stolen some money out of the doctor's wallet during a visit a month or two earlier, that he wanted to start repaying it and would pay the rest back when he earned enough from a part-time job.

If you think your son or daughter may be going through an adolescent depression, the first thing you should do is re-establish positive communications with a loving and accepting attitude. Compare your family rules to those of other Christian families. Frequently, parents of depressed adolescents are either too strict or too lenient. As parents, you can also totally eliminate nagging and other negative communications by heeding the following advice.

Have a two-hour family session involving only the teenager and both parents. Re-evaluate all the rules, chores, and punishments objectively. Have the teenager draw a line down the middle of a blank sheet of paper. Tell him to put specific rules and chores he thinks he should have on the left side of the line, and the punishments he thinks he should receive for breaking each of the rules on the right side. (Surprisingly, most teenagers will be harder on themselves than their parents would have been. Wanting more controls, teenagers frequently break rules so the parents will make them a little stricter.) Then go over each of the rules, chores, and punishments he has listed and discuss them. If they are reasonable, leave them as they are. If they are too strict or too lenient,

---

12. I have found Triavil 2-25, one tablet four times per day, to be especially helpful in speeding recovery, although medications are usually not necessary. The medicine, which is not addictive, is then gradually withdrawn over the next three to six months.

change the ones you must. As usual, the father should have the ultimate say. When you have completed the list, both parents should sign it and the teenager should also sign it and date it. This becomes a contract between the teenager and his parents. When he lists the chores, tell him to be specific about the day of the week on which he plans to do each chore. If he lives up to his part of the contract, there will be absolutely no need to nag him. If he doesn't keep his part of the bargain, you still won't need to nag—just automatically give him the consequence he listed on the right side of the line. If he breaks a rule, he suffers the consequence he agreed upon. Make the contract good for about a two-month period, and have weekly family meetings to discuss how things are going. Show respect for the teenager as a young adult, and listen to what he has to say, even if you disagree with him. When the two months are up, renegotiate the contract. If he has done a good job, give him a little more freedom in the new contract. If he has done a poor job, make the new contract a little stricter. But do your best to keep the communications constructive and positive, and be sure to compliment your teenager for showing responsibility. I have used this technique scores of times with teenagers and their parents, and the families have usually felt that it helped eliminate much of the negative communications between the parents and the teenager. It also helps put the brakes on the traditional parent-teenager power struggle, and at the same time acknowledges the teenager as a person by valuing his opinions on the rules he ought to have.[13]

---

13. This is my standard approach to treating cases of adolescent depression and adolescent rebellion, and it works most of the time. Interestingly, when it doesn't work, it is seldom the fault of the teenager, but rather of the parents, who fail to enforce the rules when the teenager tests them. Some parents come to my office expecting *me* to cure their family conflicts, and do not want to hear about ways that *they* themselves can cure these conflicts. Abraham Lincoln once said, "Most people are about as happy as they choose to be." What a wise statement! For other approaches to the treatment of depression, see bibliography references 127, 207, 323, 350, 355, and standard psychiatry textbooks.

# 16

## Mid- and Late Adolescence

Most of the problems discussed in the chapter on early adolescence also apply to mid- and late adolescence, and vice versa, especially since there is so much variability from individual to individual in the age of onset of adolescence and the rate of maturation.

### A. Developmental adaptations of mid- and late adolescence.

Before he enters adolescence, a child's allegiance is to his parents. He wants very much for his parents to love him, so he does a fairly good job of staying in line with their wishes. But in adolescence, especially in mid- and late adolescence, his allegiance is switched from his parents to his peers. To some extent, his peers' morals become his own. *However, if the parents have brought him up right so far, he will almost always choose peers who believe the things he does.* Whom he chooses for his associates is very important, because in craving popularity and social acceptance, he conforms to his peer-group ideologies, loyalties, and standards. This is often difficult for parents, because parents have little or no control over the friends their children choose to associate with away from the house. All parents can do is dictate who is allowed in the home, and tell their teenagers whom they shouldn't associate with, hoping they will obey. That's just one more reason why it's important to keep the lines of communication open—so that when you give your teenager guidance he will respect your opinion. The interpersonal relationships he develops during adolescence are more important, in my opinion, than what he learns scholastically. B. E. Segal, after reviewing the literature on adolescent socialization, made the comment that "every major social psychiatry study in the past decade has called attention to the probability that an absence of satisfying interpersonal relationships is a cause, and not just a result, of emotional disturbance."[1]

Mid- and late adolescence is also a time when girls increasingly give up their tomboy habits to accept a more feminine role. I don't know as yet how much the Women's Liberation Movement will change this. The girl's menstrual cycle also becomes more and more regular, with estrogen predominating the first two weeks of the cycle, influencing her to want to share her love with others. During the next two weeks, when progesterone predominates, she is less secure and needs to know that others love her. Then come the two days before menses starts again. At this time she will probably be more irritable, moody, and hard to get along with.[2] But it's best not to pamper her too much, even during those two days. If she learns to endure them in adolescence, it'll be much easier for her the rest of her life.

In males, androgens reach their peak level at about age seventeen or eighteen, so that's when the sex drive is greatest. In women, the sex drive is greatest at about the age of thirty. According to the Kinsey reports, about 90 percent of males and about 50 percent of females have experimented with sexual intercourse by age twenty-one. The social acceptability of it in American society today makes it even harder for Christian young people to save themselves for marriage, as God commanded them to. Children should know the facts of life by the time they are ten years old, but continued discussions from time to time, with the parent of the same sex, will help the Christian teenager maintain his determination to live up to God's sexual standards. And that will be best for him and his future marriage, also. But don't force these discussions on your teenager—wait for him to bring up the subject. If the teenager never brings it up, look for opportunities to get into a discussion on this important aspect of life.

---

1. B. E. Segal, et al., "Work, Play and Emotional Disturbances," p. 173.
2. J. Robert Willson, et al., *Obstetrics and Gynecology*, pp. 59-71.

There are three major ways in which parents view their teenage son or daughter. Some parents use projection, meaning that they project their own sinful impulses onto their teenager, suspecting him of doing things he's not guilty of. Other parents use identification, meaning that they automatically assume that their teenager is an extension of themselves in his way of thinking. This is also unrealistic. The third (and the healthy) way is for parents to empathize with their teenager, accepting him as a separate individual, and trying to understand him and his struggles. So in discussing sexual matters with your teenager, be sure you are not projecting unwarranted suspicion, or assuming that he thinks exactly the same way as you do.

I'll share with you a few of my views on dating for teenagers, but I think you should set up your own rules according to whatever you feel is right, whether you agree with me or not. In Proverbs 30, Agur (some theologians think Agur was the childhood name of Solomon) was inspired by God to describe four activities of nature that are extremely beautiful. Agur calls them "too wonderful for me." One of them is "the way of a man with a maid" (Prov. 30:19). Today, nearly three thousand years later, the same holds true. The majority of songs, books, and movies are about the love relationships between a male and a female. Dating is an important time in anyone's life. A person should date as many members of the opposite sex as possible in order to evaluate what type of mate would suit him best. But Christians should keep in mind Paul's instructions: "Be ye not unequally yoked together with unbelievers" (II Cor. 6:14). A teenage boy doesn't have to date a girl of loose morals in order to decide whether or not he would want to marry one. A good rule is to limit dating to those who might be considered as a potential mate. I don't think Christian teenagers should be allowed to date until they have reviewed the Scriptures and written out a personal list of dating rules that are in agreement with Scripture. They should then determine in their hearts that they will never violate these rules for any reason, even if it means losing some dates. Teenagers frequently fail to realize that every individual they date will some day be someone else's mate—or maybe even their own. What a teenager does or doesn't do during his dating years can significantly influence his future husband-wife relationships.

Parents frequently ask me at what age I think a teenager is

old enough to date. I'll tell you what I tell them. It all depends upon his emotional and spiritual maturity. If your teenager is of average or above average maturity for his age, a fairly good rule of thumb is that he will probably be ready for group dating at age thirteen or fourteen, double dating at age fifteen, and single dating at age sixteen. By group dating, I mean activities like a young people's party at church where some of the boys and girls may pair off after they arrive to sit together or participate in games together. In early adolescence, boys and girls are primarily trying to figure out what the opposite sex is all about, but as they mature in late adolescence, genuine love for someone of the opposite sex becomes possible in mature individuals.

In the sexual area, and in other areas as well, mid- and late adolescence is also a time for a process known as delimitation— setting limits. In early adolescence the limits individuals set for themselves are vague and sometimes bendable. But toward the end of adolescence, the individual is searching for self-identity, and this includes his moral identity, so he begins to fix or mark his limits. If he sticks to these limits, he will like himself. If he doesn't, he will experience guilt and a lowering of his self-esteem.

Late adolescence is a time when many individuals are ready emotionally to make meaningful commitments to Jesus Christ, and to call upon God's help to free them from the bondage of sin so that they *can* stay within those limits they have set for themselves. Late adolescence is also a time when young men begin thinking very seriously about what career they want to go into, and what they hope to accomplish in their lifetime. Girls think more about what type of man they want to spend the rest of their life with, and how they can develop their own God-given talents. *Many late adolescents become quite critical of their parents. This is because their self-goals, which are frequently idealistic and unattainable, are projected onto and expected of others—such as their parents. The teenager therefore becomes critical of his parents because they are not living up to the expectations he hopes to attain some day. The older and wiser he gets, the more accepting he will become of his parents.*

Many other aspects of his outlook on life also mature in late adolescence. He becomes less introspective and more goal-oriented. At least, this was true in the past. William Glasser, the author of the book *Reality Therapy,* talked about this at a seminar I attended in California.[3] He said the youth today are much less goal-oriented than the youth of a generation ago. The youth of today are generally more pleasure- and experience-oriented, living each day for the fun of that day.[4] I have also found this to be true in my own experience with teenagers. When I ask most young people —especially non-Christian young people—what they are living for, they either have a blank look, as though they had never thought about that before, or else they say, "Myself, of course!" But there's a real difference in the healthy evangelical community.[5] Those young people generally have godly ideals, and are willing to sacrifice themselves in many cases for the furtherance of the gospel. Another difference between evangelical and non-evangelical youth is that evangelical Christian young people are more likely to see themselves as pilgrims for a short time on a small piece of earth that will some day be destroyed by God when He creates a new heaven and a new earth. The non-evangelical youth in his late teens is likely to have a smaller view of the world, thinking for all practical purposes that his own lifespan must be half of history, and that the United States is at least half of the world.

## B.   Special problems of mid- and late adolescence.

This is a very difficult topic to summarize. Adolescents today face many special problems that didn't exist to any significant extent just one generation ago—like drugs and the occult. I already talked about how to produce a drug addict and how to treat one in Chapter Five, so I'll refer you back to that chapter for a discussion of the drug problem. I have studied demon-possession extensively and have hundreds of pages of notes on the subject. I have also discussed it with many missionaries who have cast out demons, usually through quiet prayer. I believe in demon-possession, but have never seen an indisputable case of it. I have had several psychotic or severely hysterical patients who claimed to be demon-possessed, but with brief psychotherapy and/or tranquilizers their

---

3. William Glasser, Seminar: Institute for Reality Therapy.

4. An excellent Christian book on generational trends and philosophies is Os Guinness' *The Dust of Death*. See also bibliography references 17, 144, 259, 297, 436.

5. I highly recommend that every Christian leader read the excellent article by Armand Nicholi (a Christian psychiatrist at Harvard), "A New Dimension of the Youth Culture."

"demons" rapidly disappeared. Given the occult trends today I probably will see a few genuine cases of it in the future.

I have also read some interesting research on student activism, but that was more of a problem in the late '60s.[6] Today's adolescents are characterized much more by student apathy than by student activism. They have a void in their lives, and are trying to fill the void with hallucinogenic drugs and other wild experiences.[7] Unfortunately, many Christian teenagers are also bored and apathetic, and are more concerned with narcissistic emotional experiences than with spreading the gospel of Jesus Christ.[8] But in the midst of all this apathy, large evangelical groups like the Navigators, Fellowship of Christian Athletes, Campus Crusade, Inter-Varsity, and Young Life are filling the void for today's youth, winning many of them to a personal acceptance of Jesus Christ as Savior and Lord.

Teenage pregnancies remain a problem for today's youth, but they have the additional problem of ready access to the local abortion clinic.[9] Abortions are granted to almost any pregnant teenager who thinks having the baby would cause her to have emotional problems, but studies have shown that the girls who have abortions end up with the same number of emotional problems as those who go ahead and have the babies. And venereal disease is epidemic among today's youth. I had one teenage patient not too long ago who received treatment for venereal disease one week and became reinfected again a week or two later.

Running away is also a common teenage problem. Psychiatrists can tell a good deal about the teenager and his or her family on the basis of running-away patterns. The spoiled, overly dependent teenager (usually a girl) will run away in order to punish her mother for not letting her have her own way. But these dependent runaways will always see to it that they are caught, usually within twenty-four to forty-eight hours.[10] They can't bear to be away from their mothers for any longer than that. The mother of one of my hysterical teenage patients called me at my office one day.

6. Robert S. Berns, et al., "Research on Student Activism."
7. See Guinness, *The Dust of Death.*
8. Francis A. Schaeffer, *The New Superspirituality.*
9. Eugene P. Shatkin, "Teenage Pregnancy: The Family Background."
10. Helm Stierlin, "A Family Perspective on Adolescent Runaways," p. 57.

She was very worried and concerned because her daughter had run away that morning. I knew the daughter quite well, so I asked the mother what time her daughter had run away. When she told me, I glanced at my watch and told the mother not to worry about the daughter because she would probably be returning home any minute. Just as I was saying that I heard some crying over the phone, and sure enough, her dependent daughter had returned.

Teenagers that run away and stay away are really much healthier than the ones who run away for only a day or two. On some occasions I think a teenager might mature more by running away than by staying in his mentally unstable home.[11] I know one man, for instance, who ran away from a very poor home situation at the age of fourteen. He got a job, worked his way through high school, college, and medical school, and became an outstanding pediatrician. If your daughter does run away in order to make you feel guilty for mistreating her, be sure you don't reward her when she returns. If it's a repeated problem, I would recommend family counseling to figure out what the family's psychodynamics are. Dr. Helm Stierlin states that between six hundred thousand and one million teenagers run away from home each year here in America. More than half of them are girls, mostly from the white suburbs.[12] Stierlin notes that

> the more a binding [smothering] parent gratifies, indulges, and spoils his child, the more conflicted, insatiable, and monster-like the child becomes. This interpersonal scenario—quick disillusionment with peers, heightened conflicts with parents—explains why a good many of these adolescents run away, yet return home quickly as abortive runaways.[13]

He says the task of the therapist is to encourage the parent and child to become more independent of each other, and comments that "an offspring's successful running away can signal progress rather than a setback, as it reflects this adolescent's (and his parents') increasing ability to live apart from, and independently of, each other."[14]

---

11. I would certainly never recommend running away, however, since better ways of handling the situation can always be found.

12. Stierlin, "Adolescent Runaways," p. 56.

13. Ibid., p. 59.

14. Ibid., p. 61.

## C.  When to let go of the leash.

Many Christian parents don't know when to let go of the leash. When a baby robin reaches a certain stage, its mother pushes it out of the nest, and the young robin learns how to fly on its way down toward the ground. Without adversity and independence, no teenager will grow up and learn how to fly. I am continually amazed at how many of my neurotic and inadequate patients are still living with their parents at age twenty, thirty, or even older. This is especially true of young adults who eventually become schizophrenic. It is also true of alcoholics, many of whom marry several mother-types before divorcing for the last time and moving back to mother to finish their short lives.

I sometimes recommend that teenagers who have graduated from high school go several hundred miles away—out of the nest— to develop their God-given talents (preferably but not neces- sarily at a Christian college), and learn the hard lessons of life by making the necessary mistakes—and then correcting them. If the parents reared the child by God's standards during those crucial first six years of life, when about 85 percent of his personality was formed, he'll do just fine. Trust him. And if the parents haven't reared their child by God's principles, most attempts to teach an eighteen-year-old something he should have learned when he was three years old will be utterly futile. Let him move out to learn from life's hard knocks, and pray that God will mature him. The greatest freedom the late adolescent can have is the freedom to fail. This is the freedom to make a mistake and to go on from there, having learned a valuable lesson by the experience. Don't kick him when he is down. He'll probably kick himself enough when no one is looking. If he can learn to lose his fear of failure, he has learned a big lesson. God's Word tells us, *"There is no fear in love; but perfect love casteth out fear"* (I John 4:18).

# 17

## A Final Challenge

### A. Paul's competitive spirit.

The Apostle Paul revealed his competitive spirit when he wrote to the Corinthians, "Know ye not that they which run in a race run all, but one receiveth the prize? *So run, that ye may obtain"* (I Cor. 9:24). I love Paul's competitive spirit, and I believe strongly that we, as Christian parents, should consider ourselves in competition with the world, especially in producing children who become the *very best* in emotional and spiritual maturity.

### B. God's pro draft for Christian parents.

Since I am an avid sports fan, I wait eagerly each year to see who will be selected in the pro draft as the best college football players. I was thinking about this one time, and I started wondering what would happen if God had a pro draft each year to select the very best Christian parents to raise our children. Which round would you be selected in—or would you be selected at all? Paul says, *"So run, that ye may obtain."* If you feel that you have made a great many mistakes in the past, well, welcome to the human race! But there is no use in dwelling on the past. Let's pick up the pieces where we are right now, and develop ourselves into the very best parents our children can possibly have. Children can tolerate many parental mistakes. We cause psychological and spir-

itual handicaps in our children only when we consistently refuse
to cooperate with God's plan and principles.

### C.  Children are a gift from God.

God's Word tells us, "Behold, children are a gift of the Lord.
The fruit of the womb is a reward" (Ps. 127:3, NASV). If the Lord
tarries, there is nothing I want more when I get older than to
see my own children and grandchildren still growing in the Lord
and still excited about life!

### D.  Good children are an honor.

Solomon said, "My son, how happy I will be if you turn out
to be sensible! It will be a public honor to me" (Prov. 27:11, LB).
Well, I feel the same way about my children.

### E.  Don't let the world squeeze you into its mold!

Paul urges us on with the words,

> I beseech you therefore, brethren, by the mercies of God, that
> ye present your bodies a living sacrifice, holy, acceptable unto
> God, which is your *reasonable* [not exceptional, but *reason-
> able*] service. And be not conformed to this world [the Phillips
> translation says, "Don't let the world squeeze you into its
> mold"]: but be ye transformed by the renewing of your mind,
> that ye may prove what is that good, and acceptable, and
> perfect will of God.                    —Rom. 12:1-2

### F.  God will help us.

Christian parents, let's dedicate ourselves to God, so He can
accomplish what He wants to accomplish in our children through
us. He has promised to help us to be the kind of parents He has
called us to be. Paul promised us, "Faithful is he that calleth you,
*who also will do it*" (I Thess. 5:24). Moreover, we have the Old
Testament assurance: "For the eyes of the Lord search back and
forth across the whole earth, looking for people whose hearts are
perfect toward him, *so that he can show his great power in helping
them*" (II Chron. 16:9, LB).

### G.  Confess past mistakes.

I would encourage you to confess your past mistakes to God,
remembering His promise that "if we confess our sins, he is

faithful and just to forgive us our sins, and to cleanse us from *all* unrighteousness" (I John 1:9).

## H.  Forget the past and move on toward that prize.

Forgive yourself for past mistakes, and move on from there with the attitude that the Apostle Paul had when he wrote, *"Forgetting those things which are behind, and reaching forth unto those things which are before,* I press toward the mark for the prize of the high calling of God in Christ Jesus" (Phil. 3:13-14). May God reward you richly for turning from the selfish ambitions of this world and totally committing yourself to God's *highest* calling— being a wise, strong, loving, and godly Christian parent.

# Bibliography

1. Adams, Paul L. "Family Characteristics of Obsessive Children." *American Journal of Psychiatry.* 128:1414-17, May, 1972.

2. Aitken, R. C., et al. "Psychological and Physiological Measures of Emotion in Chronic Asthmatic Patients." *Journal of Psychosomatic Research.* 13:289-97, Sept., 1969.

3. Aldrich, C. Knight. *An Introduction to Dynamic Psychiatry.* New York: McGraw-Hill Book Company, 1966.

4. Alexander, Franz, and Sheldon Selesnick. *The History of Psychiatry.* New York: Harper and Row, 1966.

5. Alexander, James F. "Defensive and Supportive Communications in Normal and Deviant Families." *Journal of Consulting Clinical Psychology.* 40:223-31, April, 1973.

6. Allison, Joel. "Recent Empirical Studies of Religious Conversion Experiences." *Pastoral Psychology.* Sept., 1966, pp. 21-28.

7. Anderson, W. Ferguson. "A Death in the Family: A Professional View." *British Medical Journal.* 1:31-32, Jan. 6, 1973.

8. "Anorexia Nervosa Males." *British Medical Journal.* 4:686, Dec. 23, 1972.

9. Apolito, Amaldo. "Psychoanalysis and Religion." *American Journal of Psychoanalysis.* 30:115-23, 1970.

10. Argyle, M. "Seven Psychological Roots of Religion." *Theology.* 67:1-7, 1964.

11. Arieti, Silvano. "An Overview of Schizophrenia from a Predominantly Psychological Approach." *American Journal of Psychiatry.* 131:241-49, March, 1974.

12. Arnold, Magda B. (editor). *Feelings and Emotions.* New York: Academic Press, 1970.

13. Aston, P. Jean, and Gillian Dobson London. "Family Interaction and Social Adjustment in a Sample of Normal School Children." *Journal of Child Psychology and Psychiatry.* 13:77-89, June, 1972.

14. Bader, L. "The Therapeutic Value of Realistic Hope." *International Journal of Psychiatry.* 6:385-86, Nov., 1968.

15. Bahnson, M. B., et al. "Ego Defenses in Cancer Patients." *Annals of the New York Academy of Science.* 164:546-59. Oct. 14, 1969.

16. Barcai, Avner. "Family Therapy in the Treatment of Anorexia Nervosa." *American Journal of Psychiatry.* 128:286-90, Sept., 1971.

17. Barker, Graham. "Adolescent Counseling and the Problem of Identity." Unpublished Master's Thesis. Trinity Evangelical Divinity School, Deerfield, Illinois, June, 1975.

18. Barlow, Jim. "Freedom to Love in the Male-male Relationship." *Christian Medical Society Journal.* Summer, 1973, pp. 1-7, 32.

19. Barnes, Grant. Notes from his grand rounds at Duke University and residents' meeting afterward. May 2, 1974.

20. Beck, R. N. "Hall's Genetic Psychology and Religious Conversion." *Pastoral Psychology.* 16:45-51, Sept., 1965.

21. Belgum, David (editor). *Religion and Medicine.* Ames, Iowa: Iowa State University Press, 1967.

22. Belmont, Lillian, and Francis A. Marolla. "Birth Order, Family Size and Intelligence." *Science.* 182:1096-1101, Dec. 14, 1973.

23. Bemporad, Jules R., et al. "Characteristics of Encopretic Patients and Their Families." *Journal of the American Academy of Child Psychiatry.* 10:272-92, April, 1971.

24. Bennett, Eaton Wesley. "The Human Psyche: A Study of the Struggle to Achieve Emotional Maturity." Lecture delivered at Arkansas State Hospital, Little Rock, Arkansas, Nov., 1968.

25. ———. Lecture on personality. Arkansas State Hospital, Little Rock, Arkansas, Jan. 7, 1971.

26. ———. Lecture on spiritual development in the child. Arkansas State Hospital, Little Rock, Arkansas, Jan. 21, 1971.

27. Bentovim, Arnon. "Handicapped Pre-school Children and Their Families—Effects on the Child's Early Emotional Development." *British Medical Journal.* 3:634-73, Sept. 9, 1972.

28. Berg, Ian, Alan Butter, and Ralph McGuire. "Birth Order and Family Size of School-phobic Adolescents." *British Journal of Psychiatry.* 121:509-14, Nov., 1972.

29. Bergstrom, K., P. O. Lundberg, and A. Sjövall. "The Volume of the Sella Turcica in Patients with Anorexia Nervosa." *European Neurology.* 9:183-89, 1973.

30. Berns, Robert S., Daphne E. Bugental, and Geraldine P. Berns. "Research on Student Activism." *American Journal of Psychiatry.* 128:1499-1504, June, 1972.

31. Bernstein, Lewis, and Richard H. Dana. *Interviewing and the Health Professions.* New York: Meredith Corporation, 1970.

32. Berry, George Ricker. *The Interlinear Literal Translation of the Greek New Testament.* Grand Rapids: Zondervan Publishing House, 1956.

33. Beumont, P. J. V., C. J. Beardwood, and G. F. M. Russell. "The Occurrence of the Syndrome of Anorexia Nervosa in Male Subjects." *Psychological Medicine.* 2:216-31, Aug., 1972.

34. Bindelglas, Paul M., George H. Dee, and Francis A. Enos. "Medical and Psychosocial Factors in Enuretic Children Treated with Imipramine Hydrochloride." *American Journal of Psychiatry.* 124:1107-12, Feb., 1968.

35. Binger, C. M., et al. "Childhood Leukemia. Emotional Impact on Patient and Family." *New England Journal of Medicine.* 280:414-18, Feb. 20, 1969.

36. Bisagno, John. *The Power of Positive Praying.* Grand Rapids: Zondervan Publishing House, 1965.

37. Black, Perry (editor). *Physiological Correlates of Emotion.* New York: Academic Press, 1970.

38. Bleuler, Eugen. *Dementia Praecox.* New York: International Universities Press, 1950.

39. Block, J. "Parents of Schizophrenic, Neurotic, Asthmatic, and Congenitally Ill Children: A Comparative Study." *Archives of General Psychiatry.* 20:659-74, 1969.

40. Bonine, Walter. *The Clinical Use of Dreams.* New York: Basic Books, 1962.

41. Bounds, E. M. *Power Through Prayer.* Chicago: Moody Press, n.d.

42. Boyle, Ivy, and Harold Narius. Grand rounds on school refusal. Duke University, 1975.

43. Brambilla, F., F. Viani, and V. Rossotti. "Endocrine Aspects of Child Psychoses." *Diseases of the Nervous System.* 30:627-32, 1969.

44. Brandes, N. S. "Influence of Emotionally Disturbed Teachers on Schoolchildren." *Mental Hygiene.* 53:606-10, Oct., 1969.

45. Brenner, B. "Patterns of Alcohol Use, Happiness and the Satisfaction of Wants." *Journal of Studies on Alcoholism.* 28:667-75, Dec., 1967.

46. Brenner, Charles. *An Elementary Textbook of Psychoanalysis.* Garden City, New York: Doubleday and Company, 1957.

47. Bright, Bill. *How to Experience God's Love and Forgiveness.* Arrowhead Springs, California: Campus Crusade for Christ, Incorporated, 1971.

48. Broadhurst, P. L. "Psychogenics of Emotionality in the Rat." *Annals of the New York Academy of Science.* 159:806-24, July 30, 1969.

49. Bronfenbrenner, Urie. "The Next Generation of Americans." Paper from the 1975 Annual Meeting of the American Association of Advertising Agencies. Dorado, Puerto Rico, March 19-22, 1975.

50. Brown, F., et al. "Childhood Bereavement and Subsequent Crime." *British Journal of Psychiatry.* 112:1043-48, Oct., 1966.

51. Bruch, Hilda. "Anorexia Nervosa in the Male." *Psychosomatic Medicine.* 33:31-47, Jan.-Feb., 1971.

52. ———. "Death in Anorexia Nervosa." *Psychosomatic Medicine.* 33:135-44, March-April, 1971.

53. ———. "Family Transactions in Eating Disorders." *Comprehensive Psychiatry*. 12:238-48, May, 1971.

54. Brussel, James A. *The Physician's Concise Handbook of Psychiatry*. New York: Brunner/Mazel, Incorporated, 1969.

55. Busse, Ewald W., and Eric Pfeiffer. *Mental Illness in Later Life*. Washington, D.C.: American Psychiatry Association, 1973.

56. Cannon, Walter B. *The Wisdom of the Body*. New York: W. W. Norton and Company, 1932.

57. Chafetz, Morris E., Howard T. Blane, and Marjorie J. Hill. "Children of Alcoholics. Observations in a Child Guidance Clinic." *Quarterly Journal of Studies on Alcoholism*. 32:687-98, Sept., 1971.

58. Chandler, Caroline A., Reginald S. Laurie, and Anne DeHuff Peters. *Early Child Care*. New York: Atherton Press, 1968.

59. Chess, Stella, and Alexander Thomas. *Annual Progress in Child Psychiatry and Child Development*. New York: Brunner/Mazel Publishers, 1971.

60. Christensen, C. W. "Religious Conversion." *Archives of General Psychiatry*. 9:207-16, Sept., 1963.

61. ———. "Religious Conversion in Adolescence." *Pastoral Psychology*. 16: 17-28, Sept., 1965.

62. Christensen, Larry. *The Christian Family*. Minneapolis: Bethany Fellowship, 1970.

63. Clark, W. H. "William James: Contributions to the Psychology of Religious Conversion." *Pastoral Psychology*. 16:29-36, Sept., 1965.

64. Clavan, Silvia, and Ethel Vatter. "The Affiliated Family: A Device for Integrating Old and Young." *Gerontologist*. 12:407-12, Winter, 1972.

65. Cleckley, H. M. *Mask of Sanity*. St. Louis: C. V. Mosby Company, 1941.

66. Clemes, S. R., et al. "Effect of REM Sleep Deprivation on Psychological Functioning." *Journal of Nervous and Mental Disorders*. 144:485-91, June, 1967.

67. Cline, David W., and Jack C. Westman. "The Impact of Divorce on the Family." *Child Psychology and Human Development*. 2:78-83, Winter, 1971.

68. Cohen, S. I. "Psychoneurophysiologic Consideration of Emotions: I." *Postgraduate Medicine*. 47:79-87, May, 1970.

69. ———. "Psychoneurophysiologic Consideration of Emotions: II." *Postgraduate Medicine*. 47:91-95, June, 1970.

70. Coleman, Robert E. *The Master Plan of Evangelism*. Old Tappan, New Jersey: Fleming H. Revell, 1964.

71. Collins, Gary R. *Search for Reality*. Wheaton, Illinois: Key Publishers, 1969.

72. ———. *Living in Peace*. Wheaton, Illinois: Key Publishers, 1970.

73. ———. *Man in Transition: The Psychology of Human Development*. Carol Stream, Illinois: Creation House, 1971.

74. ———. *Effective Counseling*. Carol Stream, Illinois: Creation House, 1972.

75. ———. *Fractured Personalities*. Carol Stream, Illinois: Creation House, 1972.

76. ———. *Man in Motion*. Carol Stream, Illinois: Creation House, 1973.

77. Crisp, A. H., G. W. Fenton, and L. Scotton. "The Electroencephalogram in Anorexia Nervosa." *Electroencephalography and Clinical Neurophysiology*. 23:490, Nov., 1967.

78. ———. "A Controlled Study of the Electroencephalogram in Anorexia Nervosa." *British Journal of Psychiatry*. 114:1149-60, Sept., 1968.

79. Crisp, Arthur H. "Primary Anorexia Nervosa." *Gut*. 9:370-72, 1968.

80. ———. "Premorbid Factors in Adult Disorders of Weight, with Particular Reference to Primary Anorexia Nervosa (Weight Phobia). A Literature Review." *Journal of Psychosomatic Research*. 14:1-22, March, 1970.

81. ———. "Reported Birth Weight and Growth Rates in a Group of Patients with Primary Anorexia Nervosa (Weight Phobia)." *Journal of Psychosomatic Research*. 14:23-50, March, 1970.

82. Crisp, Arthur H., Edward Stonehill, and George W. Fenton. "The Relationship Between Sleep, Nutrition and Mood: A Study of Patients with Anorexia Nervosa." *Postgraduate Medical Journal*. 47:207-13, April, 1971.

83. Crisp, Arthur H., and D. A. Toms. "Primary Anorexia or Weight Phobia in the Male: Report on Thirteen Cases." *British Medical Journal*. 1:334-38, 1972.

84. Danowski, R. S., E. Livstone, A. R. Gonzales, Y. Jung, and R. C. Khurana. "Fractional and Partial Hypopituitarism in Anorexia Nervosa." *Hormones*. 3:105-18, 1972.

85. Delgado, J. M., et al. "Fragmental Organization of Emotional Behavior in the Monkey Brain." *Annals of the New York Academy of Science*. 159:731-51, July 30, 1969.

86. Dennehy, C. M. "Childhood Bereavement and Psychiatric Illness." *British Journal of Psychiatry*. 112:1049-69, Oct., 1966.

87. Detrie, Thomas P., and Henry G. Jarecki. *Modern Psychiatric Treatment*. Philadelphia: J. B. Lippincott Company, 1971.

88. *Diagnostic and Statistical Manual of Mental Disorders*. Washington, D.C.: American Psychiatric Association, 1968.

89. Dickens, J. A. "Concurrence of Turner's Syndrome and Anorexia Nervosa." *British Journal of Psychiatry*. 117:237, Aug., 1970.

90. Dobson, James. *Dare to Discipline*. Wheaton, Illinois: Tyndale House Publishers, 1971.

91. Dollar, George W. *A History of Fundamentalism in America*. Greenville, South Carolina: B.J.U. Press, 1973.

92. Dorcus, Roy, and G. Wilson Shaffer. *Abnormal Psychology*. Baltimore: The Williams and Wilkins Company, 1950.

93. Drakeford, J. W. *Psychology in Search of a Soul*. Nashville: Broadman, 1964.

94. Draper, Edgar, et al. "On the Diagnostic Value of Religious Ideation." *Archives of General Psychiatry*. 13:202-07, Sept., 1965.

95. *Drug Dependence*. Chicago: American Medical Association, 1969.

96. Dumermuth, G. "EEG-untersuchungen beim Jugendlichen Klinefelter Syndrom." *Helvetica Paediatrica Acta.* 16:702-10, 1961.

97. Dutton, G. "The Growth Patterns of Psychotic Boys." *British Journal of Psychology.* 110:101-03, 1964.

98. Duty, Guy. *Divorce and Remarriage.* Minneapolis: Bethany Fellowship, 1967.

99. Dykman, Roscoe A., John E. Peters, and Peggy T. Ackerman. "Experimental Approaches to the Study of Minimal Brain Dysfunction: A Follow-up Study." *Annals of the New York Academy of Sciences.* 205:93-108, Feb. 28, 1973.

100. Easson, William M. "The Family of the Dying Child." *Pediatric Clinics of North America.* 19:1157-65, Nov., 1972.

101. Eaton, Merrill T., and Margaret H. Peterson. *Psychiatry.* New York: Medical Examination Publishing Company, 1969.

102. Edelson, S. R. "A Dynamic Formulation of Childhood Schizophrenia." *Diseases of the Nervous System.* 27:610-15, 1966.

103. *Education for the Culturally Disadvantaged.* South Central Region Educational Laboratory, United States Office of Education, 1967.

104. Eisenberg, J. F. "Social Organization and Emotional Behavior." *Annals of the New York Academy of Science.* 159:752-59, July 30, 1969.

105. "Epidemiology of Anorexia Nervosa." *British Medical Journal.* 3:556, Sept. 15, 1973.

106. Evans, Sue L., John B. Reinhart, and Ruth A. Succop. "Failure to Thrive. A Study of 45 Children and Their Families." *Journal of the American Academy of Child Psychology.* 11:440-57, July, 1972.

107. Fagen, Joen, and Irma Lee Shepherd. *Gestalt Therapy Now.* Palo Alto, California: Science and Behavior Books, Incorporated, 1970.

108. Falliers, C. J. "Environmental and Psychological Influences on Allergic Diseases." *Postgraduate Medicine.* 46:127-32, July, 1969.

109. Fehr, F. S., et al. "Peripheral Physiological Variables and Emotion: The James-Lange Theory Revisited." *Psychological Bulletin.* 74:411-24, Dec., 1970.

110. Fenton, George W., and T. M. Elphicke. "Sleep Patterns in Malnutrition: A Longitudinal Study of Anorexic Patients." *Electroencephalography and Clinical Neurophysiology.* 27:681, Sept., 1969.

111. Ferm, R. O. *The Psychology of Christian Conversion.* Old Tappan, New Jersey: Fleming H. Revell, 1959.

112. Fish, B., et al. "The Prediction of Schizophrenia in Infancy: II. A Ten-year Follow-up Report of Predictions Made at One Month of Age." *Psychopathology of Schizophrenia.* Edited by P. H. Hoch and J. Zubin. New York: Grune and Stratton, 1966.

113. Fish, F. J. *Schizophrenia.* Baltimore: The Williams and Wilkins Company, 1962.

114. Florence, Varina Sue. "The Responsibility of the Church to Parents of the Retarded." Unpublished Master's Thesis. Trinity Evangelical Divinity School, Deerfield, Illinois, June, 1975.

115. Flynn, W. E. "Managing the Emotional Aspects of Peptic Ulcer and Ulcerative Colitis." *Postgraduate Medicine*. 47:119-22, May, 1970.

116. Ford, Frederick R., and Joan Herrick. "Family Rules: Family Life Styles." *American Journal of Orthopsychiatry*. 44:61-69, Jan., 1974.

117. Formby, D. "Maternal Recognition of Infant's Cry." *Developmental Medicine and Child Neurology*. 9:293-98, June, 1967.

118. Forssman, Hans, Gunnel Mellbin, and Jan Walinder. "Concurrence of Turner's Syndrome and Anorexia Nervosa." *British Journal of Psychiatry*. 116:221-23, Feb., 1970.

119. Fowle, A. M. "Atypical Leukocyte Pattern of Schizophrenic Children." *Archives of General Psychiatry*. 18:666-80, 1968.

120. Fowler, P. B. S., S. O. Banin, and Hamid Ikram. "Prolonged Ankle Reflex in Anorexia Nervosa." *Lancet*. 2:307-08, Aug. 12, 1972.

121. Framrose, R. "First 70 Admissions to Adolescent Unit: General Characteristics and Treatment Outcome." *British Journal of Psychiatry*. 126:380-89, 1975.

122. Frank, J. D. *Persuasion and Healing*. New York: Schocken Books, 1974.

123. Freedman, Alfred M., and Harold I. Kaplan (editors). *Comprehensive Textbook of Psychiatry*. Baltimore: The Williams and Wilkins Company, 1967.

124. Freedman, Alfred M., Harold I. Kaplan, and Benjamin J. Sadock. *Modern Synopsis of Psychiatry*. Baltimore: The Williams and Wilkins Company, 1972.

125. Freud, Anna. *The Ego and the Mechanisms of Defense*. London: Hogarth Press, 1937.

126. Friedman, C. Jack, and Alfred S. Friedman. "Sex Concordance in Psychogenic Disorders. Psychosomatic Disorders in Mothers and Schizophrenia in Daughters." *Archives of General Psychiatry*. 27:611-17, Nov., 1972.

127. Gallemore, J. L., William P. Wilson, and J. M. Rhoads. "The Religious Life of Patients with Affective Disorders." *Diseases of the Nervous System*. 30:483-86, July, 1969.

128. Garattini, S., and L. Valzelli. *Serotonin*. New York: Elsevier Publishing Company, 1965.

129. Garfinkel, Paul E., Stephen A. Kline, and Harvey S. Stancer. *Journal of Nervous and Mental Disorders*. 157:428-33, Dec., 1973.

130. Gerber, Gwendolyn L. "Psychological Distance in the Family as Schematized by Families of Normal, Disturbed and Learning-problem Children." *Journal of Consulting and Clinical Psychology*. 40:139-47, Feb., 1973.

131. Getz, Gene A. *The Christian Home in a Changing World*. Chicago: Moody Press, 1972.

132. ———. *Sharpening the Focus of the Church*. Chicago: Moody Press, 1974.

133. ———. *The Measure of a Church*. Glendale, California: G/L Publications, 1975.

134. Gibbs, F. A., and E. Gibbs. *Atlas of Electroencephalography.* Vol. III, p. 450.

135. Giele, Janet Zollinger. "Changes in the Modern Family: Their Impact on Sex Roles." *American Journal of Orthopsychiatry.* 41:757-66, Oct., 1971.

136. Gilder, George. "In Defense of Monogamy." *Commentary.* Nov., 1974, pp. 31-36.

137. Gilmore, Susan K. "Personality Differences Between High and Low Dogmatism Groups of Pentecostal Believers." *Journal for the Scientific Study of Religion.* 8:161-64, 1969.

138. Ginott, Haim G. *Between Parent and Child.* New York: Avon Books, 1965.

139. Gittleman, M., and H. G. Birch. "Childhood Schizophrenia: Intellect, Neurologic Status, Perinatal Risk, Prognosis, and Family Pathology." *Archives of General Psychiatry.* 17:16-25, 1967.

140. Glass, David C. (editor). *Neurophysiology and Emotion.* New York: The Rockefeller University Press, 1967.

141. Glasser, William. *Mental Health or Mental Illness.* New York: Harper and Row, 1960.

142. ———. *Reality Therapy.* New York: Harper and Row, 1965.

143. ———. *Schools Without Failure.* New York: Harper and Row, 1969.

144. ———. *The Identity Society.* New York: Harper and Row, 1972.

145. ———. Seminar: Institute for Reality Therapy. Los Angeles, California, Aug., 1973.

146. Gold, S., and M. J. Seller. "An Epileptic Factor in the Serum of Psychotic Children." *The Medical Journal of Australia.* 2:876-77, 1965.

147. Goldfarb, C., et al. "Psychophysiologic Aspects of Malignancy." *American Journal of Psychiatry.* 123:1545-52, June, 1967.

148. Goldfarb, W. "An Investigation of Childhood Schizophrenia." *Archives of General Psychiatry.* 11:620-34, 1964.

149. Goldman, P. S. "The Relationship Between the Amount of Stimulation in Infancy and Subsequent Emotionality." *Annals of the New York Academy of Science.* 159:640-50, July 30, 1969.

150. Goor, C. "EEG in Anorexia Nervosa." *Electroencephalography and Clinical Neurophysiology.* 6:351, 1954.

151. Gordon, A. I. *The Nature of Conversion.* Boston: Beacon Press, 1967.

152. Gothard, Bill. Seminar: Institute in Basic Youth Conflicts. Kansas City, Missouri, Nov., 1972.

153. ———. Seminar: (Advanced) Institute in Basic Youth Conflicts. Los Angeles, California, Aug., 1973.

154. Granberg, Lars I. *Marriage Is for Adults Only.* Grand Rapids: Zondervan Publishing House, 1971.

155. Green, Richard S., and John H. Rau. "Treatment of Compulsive Eating Disturbances with Anticonvulsant Medication." *American Journal of Psychiatry.* 131:428-32, April, 1974.

156. Greenbaum, Henry. "Marriage, Family and Parenthood." *American Journal of Psychiatry.* 130:1262-65, Nov., 1973.

157. Griffith, R. "Philosophy of Psychotherapy of Juvenile Delinquency." *Psychotherapy and Psychosomatics.* 25:134-37, 1975.

158. Guinness, Os. *The Dust of Death.* Downers Grove, Illinois: Inter-Varsity Press, 1973.

159. Gull, Sir William W. "Anorexia Nervosa (Apepsia Hysterica)." *British Medical Journal.* 2:527, 1873.

160. Gunderson, John G., et al. "Special Report: Schizophrenia, 1974." *Schizophrenia Bulletin.* 9:16-54, Summer, 1974.

161. Gunderson, John G., and Margaret T. Singer. "Defining Borderline Patients: An Overview." *The American Journal of Psychiatry.* 132:1-10, Jan., 1975.

162. Gundlach, Ralph H. "Data on the Relation of Birth Order and Sex of Sibling of Lesbians Oppose the Hypothesis That Homosexuality Is Genetic." *Annals of the New York Academy of Science.* 197:179-81, May 25, 1972.

163. Guze, Samuel B., Robert A. Woodruff, and Paul J. Clayton. "Sex, Age, and the Diagnosis of Hysteria." *American Journal of Psychiatry.* 129:745-48, Dec., 1972.

164. Hall, Calvin S. *A Primer of Freudian Psychology.* New York: New American Library, 1954.

165. Hall, Calvin S., and Gardner Lindzey. *Theories of Personality.* New York: John Wiley and Sons, 1970.

166. Halmi, Katherine A., and Constantine Riggs. "Urogenital Malformations Associated with Anorexia Nervosa." *British Journal of Psychiatry.* 122: 79-81, Jan., 1973.

167. Halmi, K. A., et al. "Familial Alcoholism in Anorexia Nervosa." *British Journal of Psychiatry.* 123:53-54, July, 1973.

168. Hamilton, Floyd E. *The Basis of Christian Faith.* New York: Harper and Row, 1964.

169. Hancock, Sheila. "A Death in the Family: A Lay View." *British Medical Journal.* 1:29-30, Jan. 6, 1973.

170. Harlow, Harry F., and Margaret K. Harlow. *The Affectional Systems in Behavior of Non-Human Primates.* Edited by A. M. Schrier, et al. Volume II. New York: Academic Press, 1965.

171. Harris, Thomas A. *I'm O.K.—You're O.K.* New York: Harper and Row, 1969.

172. Hartshorne, H., and M. A. May. "A Summary of the Work of the Character Education Inquiry." *Religious Education.* 25:607-19, 754-62, 1930.

173. Hartup, Willard W., and Nancy L. Smothergill (editors). *The Young Child.* Washington, D.C.: National Association for the Education of Young Children, 1967.

174. Harvey, A. McGehee, et al. (editors). *The Principles and Practice of Medicine.* New York: Meredith Corporation, 1968.

175. Hawkins, David. Grand rounds on treatment of the male hysteric. Duke University Medical Center, Durham, North Carolina. Jan. 16, 1975.

176. Hays, Peter. "Determination of the Obsessional Personality." *American Journal of Psychiatry*. 129:217-19, Aug., 1972.

177. Heidrich, R., and H. Schmidt-Matthias. "Encephalographische Befunde bei Anorexia Nervosa." *Arch. Psychiat. Neuroenkr*. 202:183-201, 1961.

178. Heimstra, N. W., et al. "Effects of Operator Mood on Performance in a Simulated Driving Task." *Perceptual Motor Skills*. 25:729-35, Dec., 1967.

179. Hennig, Margaret M. "Family Dynamics for Developing Positive Achievement Motivation in Women: The Successful Woman Executive." *Annals of the New York Academy of Science*. 208:76-81, March 15, 1973.

180. Hersey, William J., Jr., and Karin R. Lapidus. "Restoring the Balance." *Pediatric Clinics of North America*. 20:221-31, Feb., 1973.

181. Hill, William S. "The Psychology of Conversion." *Pastoral Psychology*. 6:43-46, Nov., 1955.

182. Hiltner, S. "Toward a Theology of Conversion in the Light of Psychology." *Pastoral Psychology*. 17:35-42, Sept., 1966.

183. Hine, Frederick R. *Introduction to Psychodynamics: A Conflict-Adaptational Approach*. Durham, North Carolina: Duke University Press, 1971.

184. Hine, Frederick R., and Eric Pfeiffer. *Behavioral Science: A Selective View*. Boston: Little, Brown and Company, 1972.

185. Hoag, Jean Marie, et al. "The Encopretic Child and His Family." *Journal of the American Academy of Child Psychiatry*. 10:242-56, April, 1971.

186. Hoerr, Narmand L., et al. (editors). *Blakiston's New Gould Medical Dictionary*. New York: McGraw-Hill Book Company, 1956.

187. Hoffman, H., et al. "Emotional Self-Description of Alcoholic Patients After Treatment." *Psychological Reports*. 26:892, June, 1970.

188. ———. "Analysis of Moods in Personality Disorders." *Psychological Reports*. 27:187-90, Aug., 1970.

189. Hollenweger, Walter J. *The Pentecostals*. Minneapolis: Augsburg Publishing House, 1972.

190. Hooper, Douglas, Roger Gill, Peter Powesland, and Bernard Ineichen. "The Health of Young Families in New Housing." *Journal of Psychosomatic Research*. 16:367-74, Aug., 1972.

191. Hoover, Carol F., and Juliana Day Franz. "Siblings in the Families of Schizophrenics." *Archives of General Psychiatry*. 26:334-42, April, 1972.

192. Hopkins, Henry U. *Leopold's Principles and Methods of Physical Diagnosis*. Philadelphia: W. B. Saunders Company, 1966.

193. Horton, Paul C. "A Mystical Experience as a Suicide Preventive." *American Journal of Psychiatry*. 130:294-96, March, 1973.

194. Howell, Mary C. "Employed Mothers and Their Families." *Pediatrics*. 52:252-63, Aug., 1973.

195. Hunt, David. *Parents and Children in History*. New York: Basic Books, 1970.

196. Hunt, Gladys. *Ms. Means Myself*. Grand Rapids: Zondervan Publishing House, 1972.

197. Husband, Peter, and Pat E. Hinton. "Families of Children with Repeated Accidents." *Archives of Diseases of Children.* 47:396-400, June, 1972.

198. Hyder, O. Quentin. *The Christian's Handbook of Psychiatry.* Old Tappan, New Jersey: Fleming H. Revell Company, 1971.

199. Ironside, Harry A. *Notes on the Book of Proverbs.* Neptune, New Jersey: Loizeaux Brothers, 1908.

200. Isbister, Clair. "The Family: Past, Present and Future." *Medical Journal of Australia.* 1:762-64, April 14, 1973.

201. Jacobson, Edmund. *Biology of Emotions.* Springfield, Illinois: Charles C. Thomas, 1967.

202. James, Muriel, and Dorothy Jongeward. *Born to Win.* Reading, Massachusetts: Addison-Wesley Publishing Company, 1971.

203. James, William. *The Varieties of Religious Experience.* New York: Signet, 1958.

204. James, William H. "Age at Menarch, Family Size and Birth Order." *American Journal of Obstetrics and Gynecology.* 116:292-93, May 15, 1973.

205. Janowski, D. S., et al. "The Menstrual Cycle." *Archives of General Psychiatry.* 17:459-69, Oct., 1967.

206. Jensen, G. D., and M. Womack. "Operant Conditioning Techniques Applied in the Treatment of an Autistic Child." *American Journal of Orthopsychiatry.* 37:30-35, 1967.

207. Jensen, Nancy. "Adolescent Depression." Unpublished Master's Thesis. Trinity Evangelical Divinity School, Deerfield, Illinois. Jan., 1976.

208. Joffe, J. M. "Perinatal Determinants of Emotionality." *Annals of the New York Academy of Science.* 159:668-80, July 30, 1969.

209. Jones, E. Stanley. *Conversion.* Nashville: Abingdon Press, 1959.

210. Kahn, R. M., and M. A. Arbib. "A Cybernetic Approach to Mental Development, with Some Comments on Infantile Autism and the Childhood Schizophrenias." Presented at the American Orthopsychiatric Association, 1968.

211. Kanner, L. "Infantile Autism and the Schizophrenias." *Behavioral Science.* 10:412-20, 1965.

212. Kantzer, Kenneth. Lecture notes from systematic theology course on the charismatic movement. Trinity Evangelical Divinity School, Deerfield, Illinois. Fall, 1975.

213. Kaufman, I. C., et al. "Effects of Separation from Mother on the Emotional Behavior of Infant Monkeys." *Annals of the New York Academy of Science.* 159:681-95, July 30, 1969.

214. Kaufman, K. K. "Emotional Imbalance and Chronic Disease in the Male." *Journal of the American Geriatric Society.* 17:894-98, Sept., 1969.

215. Kay, D. W. K., and Denis Leigh. "The Natural History, Treatment and Prognosis of Anorexia Nervosa, Based on a Study of 38 Patients." *Journal of Mental Science.* 100:411-31, 1954.

216. Kildahl, J. P. "The Personalities of Sudden Religious Converts." *Pastoral Psychology.* 16:37-44, Sept., 1965.

217. Klatskin, E. H., et al. "Projective Test Content During Pregnancy and Postpartum Adjustment." *Psychosomatic Medicine.* 32:487-93. Sept.-Oct., 1970.

218. Knight, J. A. "Psychodynamics of the Allergic Eczemas." *Annals of Allergy.* 25:392-96, July, 1967.

219. Kogelschatz, Joan L., Paul L. Adams, and Daniel Tucker. "Family Styles of Fatherless Households." *Journal of the American Academy of Child Psychiatry.* 11:365-83, April, 1972.

220. Krell, Robert. "Problems of the Single-parent Family Unit." *Canadian Medical Association Journal.* 107:867-68, Nov. 4, 1972.

221. Kübler-Ross, Elisabeth. *On Death and Dying.* New York: The Macmillan Company, 1969.

222. Kuo, You-Yuh. "Family Constellation in the Chinese Language." *Journal of Individual Psychology.* 27:181-84, Nov., 1971.

223. LaBaw, W., et al. "Use of Self-hypnosis by Children with Cancer." *American Journal of Clinical Hypnosis.* 17:233-38, 1975.

224. Landau, Rita, et al. "The Influence of Psychotic Parents on Their Children's Development." *American Journal of Psychiatry.* 129:38-43, July, 1972.

225. Lewin, K., et al. "Anorexia Nervosa Associated with Hypothalmic Tumour." *British Medical Journal.* 2:629-30, June 10, 1972.

226. Lewis, C. S. *Mere Christianity.* New York: Macmillan Company, 1952.

227. ———. *The Problem of Pain.* New York: Macmillan Company, 1962.

228. Lidz, Theodore. *The Person.* New York: Basic Books, 1968.

229. ———. "The Nature and Origins of Schizophrenic Disorders." *Annals of Internal Medicine.* 77:639-45, Oct., 1972.

230. Liebman, Ronald, Salvador Minuchin, and Lester Baker. "An Integrated Treatment Program for Anorexia Nervosa." *American Journal of Psychiatry.* Vol. 131, No. 4, pp. 432-36, April, 1974.

231. Liljefors, I., et al. "An Identical Twin Study of Psychosocial Factors in Coronary Heart Disease in Sweden." *Psychosomatic Medicine.* 32:523-42, Sept.-Oct., 1970.

232. Liston, E. H., et al. "Concurrence of Anorexia Nervosa and Gonadal Dysgenesis. A Critical Review with Practical Considerations." *Archives of General Psychiatry.* 29:834-36, Dec., 1973.

233. Little, Paul E. *Know What You Believe.* Wheaton, Illinois: Scripture Press, 1971.

234. ———. *Know Why You Believe.* Downers Grove, Illinois: Inter-Varsity Press, 1973.

235. Lloyd-Jones, D. M. *Conversions, Psychological and Spiritual.* Downers Grove, Illinois: Inter-Varsity Press, 1959.

236. London, Shirley L. "Socio-economics of the Family with Multiple Allergic Children." *Annals of Allergy.* 28:153-58, April, 1970.

237. Low, Jolanda E. "Successful Women in the Sciences: An Analysis of Determinants." *Annals of the New York Academy of Science.* 208:98-106, March 15, 1973.

238. Lowe, L. H. "Families of Children with Early Childhood Schizophrenia." *Archives of General Psychiatry.* 14:26-30, 1966.

239. Luban-Plozza, B., and A. Comazzi. "The Family as a Factor in Psychosomatic Disturbances." *Psychotherapy and Psychosomatics.* 22:372-77, 1973.

240. Lubowe, Irwin I. "The Pathogenesis of Acne." *Medical Times.* 97:194-98, Jan., 1969.

241. Ludwig, Arnold M. "The Proper Domain of Psychiatry." *Psychiatry Digest.* Jan., 1976, pp. 15-24.

242. Lundberg, Olov, and Jan Walinder. "Anorexia Nervosa and Signs of Brain Damage." *International Journal of Neuropsychiatry.* 3:165-73, 1967.

243. Lundberg, P. O., Jan Walinder, I. Werner, and L. Wide. "Effects of Thyrotrophin-releasing Hormone on Plasma Levels of TSH, FSH, LH and GH in Anorexia Nervosa." *European Journal of Clinical Investigation.* 2:150-53, March, 1972.

244. Luria, Z., et al. "Children's Conceptions of Events Before and After Confession of Transgression." *Child Development.* 40:1055-61, Dec., 1969.

245. Lynch, H. T., et al. "Heredity, Emotions and Cancer Control." *Postgraduate Medicine.* 43:134-38, Feb., 1968.

246. Lynch, M., D. Steinberg, and C. Ounsted. "Family Unit in Children's Psychiatric Hospital." *British Medical Journal.* 2:127-29, 1975.

247. Mallory, James D. *The Kink and I.* Grand Rapids: Zondervan Publishing House, 1965.

248. Mant, M. J., et al. "The Haematology of Anorexia Nervosa." *British Journal of Haematology.* 23:737-49, Dec., 1972.

249. *Manual on Alcoholism.* Chicago: American Medical Association, 1970.

250. Marcotte, D. B., et al. "Psychophysiologic Changes Accompanying Oral Contraceptive Use." *British Journal of Psychiatry.* 116:165-67, Feb., 1970.

251. Mark, Vernon H., and Frank R. Ervin. *Violence and the Brain.* New York: Harper and Row, 1970.

252. Marks, Isaac M. *Fears and Phobias.* New York: Academic Press, 1969.

253. Marks, Philip A., William Seeman, and Deborah L. Haller. *The Actuarial Use of the MMPI with Adolescents and Adults.* Baltimore: The Williams and Wilkins Company, 1974.

254. Marshall, J. R. "Treatment of Night Terrors Associated with Post-traumatic Syndrome." *American Journal of Psychiatry.* 132:293-95, 1975.

255. Martin, F. "Pathologie des Aspects Neurologiques et Psychiatriques dans Quelques Manifestations Carentielles avec Troubles Digestifs et Neuroendocriniens." *Helvetica Medica Acta.* 22:522-29, 1955.

256. Maslow, Abraham. "Comments on Religions, Values and Peak Experiences." In *The Farther Reaches of Human Nature.* New York: Viking Press, 1971.

257. ———. "Religion and Peak Experience." In *Psyche and Spirit.* Edited by J. J. Heaney. New York: Paulist Press, 1973.

258. Mason, S. A. "Emotional Aspects of Allergy." *Review of Allergy.* 23:556-60, July, 1969.

259. May, Rollo. *Existence.* New York: Basic Books, 1958.

260. Mayo, C. C., et al. "MMPI Correlates of Religiousness in Late Adolescent College Students." *Journal of Nervous and Mental Disease.* 149:381-85, Nov., 1969.

261. McCall, Raymond J. "The Defense Mechanisms Re-examined: A Logical and Phenomenal Analysis." *Catholic Psychological Research.* 1:44-64, 1963.

262. McCandless, Boyd R. *Children: Behavior and Development.* New York: Holt, Rinehart and Winston, 1967.

263. McDanald, Eugene. "Emotional Growth of the Child." *Texas Medicine.* 63:73-79, April, 1967.

264. McDonald, R. L. "The Role of Emotional Factors in Obstetric Complications." *Psychosomatic Medicine.* 30:222-43, March-April, 1968.

265. McGrade, B. J. "Newborn Activity and Emotional Response at Eight Months." *Child Development.* 39:1247-52, Dec., 1968.

266. McIsaac, W. M. "A Biochemical Concept of Mental Disease." *Postgraduate Medicine.* 30:111-18, Aug., 1961.

267. McKenzie, J. G. *Psychology, Psychotherapy and Evangelicalism.* London: George Allen, 1940.

268. McKibbin, Elsie H. "An Interdisciplinary Program for Retarded Children and Their Families." *American Journal of Occupational Therapy.* 26: 125-29, April, 1972.

269. McLean, James A., and Alfred Y. T. Ching. "Follow-up Study of Relationships Between Family Situation and Bronchial Asthma in Children." *Journal of the American Academy of Child Psychiatry.* 12:142-61, Jan., 1973.

270. McMillen, S. I. *None of These Diseases.* Old Tappan, New Jersey: Fleming H. Revell, 1963.

271. McNichol, Ronald W. *The Treatment of Delirium Tremens and Related States.* Springfield, Illinois: Charles C. Thomas, 1970.

272. McPherson, Sigrid R., et al. "Who Listens? Who Communicates? How? Styles of Interaction Among Parents and Their Disturbed Adolescent Children." *Archives of General Psychiatry.* 28:393-99, March, 1973.

273. Mednick, Birgitte R. "Breakdown in High-Risk Subjects: Familial and Early Environmental Factors." *Journal of Abnormal Psychology.* 82:469-75, Dec., 1973.

274. Meier, Paul D. "The Cardiovascular Effects of 5-Hydroxytryptamine (Serotonin)." Unpublished Master's Thesis. Michigan State University, East Lansing, Michigan, 1969.

275. ———. "Divorce Is Never Necessary." *Action.* 34:15-17, Fall, 1975.

276. ———. "Self-Acceptance Leads to Mate-Acceptance." *Christian Life,* Spring, 1976.

277. Mellbin, G. "Neuropsychiatric Disorders in Sex Chromatin Negative Women." *British Journal of Psychiatry.* 112:145-48, 1966.

278. Melzack, R. "The Role of Early Experience in Emotional Arousal." *Annals of the New York Academy of Science.* 159:721-30, July 30, 1969.

279. *Mental Retardation.* Chicago: American Medical Association, 1969.

280. Meredith, Don, Tim Timmons, and Jody Dillow. Christian Family Life Seminar. Dallas, Texas, 1973.

281. Meyer, J. E. "Das Syndrom der Anorexia Nervosa." *Archiv. für Psychiatrie und Nervenkrankheiten.* 202:31-59, 1961.

282. Meyers, Frederick H., Ernest Jawetz, and Alan Goldfein. *Review of Medical Pharmacology.* Los Altos, California: Lange Medical Publications, 1968.

283. Minard, J. G., et al. "Psychological Differentiation and Perceptual Defense: Studies of the Separation of Perception from Emotion." *Journal of Abnormal Psychology.* 74:131-39, April, 1969.

284. Minc, S. "Emotions and Ischemic Heart Disease." *American Heart Journal.* 73:713-15, May, 1967.

285. Minde, Klaus K., J. D. Hackett, D. Killou, and S. Silver. "How They Grow Up: 41 Physically Handicapped Children and Their Families." *American Journal of Psychiatry.* 128:1554-60, June, 1972.

286. Minirth, Frank B. "Hysteria—Clarification of Definitions and Dynamics." *The Journal of the Arkansas Medical Society.* 72:159-62, Sept., 1975.

287. Moos, R. H., et al. "Fluctuations in Symptoms and Moods During the Menstrual Cycle." *Journal of Psychosomatic Research.* 13:37-44, March, 1969.

288. Mosak, Harold H. "Life Style Assessment: A Demonstration Focused on Family Constellation." *Journal of Individual Psychology.* 28:232-47, Nov., 1972.

289. Muslin, H. L., et al. "Separation Experience and Cancer of the Breast." *Annals of the New York Academy of Science.* 125:802-06, Jan. 21, 1966.

290. Narramore, Clyde M. *How to Tell Your Children About Sex.* Grand Rapids: Zondervan Publishing House, 1958.

291. ———. *Encyclopedia of Psychological Problems.* Grand Rapids: Zondervan Publishing House, 1966.

292. ———. *How to Succeed in Family Living.* Glendale, California: Regal Books, 1968.

293. Nay, G. G. "The Psychodynamics of Spirituality." *Journal of Pastoral Care.* June, 1974, pp. 84-91.

294. Nee, Watchman. *The Normal Christian Worker.* Kowloon, Hong Kong: Church Book Room, 1965.

295. Nelson, Marion H. *Why Christians Crack Up.* Chicago: Moody Press, 1960.

296. Newman, Morton B., and Mary San Martino. "The Child and the Seriously Disturbed Parent. Treatment Issues." *Journal of the American Academy of Child Psychiatry.* 12:162-81, Jan., 1973.

297. Nicholi, Armand. "A New Dimension of the Youth Culture." *American Journal of Psychiatry.* 131:396-401, April, 1974.

298. Nichtern, Sol. "The Children of Drug Users." *Journal of the American Academy of Child Psychiatry.* 12:24-31, Jan., 1973.

299. Oates, Wayne E. "Conversion and Mental Health." *Pastoral Psychology.* 17:43-48, Sept., 1966.

300. ———. *The Psychology of Religion.* Waco, Texas: Word Books, 1973.

301. Oberleder, M. "Emotional Breakdowns in Elderly People." *Hospital and Community Psychiatry.* 20:191-96, July, 1969.

302. Odom, Linda, Julius Seeman, and J. R. Newbrough. "A Study of Family Communication Patterns and Personality Integration in Children." *Child Psychiatry and Human Development.* 1:275-85, Summer, 1971.

303. Osborn, D. K., and M. Endsley. "Emotional Reactions of Young Children to T.V. Violence." *Child Development.* 42:321-31, March, 1971.

304. *Partners for Life.* Grand Rapids: Baker Book House, 1958.

305. Peters, John. *Lectures on Piaget.* University of Arkansas Child Study Center, Little Rock, Arkansas. July, 1973.

306. Peters, John E., Joanna S. Davis, Cleo M. Goolsby, and Sam D. Clements. *Physician's Handbook: Screening for MBD.* CIBA, 1973.

307. Piaget, Jean. *The Moral Judgment of the Child.* Glencoe, Illinois: The Free Press, 1948.

308. ———. *The Origins of Intelligence in Children.* New York: International Universities Press, 1952.

309. ———. *The Construction of Reality in the Child.* New York: Basic Books, 1954.

310. ———. *Logic and Psychology.* New York: Basic Books, 1957.

311. ———. *The Language and Thought of the Child.* New York: Humanities Press, 1959.

312. ———. *Play, Dreams and Imitation in Childhood.* New York: Norton, 1962.

313. ———. *The Mechanisms of Perception.* New York: Basic Books, 1969.

314. Pintner, Rudolf, et al. *Educational Psychology.* New York: Barnes and Noble, 1962.

315. Pitfield, M., and A. N. Oppenheim. "Childrearing Attitudes of Mothers of Psychotic Children." *Journal of Child Psychology and Psychiatry.* 5:51-57, 1964.

316. Plath, David W. "Japanese Psychology Through Japanese Literature." *Journal of Nervous Mental Disease.* 157:346-57, Nov., 1973.

317. Pollack, M., and R. K. Gittelman. "The Siblings of Childhood Schizophrenics: A Review." *American Journal of Orthopsychiatry.* 34:868-73, 1964.

318. Pollack, M., and M. G. Woerner. "Pre- and Peri-natal Complications and 'Childhood Schizophrenia': A Comparison of Five Controlled Studies." *Journal of Child Psychology and Psychiatry.* 7:235-42, 1966.

319. Pribram, K. H. "The New Neurology and the Biology of Emotion: A Structural Approach." *American Psychologist.* 22:830-38, Oct., 1967.

320. Pruyser, Paul W. *A Dynamic Psychology of Religion.* New York: Harper and Row, 1968.

321. Quaade, N. *Obese Children: Anthropology and Environment.* Copenhagen: Danish Science Press, 1955.

322. Ravenscroft, Kent, Jr. "Normal Family Regression at Adolescence." *American Journal of Psychiatry.* 131:31-35, Jan., 1974.

323. Reese, William G. "The Major Cause of Death." *Texas Medicine.* 66: 56-61, Sept., 1970.

324. ———. Lecture to medical students. University of Arkansas Medical Center, Dec. 15, 1970.

325. Reiss, D. "Intimacy and Problem-solving." *Archives of General Psychiatry.* 25:442-55, 1971.

326. Rice, G., J. G. Kepecs, and I. Yahalom. "Differences in Communicative Impact Between Mothers of Psychotic and Nonpsychotic Children." *American Journal of Orthopsychiatry.* 36:363-77, Sept., 1971.

327. Robson, K. S., et al. "Patterns and Determinants of Maternal Attachments." *Journal of Pediatrics.* 77:976-85, Dec., 1970.

328. Rollins, Nancy, Joseph P. Lord, Ethel Walsh, and Geraldine R. Weil. "Some Roles Children Play in Their Families. Scapegoat, Baby, Pet and Peacemaker." *Journal of the American Academy of Child Psychiatry.* 12: 511-30, July, 1973.

329. Rossi, Alice S. "Family Development in a Changing World." *American Journal of Psychiatry.* 128:1057-66, March, 1972.

330. Rothchild, E. "Emotional Aspects of Sexual Development." *Pediatric Clinics of North America.* 16:415-28, May, 1969.

331. Rothman, E. P. "Work as Therapy for Emotionally Disturbed Girls." *Mental Hygiene.* 53:269-79, April, 1969.

332. Rousell, Charles H., and Carl N. Edwards. "Some Developmental Antecedents of Psychopathology." *Journal of Personality.* 39:362-77, Sept., 1971.

333. Royce, James E. *Personality and Mental Health.* Milwaukee: The Bruce Publishing Company, 1955.

334. Russell, G. F. M. "Clinical and Endocrine Features of Anorexia Nervosa." *Transactions of the Medical Society of London.* 87:40-50, 1971.

335. ———. "Premenstrual Tension and 'Psychogenic' Amenorrhoea: Psychophysical Interactions." *Journal of Psychosomatic Research.* 16:279-87, 1972.

336. Sadler, H. H., et al. "The Complementary Relationship Between the Emotional State and the Function of the Ileum in a Human Subject." *American Journal of Psychiatry.* 124:1375-84, April, 1968.

337. Salzman, Leon. "Types of Religious Conversion." *Pastoral Psychology.* Sept., 1966, pp. 8-20.

338. ———. *The Obsessive Personality.* New York: Jason Aronson, 1973.

339. Sanders, R. Wyman. "Resistance to Dealing with Parents of Battered Children." *Pediatrics.* 50:853-57, Dec., 1972.

340. Sandler, B. "Emotional Stress and Infertility." *Journal of Psychosomatic Research.* 12:51-59, June, 1968.

341. Sankar, D. V., et al. "Effect of Administration of LSD on Serotonin Levels in the Body." *Nature* (London). 191:499-500, July 29, 1961.

342. Sassin, J. F., D. C. Parker, J. W. Mace, R. W. Gotlin, L. C. Johnson, and L. G. Rossman. *Science.* 165:513-15, 1969.

343. Saunders, Cicely. "A Death in the Family: A Professional View." *British Medical Journal.* 1:30-31, Jan. 6, 1973.

344. Schaeffer, Edith. *Hidden Art.* Wheaton, Illinois: Tyndale House, 1971.

345. Schaeffer, Francis A. *Escape from Reason.* Downers Grove, Illinois: Inter-Varsity Press, 1968.

346. ———. *The God Who Is There.* Downers Grove, Illinois: Inter-Varsity Press, 1968.

347. ———. *The Church at the End of the 20th Century.* Downers Grove, Illinois: Inter-Varsity Press, 1970.

348. ———. *Art and the Bible.* Downers Grove, Illinois: Inter-Varsity Press, 1973.

349. ———. *The New Superspirituality.* Downers Grove, Illinois: Inter-Varsity Press, 1973.

350. Schildkraut, J. J., et al. "Norepinephrine Metabolism and Drugs Used in the Affective Disorders: A Possible Mechanism of Action." *American Journal of Psychiatry.* 124:600-08, Nov., 1967.

351. Schuckit, Marc Alan. "Family History and Half-sibling Research in Alcoholism." *Annals of the New York Academy of Science.* 197:121-25, May 25, 1972.

352. Schwartz, J. L., et al. "Changes in Anxiety, Mood and Self-Esteem Resulting from an Attempt to Stop Smoking." *American Journal of Psychiatry.* 124:1580-84, May, 1968.

353. Scott, J. P. "The Emotional Basis of Social Behavior." *Annals of the New York Academy of Science.* 159:777-90, July 30, 1969.

354. Segal, B. E., et al. "Work, Play and Emotional Disturbance." *Archives of General Psychiatry.* 16:173-79, Feb., 1967.

355. Shannon, Robert F., and Joe T. Backus. "Depression." *The Journal of the Arkansas Medical Society.* July, 1973.

356. Shapiro, Arthur K., Elaine Shapiro, and Henriette Wayne. "Birth, Developmental and Family Histories and Demographic Information in Tourette's Syndrome." *Journal of Nervous Mental Disease.* 155:335-44, Nov., 1972.

357. Shatin, L. "Alteration of Mood via Music: A Study of the Vectoring Effect." *Journal of Psychology.* 75:81-86, May, 1970.

358. Shatkin, Eugene P. "Teen-age Pregnancy: The Family Background." *Pediatrics.* 50:167, July, 1972.

359. Shedd, Charlie W. *Letters to Philip on How to Treat a Woman.* Old Tappan, New Jersey: Fleming H. Revell Company, 1968.

360. Siegelman, Marvin. "Family Background of Alcoholics: Some Research Considerations." *Annals of the New York Academy of Science.* 197:226-29, May 25, 1972.

361. ———. "Birth Order and Family Size of Homosexual Men and Women." *Journal of Consulting and Clinical Psychology.* 41:164, Aug., 1973.

362. Sigler, L. H. "Emotion and Atherosclerotic Heart Disease." *British Journal of Medical Psychology.* 40:55-64, March, 1967.

363. Simmons, J. Q., and O. I. Lovaas. "Use of Pain and Punishment as Treatment Techniques with Childhood Schizophrenics." *American Journal of Psychotherapy.* 23:23-35, 1969.

364. Simon, G. B., and S. M. Gillies. "Some Physical Characteristics of a Group of Psychotic Children." *British Journal of Psychiatry.* 110:104-07, 1964.

365. Singh, B., B. K. Anand, C. L. Malhotra, and S. Dua. "Stress as an Aetiological Factor in the Causation of Anorexia Nervosa." *Neurol.* (India). 4:50-52, 1958.

366. Smart, Reginald G., and Dianne Fejer. "Drug Use Among Adolescents and Their Parents: Closing the Generation Gap in Mood Modification." *Journal of Abnormal Psychology.* 79:153-60, April, 1972.

367. Sokoloff, B. "The Biological Activity of Serotonin." *Growth.* 28:113-26, June, 1964.

368. Solomon, G. F. "Emotions, Stress, the Central Nervous System and Immunity." *Annals of the New York Academy of Science.* 164:335-43, Oct. 14, 1969.

369. Southam, C. M. "Emotions, Immunology, and Cancer: How Might the Psyche Influence Neoplasia?" *Annals of the New York Academy of Science.* 164:473-75, Oct., 1969.

370. Spitz, René A. "Hospitalism: An Inquiry into the Genesis of Psychiatric Conditions in Early Childhood." *The Psychoanalytic Study of the Child.* Volume I. New York: International Universities Press, 1945, pp. 53-74.

371. Spivack, G., and M. Levine. "The Devereux Child Behavior Rating Scale: A Study of Symptom Behavior in Latency Age Atypical Children." *American Journal of Mental Deficiency.* 68:700-17, 1964.

372. Stabenau, James R. "Heredity and Environment in Schizophrenia." *Archives of General Psychiatry.* 18:458-63, April, 1968.

373. Stanbury, John B., James B. Wyngaarder, and Donald S. Fredrickson. *The Metabolic Basis of Inherited Disease.* New York: McGraw-Hill, 1972.

374. Starbuck, Edwin Diller. "A Study of Conversion." *American Journal of Psychology,* 1897, pp. 268-308.

375. State, D. "Gastrointestinal Hormones in the Production of Peptic Ulcer." *Journal of the American Medical Association.* 187:410-12, Feb. 8, 1964.

376. Stedman, Ray C. *Body Life.* Glendale, California: Regal Books, 1972.

377. Stein, Stefan P., and Edward Charles. "Emotional Factors in Juvenile Diabetes Mellitus: A Study of Early Life Experiences of Adolescent Diabetics." *American Journal of Psychiatry.* 128:200-04, Dec., 1971.

378. Stephan, F., P. Reville, R. Thierry, and J. L. Schlienger. "Correlations Between Plasma Insulin and Body Weight in Obesity, Anorexia Nervosa and Diabetes Mellitus." *Diabetologia.* 8:196-201, July, 1972.

379. Stierlin, Helm. "A Family Perspective on Adolescent Runaways." *Archives of General Psychiatry.* 29:56-62, July, 1973.

380. Stone, H. "The Birth of a Child with Down's Syndrome: A Medico-social Study of Thirty-one Children and Their Families." *Scottish Medical Journal.* 18:182-87, Nov., 1973.

381. Sugar, M., et al. "Use of College-student Companions for Psychotic Children to Avoid Hospitalization." *Journal of Child Psychiatry.* 14:249-66, 1975.

382. Taft, L. T., and W. Goldfarb. "Prenatal and Perinatal Factors in Child-hood Schizophrenia." *Developmental Medicine and Child Neurology.* 6:32-43, 1964.

383. Tate, B. G., and G. S. Baroff. "Aversive Control of Self-injurious Behavior in a Psychotic Boy." *Behavior Research and Therapy.* 4:281-87, 1966.

384. Terris, M., R. Lapouse, and M. A. Monk. "The Relation of Prematurity and Previous Fetal Loss to Childhood Schizophrenia." *American Journal of Psychiatry.* 121:476-81, 1964.

385. *The Addictive Personality.* Connecticut Postgraduate Seminar in Psychiatry and Neurology, 1972.

386. Tiebout, H. M. "Conversion as a Psychological Phenomenon." *Pastoral Psychology.* 2:28-34, April, 1951.

387. Tillich, Paul. *Dynamics of Faith.* New York: Harper and Row, 1957.

388. Tilton, J. R., M. K. DeMyer, and L. H. Loew. *Annotated Bibliography on Childhood Schizophrenia, 1955-1964.* New York: Grune and Stratton, 1966.

389. Toms, D. A., and Arthur H. Crisp. "Weight Phobia in an Adolescent Male with Stunted Development." *Journal of Psychosomatic Research.* 16: 289-95, 1972.

390. Tournier, Paul. *A Doctor's Casebook in the Light of the Bible.* New York: Harper and Row, 1960.

391. ———. *Guilt and Grace.* New York: Harper and Row, 1962.

392. ———. *The Strong and the Weak.* Philadelphia: The Westminster Press, 1963.

393. ———. *The Whole Person in a Broken World.* New York: Harper and Row, 1964.

394. ———. *The Healing of Persons.* New York: Harper and Row, 1965.

395. ———. *A Place for You.* New York: Harper and Row, 1966.

396. ———. *The Person Reborn.* New York: Harper and Row, 1966.

397. ———. *To Resist or to Surrender.* Richmond, Virginia: John Knox Press, 1968.

398. Trobisch, Walter. *I Married You.* New York: Harper and Row, 1952.

399. Underwood, A. C. *Conversion: Christian and Non-Christian.* New York: Macmillan, 1925.

400. Unger, Merrill F. *Demons in the World Today.* Wheaton, Illinois: Tyndale House, 1971.

401. Vaillant, George E. "Theoretical Hierarchy of Adaptive Ego Mechanisms." *Archives of General Psychiatry.* 24:107-18, Feb., 1971.

402. ———. "A 20-year Follow-up of New York Narcotic Addicts." *Archives of General Psychiatry.* 29:237-41, 1973.

403. ———. "Sociopathy as a Human Process." *Archives of General Psychiatry.* 32:178-83, Feb., 1975.

404. Wakeling, A., and G. F. M. Russell. "Disturbances in the Regulation of Body Temperature in Anorexia Nervosa." *Psychological Medicine.* 1:30-39, 1970.

405. Wallach, E. E., et al. "Psychodynamic Aspects of Oral Contraception." *Journal of the American Medical Association*. 203:927-31, March 31, 1968.

406. Walters, A. "Emotion and Low Back Pain." *Applied Therapy*. 8:68-71, Oct., 1966.

407. Warner, R. R. "Current Studies and Implications of Serotonin in Clinical Medicine." *Advances in Internal Medicine*. 13:241-82, 1967.

408. Warren, Michelle P., and Raymond L. Vande Wiele. "Clinical and Metabolic Features of Anorexia Nervosa." *American Journal of Obstetrics and Gynecology*. 117:435-49, Oct. 1, 1973.

409. Wattenberg, Ben J. *The Forming Families*. New York: Ziff-Davis Publishing Company, 1974.

410. Weber, A. "Crisis of Adolescence." *Schweiz. Rundschau Medicine*. 64: 383-87, 1975.

411. Weiner, Jan D., and G. A. Lindeboom. "Suprahypophyseal Involvement in Anorexia Nervosa." *British Medical Journal*. 3:236, July 22, 1972.

412. Weitzman, Elliot L., Charles A. Shamoian, and Nikolas Golosaw. "Family Dynamics in Male Transsexualism." *Psychosomatic Medicine*. 33:289-99, July-Aug., 1971.

413. Wendkos, M. H., et al. "Emotional Correlates of Angina Pectoris." *Israeli Journal of Medical Science*. 5:723-26, July-Aug., 1969.

414. Wenkart, A. "Spatiality and Human Experience." *American Journal of Psychotherapy*. 22:270-79, April, 1968.

415. Werkman, Sidney L. "Hazards of Rearing Children in Foreign Countries." *American Journal of Psychiatry*. 128:992-97, Feb., 1972.

416. White, P. T., W. DeMyer, and M. DeMyer. "EEG Abnormalities in Early Childhood Schizophrenia." *American Journal of Psychiatry*. 120:950-58, 1964.

417. White, R. K., et al. "Emotional Aspects of Disability." *Southern Medical Journal*. 63:1304-08, Nov., 1970.

418. Whittam, H., G. B. Simon, and P. J. Mittler. "The Early Development of Psychotic Children and Their Siblings." *Developmental Medicine and Child Neurology*. 8:552-60, 1966.

419. Wiegelmann, W., and H. G. Solbach. "Effects of LH-RH on Plasma Levels of LH and FSH in Anorexia Nervosa." *Hormone and Metabolic Research*. 4:404, Sept., 1972.

420. Wild, Cynthia M., Linda N. Shapiro, and Theodor Abelin. "Sampling Issues in Family Studies of Schizophrenia." *Archives of General Psychiatry*. 30:211-15, Feb., 1974.

421. Wilke, Richard B. *The Pastor and Marriage Group Counseling*. Nashville: Abingdon Press, 1974.

422. Willie, Charles V. "The Black Family and Social Class." *American Journal of Orthopsychiatry*. 44:50-60, Jan., 1974.

423. Willson, J. Robert, Clayton T. Beecham, and Elsie Reid Carrington. *Obstetrics and Gynecology*. St. Louis: The C. V. Mosby Company, 1966.

424. Wilson, William P. (editor). *Applications of Electroencephalography in Psychiatry*. Durham, North Carolina: Duke University Press, 1965.

425. Wilson, William P., et al. "Pain and Emotion." *Postgraduate Medicine*. 47:183-87, May, 1970.

426. Wilson, William P. "Mental Health Benefits of Religious Salvation." *Diseases of the Nervous System*. 33:382-86, June, 1972.

427. Wold, Patricia. "Family Structure in Three Cases of Anorexia Nervosa: The Role of the Father." *American Journal of Psychiatry*. 130:1394-97, Dec., 1973.

428. Wolf, S. "Emotions and the Autonomic Nervous System." *Archives of Internal Medicine*. 126:1024-30, Dec., 1970.

429. Wolff, Harold G. *Stress and Disease*. Springfield, Illinois: Charles C. Thomas, 1968.

430. Woodmansey, A. C. "Emotion and the Motions." *British Journal of Medical Psychology*. 40:207-24, 1967.

431. Woolley, D. W. "Serotonin in Mental Disorders." *Diseases of the Nervous System*. 21(2) Supplement: 87-96, Feb., 1960.

432. Woolley, D. W., and E. W. Shaw. "Neurophysiologic Aspects of Serotonin." *British Medical Journal*. 2:122-26, July 17, 1954.

433. Yochelson, L. "The Emotional Problems of Men in the Mature Years and Beyond." *Journal of the American Geriatric Society*. 17:855-60, Sept., 1969.

434. Ziai, Mohsen (editor). *Pediatrics*. Boston: Little, Brown and Company, 1969.

435. Zitrin, A., P. Ferbu, and D. Cohen. "Pre- and Para-natal Factors in Mental Disorders of Children." *Journal of Nervous and Mental Disease*. 139:357-61, 1964.

436. Zuck, Roy B., and Gene A. Getz. *Christian Youth, an In-Depth Study*. Chicago: Moody Press, 1968.